A Guide to Examining BUILDIN

This book is one of a series of composition/
Each level is color-coded:

Gold Level*—Grade 6
Red Level—Grade 7
Green Level—Grade 8
Orange Level—Grade 9
Blue Level—Grade 10
Yellow Level—Grade 11
Purple Level—Grade 12

As you examine this book, note the following features common to the books
for grades 7–12:

1. Organization. Like others in the series, it has two parts. The first half focuses
on writing. The second half, with page numbers printed in red, is devoted to
grammar, usage, and mechanics. For grades 6–8, the grammar and usage
section is primarily developmental; for grades 9–12, it is in a handbook format
useful for either developmental teaching or for easy reference.

2. Scope and Sequence. The book for each grade level strengthens the skills
developed at the previous level and adds additional skills and concepts.
Fundamental writing skills and concepts are emphasized at each grade level
...in particular, the sentence, the paragraph, and the composition. Other
topics are treated in some but not all levels. For complete tables of contents,
refer to the detailed brochure.

3. Readability. The reading level of each book is one to two grades below the
suggested grade level. The format is open, the type is large, and the organization is exceptionally clear. Thus, each book can be read and understood
by students with a wide range of abilities.

4. Emphasis on Composition. The series contains far more material on
composition than other leading series. It also contains two to three times as
many writing models and far more composition exercises... both important
tools by which students learn to write.

5. Additional Supporting Materials. Also available for each level are the
following: *Teacher's Manuals, Skills Practice Books, Duplicating Masters,*
and *Diagnostic & Mastery Tests.*

*Write for details about the sixth-grade book.

For more information or examination copies, write or call TOLL FREE and ask
for a BUILDING ENGLISH SKILLS Consultant.

McDougal, Littell & Company

P. O. Box 1667-X
Evanston, IL 60204

(800) 323-4345
Call between 9:00 am and 5:00 pm
Central Time. Illinois residents
call collect (312) 256-5240.

Building English Skills

Green Level

Building English Skills   Purple Level

Building English Skills   Yellow Level

Building English Skills   Blue Level

Building English Skills   Orange Level

Building English Skills   Green Level

Building English Skills   Red Level

Building English Skills

Green Level

Prepared by the Staff of
The Writing Improvement Project

McDougal, Littell & Company
Evanston, Illinois

Staff of THE WRITING IMPROVEMENT PROJECT

J. A. Christensen, East High School, Salt Lake City, Utah

Kathleen L. Bell, Lincoln Junior High School, Mount Prospect, Illinois

Donna Rae Blackall, Chairperson, English Department, Miner Junior High School, Arlington Heights, Illinois

Eric L. Kraft, Writer and Editor, Stow, Massachusetts

Joy Littell, Editorial Director, McDougal, Littell & Company

M. Rachel McKay, Writer and Editor, Chicago, Illinois

William A. Seabright, Director of Design, McDougal, Littell & Company

Project Assistant: Peggy Jo Schleker

For their cooperation in the development of the sections on grammar, usage, and mechanics, grateful acknowledgment is made to Thomas Clark Pollock, John P. Milligan, and Richard L. Loughlin.

ISBN: 0–88343–454–7

Copyright © 1978 by McDougal, Littell & Company
Box 1667, Evanston, Illinois 60204
All rights reserved. Printed in the United States of America

The twelve sections on grammar, usage, and mechanics
contain, in revised form, some materials that
appeared originally in *The Macmillan English
Series, Grade 8,* by Thomas Clark Pollock et al.,
copyright © 1963, 1960, 1954 by The Macmillan Company.
Used by arrangement.

Contents

The page numbers for the Grammar and Usage sections (the second half of this book) appear in red.

Chapter 1 **Developing Your Vocabulary** **1**

Part 1 **Learning Word Meanings from Context** **2**

Context Clue 1: Definition   3
Context Clue 2: Restatement   4
Context Clue 3: Examples   6
Context Clue 4: Comparison   8
Context Clue 5: Contrast   9

Part 2 **Gaining Precision in the Use of Words** **11**

Using Synonyms   11
Using Antonyms   13

Chapter 2 **Using the Dictionary** **17**

Part 1 **Alphabetical Order** **18**

Part 2 **Guide Words** **19**

Part 3 **Finding a Word** **23**

Part 4 **Word Division** **24**

Part 5 **Pronunciation** **25**

Accent Marks   26
Respellings   26

Part 6 **Definitions** **29**

Part 7 **Synonyms** **30**

Chapter 3 **Writing the Paragraph** **35**

Part 1 **What Is a Paragraph?** **35**

Part 2	**The Topic Sentence**	**39**
Part 3	**Writing Topic Sentences**	**43**

Narrowing the Topic 43
Writing Interesting Topic Sentences 44

Chapter 4   Developing the Paragraph   49

Part 1	**Using Specific Details**	**50**
Part 2	**Using Facts or Figures**	**53**
Part 3	**Using an Example**	**55**
Part 4	**Using a Definition**	**57**

Chapter 5   Different Kinds of Paragraphs   63

Part 1	**The Narrative Paragraph**	**64**

The First-Person Narrative Paragraph 64
The Third-Person Narrative Paragraph 66

Part 2	**The Descriptive Paragraph**	**67**

Choosing Words and Details Carefully 68
Following a Logical Order 71

Part 3	**The Explanatory Paragraph**	**75**

The "How" Paragraph 75
The "What" Paragraph 77
The "Why" Paragraph 78

Chapter 6   Writing the Composition   83

Part 1	**Parts of the Composition**	**83**
Part 2	**Finding a Subject**	**84**

Part 3   **Planning the Composition**   87

     Narrowing the Topic   88
     Putting Down Ideas   89
     Grouping Ideas   90
     Organizing Ideas   93

Part 4   **Writing the Composition**   95

     Writing the Introduction   95
     The Middle   98
     The Conclusion   101

Chapter 7   Kinds of Compositions   103

Part 1   **The Narrative Composition**   104

     First-Person Narrative   105
     Third-Person Narrative   106

Part 2   **The Descriptive Composition**   109

Part 3   **The Explanatory Composition**   111

     The "How" Composition   111
     The "What" Composition   113
     The "Why" Composition   115

Chapter 8   Writing Social and Business Letters   119

Part 1   **Writing Friendly Letters**   120

Part 2   **Social Notes**   124

     The Thank-You Note   124
     Notes of Invitation, Acceptance and Regret   126

Part 3   **Writing Business Letters**   130

     Business Letter Forms   130
     Parts of a Business Letter   133

Part 4   Types of Business Letters   134

     The Letter of Request   134
     The Order Letter   136
     The Letter of Complaint or Adjustment   138

Part 5   Preparing Your Letter for the Mail   140

     Folding Your Letter   140
     Addressing Envelopes for Friendly Letters   142
     Addressing Envelopes for Business Letters   143

Chapter 9   Thinking Clearly   145

Part 1   Separating Fact from Opinion   146
     Judgment Words   148
     Connotations of Words   149
     Slanting   151

Part 2   Checking Your Facts   153

Part 3   Making the Facts Clear   156

     Be Specific   156
     Give Your Source   158

Part 4   Logical Reasoning   159

     Generalizing   159
     Errors in Generalizing   160
     Qualifying Generalizations   161
     Giving Evidence for a Generalization   161
     Cause and Effect   164
     The Wrong-Cause Fallacy   165
     The One-Cause Fallacy   166
     Making Cause and Effect Reasoning Clear   166
     Either-Or Thinking   168

Chapter 10   The Library and How To Use It   173

Part 1   The Classification and Arrangement of Books   174

     The Classification of Books   174
     Call Numbers   176

Part 2 Using the Card Catalog **179**

The Author Card 179
The Title Card 180
The Subject Card 181
Cross Reference Cards 182
Guide Cards 183

Part 3 Using Reference Materials **185**

Dictionaries 185
Encyclopedias 188
Almanacs and Yearbooks 191
Atlases 191
Biographical References 192
The Vertical File 193
Readers' Guide to Periodical Literature 193

Chapter 11 Interviews and Group Discussions **197**

Part 1 Interviewing Others **198**

Guidelines for Conducting Interviews 198

Part 2 Group Discussion **200**

Informal Group Discussion 200
Formal Group Discussion 201

Part 3 Roles of Responsibility **204**

The Chairperson or Temporary Leader 204
The Initiator 205
The Clarifier 206
The Summarizer 206
The Evaluator 207

Each chapter opens with a letter of the alphabet. These twenty-six letters are "found" letters, photographed by Joseph D. Jachna as he encountered them in the natural world.

Grammar, Usage, and Mechanics

Section 1 **The Simple Sentence** **3**

Part 1 **Sentences and Sentence Fragments** 4

Part 2 **Subjects and Predicates** 6

Part 3 **Simple Subjects and Predicates** 8

Part 4 **The Parts of a Verb** 11

Part 5 **Subjects in Unusual Positions** 13

Sentences Beginning with *There* 13
Other Sentences with Unusual Word Order 15
Imperative Sentences 16

Part 6 **Objects of Verbs** 17

Direct Objects 18
Direct Object or Adverb? 18
Indirect Objects 19

Part 7 **Predicate Words and Linking Verbs** 22

Part 8 **Compound Sentence Parts** 24

Additional Exercises 27

Section 2 **Using Nouns** **33**

Part 1 **What Are Nouns?** 34

Part 2 **Forming the Singular and Plural of Nouns** 36

Part 3 **Forming the Possessive of Nouns** 39

Section 3 **Using Pronouns** **45**

Part 1 **Personal Pronouns** 46

Part 2   **Compound Personal Pronouns**   48

Part 3   **Indefinite Pronouns**   50

Part 4   **Demonstrative Pronouns**   52

Part 5   **Interrogative Pronouns**   52

Part 6   **The Cases of Pronouns**   53

      The Nominative Case of Pronouns 54
      The Objective Case of Pronouns 54
      The Possessive Case of Pronouns 55

Part 7   **Pronouns in Compound Sentence Parts**   57

Part 8   ***Who* and *Whom***   59

Part 9   **Possessive Pronouns and Contractions**   61

Part 10   **Special Pronoun Problems**   62

      Compound Personal Pronouns 62
      We Boys—Us Boys; We Girls—Us Girls 63
      Them and *Those* 63

Part 11   **Pronouns and Antecedents**   65

      Additional Exercises   67

Section 4   **Using Verbs**   73

Part 1   **What Verbs Are**   74

Part 2   **Helping Verbs and Main Verbs**   76

Part 3   **Progressive Forms**   78

Part 4   **The Tenses of Verbs**   79

      The Simple Tenses 79
      The Perfect Tenses 80

Part 5   **The Principal Parts of Verbs**   81

Part 6   **Irregular Verbs**   82

      Practice Pages on Irregular Verbs 85

Part 7   **Active and Passive Verbs**   100

Part 8   **Troublesome Pairs of Verbs**   102

Additional Exercises   105

Section 5   # Using Modifiers   109

Part 1   **Adjectives**   110

Adjective or Pronoun?   110
Predicate Adjectives and Proper Adjectives   111

Part 2   **Adverbs**   112

Adverbs Used with Verbs   113
Adverbs Used with Adjectives or Other Adverbs   113
Forming Adverbs   114

Part 3   **Adjective or Adverb?**   116

Adverbs and Predicate Adjectives   118
Good and *Well*   119

Part 4   **Articles**   120

Part 5   **Adjectives in Comparisons**   121

The Comparative   121
The Superlative   122

Part 6   **Adverbs in Comparison**   125

The Comparative and The Superlative   125

Part 7   **Special Problems with Modifiers**   127

Them and *Those*   127
The Extra *Here* and *There*   127
Kind and *Sort*   128
The Double Negative   128

Additional Exercises   130

Section 6   # Using Prepositions and Conjunctions   135

Part 1   **Prepositions**   136

Part 2   **Prepositional Phrases as Modifiers**   140

Part 3 **Conjunctions** 143

Coordinating and Correlative Conjunctions 144

Part 4 **Review of Parts of Speech** 146

Additional Exercises 148

Section 7 Using Compound and Complex Sentences 151

Part 1 **Review of the Simple Sentence** 152

Action Verbs and Linking Verbs 152
Compound Parts of the Simple Sentence 153
Definition of the Simple Sentence 153

Part 2 **Compound Sentences** 155

Part 3 **Compound Sentences and Compound Verbs** 159

Part 4 **Complex Sentences** 162

Main Clauses and Subordinate Clauses 163
Definition of the Complex Sentence 164

Part 5 **More About Sentence Fragments** 166

Part 6 **Adverb Clauses** 168

Part 7 **Adjective Clauses** 170

Clauses as Modifiers 171
Phrases and Clauses 171

Part 8 *Who* and *Whom* in Clauses 173

Part 9 **Noun Clauses** 175

Additional Exercises 180

Section 8 Making Subjects and Verbs Agree 185

Part 1 **Making Subjects and Verbs Agree in Number** 185

Part 2 **Compound Subjects** 188

| Part 3 | **Indefinite Pronouns** | **189** |

| Part 4 | **Other Problems of Agreement** | **191** |
| | Additional Exercises | 193 |

Section 9 Using Verbals 197

| Part 1 | **Infinitives** | **198** |

Use of the Infinitive Phrase   198
The Split Infinitive   199

| Part 2 | **Participles** | **200** |

| Part 3 | **Gerunds** | **202** |
| | Additional Exercises | 206 |

Section 10 Capitalization 209

Proper Nouns and Adjectives **210**

Names of Persons   210
Family Relationships, The Pronoun *I*, The Deity   211
Geographical Names   212
Directions and Sections   213
Names of Organizations and Institutions   215
Names of Events, Documents, and Periods of Time   215
Months, Days, and Holidays   215
Races, Languages, Nationalities, Religions   215
School Subjects   216
Ships, Trains, Airplanes, Automobiles   216

First Words **218**

Sentences and Poetry   218
Quotations and Letters   218
Outlines and Titles   219

Additional Exercises   221

Section 11 Punctuation 225

End Marks **226**

The Period   226

The Question Mark   227
The Exclamation Point   228

The Comma   229

Commas in a Series   229
Commas after Introductory Words, Phrases,
    or Clauses   231
Commas with Interrupters   232
Commas with Nouns of Direct Address   233
Commas with Appositives   233
Commas with Quotations   234
Commas in Compound Sentences   234
Commas in Dates   236
Commas in Locations and Addresses   236
Commas in Letter Parts   237
Commas with Nonrestrictive Clauses   238
Commas To Prevent Misreading   239

The Semicolon   241

The Colon   241

The Hyphen   243

The Apostrophe   245

Quotation Marks   247

Additional Exercises   254

Section 12   Spelling   263

How To Become a Better Speller   264

How To Master the Spelling of Particular Words   265

Rules for Spelling   265

The Final Silent *e*   265
Words Ending in *y*   266
The Addition of Prefixes   267
The Suffixes *-ness* and *-ly*   267
Words with the "Seed" Sound   268
Words with *ie* and *ei*   268
Doubling the Final Consonant   269

Additional Exercises   271

Chapter 1

Building Your Vocabulary

You have a group of words that you know well, use well, and feel comfortable with. These are the words that you use from day to day. You use them when you talk with friends, and your friends use them when they talk with you. This group of words that you use so comfortably in speaking is your **speaking vocabulary.**

When you sit down to write a letter or a composition, you have more time to think about the words you will use. In fact, when you are writing, you may use some words that you wouldn't use when you are speaking. You may not feel as sure of these words as you do of the words in your speaking vocabulary. You do understand them, however, and you use them when you can think about them. These words, in addition to the words in your speaking vocabulary, make up your **writing vocabulary.**

There is another group of words that you understand when you read them. You do not know these words well enough to feel comfortable about using them in speaking or in writing. But you do understand them when you come across them in your reading. These words, added to all the words in your writing vocabulary, equal your **reading vocabulary.**

The larger your reading vocabulary is, the better you will understand what you read. The larger your writing and speaking vocabularies are, the better you will be able to make people understand you. In this chapter you will learn how to make your reading vocabulary larger. You will also learn how to use words to say exactly what you mean in writing or speaking.

Part 1　Learning Word Meanings from Context

Many words have more than one meaning. For example, the word *sink* has a different meaning in each of these sentences.

> If we don't plug that leak, this boat will *sink*.
> The *sink* is full of dishes.

In one sentence, *sink* means "to go under water." In the other, it means "a tub or basin." You can easily tell which meaning fits which sentence. You can tell from the other words in each sentence.

The meaning of a word depends on its **context,** the words that come before or after it. Often the context makes the meaning clear, as it did in the two sentences above. Sometimes it does not, as in this sentence.

> We waited to see if Donna would sink it.

Here the context does not tell you whether Donna is playing golf or trying to sink a boat.

Context can tell you which meaning of a word fits what you are reading. It can also help you decide the meaning of a word you do not know. As you have seen, context will not always tell you enough to let you decide. But if you learn to look for certain clues, context can be a great help.

In this chapter you will learn how to use five kinds of context clues that will help you in your reading.

Context Clue 1: Definition

Sometimes a writer knows that a word will be unfamiliar to many readers. To make the word easier to understand, the writer may include a definition of the word in a sentence. It is as if the writer were saying to the reader, "I know you won't know the meaning of this word, so I am going to tell it to you." This context clue is the easiest one to spot, and it is the easiest to understand. Look at the following examples.

Examples:

At the zoo we saw a *gnu*, which is a large African antelope.
Helium makes the balloon *buoyant*; in other words, it floats.
The harbor is protected by a *jetty*. A jetty is a wall built out into the water.

In the first example, the writer tells you that a gnu is a large African antelope. The key words *which is* signal the definition. In the second example, the writer tells you that to be buoyant means to float. The key words *in other words* signal this definition. In the third example, the definition of *jetty* is given in a sentence of its own. The key word in this example is *is*.

Watch for the key words *which is* (or *that is*), *in other words*, and *is* when you read. These key words often signal a definition.

Exercise Definition

Number a sheet of paper from 1–10. Read each of the following sentences. Each sentence includes a definition for the italicized word. Write the meaning of each italicized word. Be ready to tell what key words helped you spot the definition.

1. We stayed in *youth hostels*, which are cheap places to stay for young people who are traveling.

2. Metal can be polished with *pumice*, which is rock formed from the lava of a volcano.

3. Clarice is *indecisive*; that is, she can't make up her mind.

4. We had to *rappel* down the face of the cliff. In other words, we had to lower ourselves on ropes.

5. I learned to use a *pantograph*. A pantograph is a mechanical gadget used to make a copy of a drawing.

6. The legs should be *perpendicular* to the top of the table. That is, they should meet the top at right angles.

7. The *marimba*, which is a kind of xylophone, is played with mallets.

8. The crops were destroyed by *locusts*. Locusts are large grasshoppers.

9. This piece of sculpture is made of *gesso*, which is a kind of plaster.

10. Our feet were tangled in a kind of seaweed called *kelp*.

Context Clue 2: Restatement

Often, you will not be lucky enough to find a definition for a word in its context. More often, you will find a restatement. A restatement tells you almost as much as a definition, but it is not as easy to spot. Look at the following examples.

Examples:

The walls were buttressed, or propped up, with sturdy logs.

We need volunteers to make *hors d'oeuvres*—appetizers—for the parents' meeting.

He had a wan look, pale and weak.

In the first example, the writer restates *buttressed* as "propped up." The writer has not directly said that *buttressed* means "propped up." Instead, the writer has written the same idea twice. The keys to spotting "popped up" as a restatement of *buttressed* are the word *or* and the commas that separate "or propped up" from the rest of the sentence.

In the second example, *hors d'oeuvres* is restated as "appetizers." Dashes separate *appetizers* from the rest of the sentence. These dashes are a key to spotting "appetizers" as a restatement of *hors d'oeuvres*.

The words *pale and weak* restate the idea of *wan* in the third example. The only key to *pale and weak* as a restatement is the comma that separates these words from the rest of the sentence.

The examples show three keys to spotting restatement as a context clue. They are the word *or*, a dash or a pair of dashes, and a comma or a pair of commas. Parentheses can also indicate a restatement.

Exercise   Restatement

Number a sheet of paper from 1–10. Read each of the following sentences. Each sentence includes a restatement of the italicized word or words. Write the meaning of each italicized word. Be ready to tell what key or keys helped you spot the restatement.

1. At first this new school seemed like a *labyrinth*—a maze —to me.

2. The meeting turned into quite a *fracas*, or uproar.

3. My favorite spot at the zoo is the *aviary*, the building where the birds are kept.

4. Colonial families cleaned house with a *besom*—a broom made of twigs tied to a handle.

5. We have to *collate* these pages—put them in the right order—before we staple them.

6. Carl led us on a *devious*, or winding, route home.

7. For short hikes you may want to use a *haversack*, a small bag that you can carry over one shoulder.

8. She has always been an *upright* person, honest and just.

9. We spent the afternoon playing *quoits*, a game like horseshoes.

10. Carbon monoxide is a *noxious* (poisonous) gas.

Context Clue 3: Examples

Examples can also give you a clue to the meaning of unfamiliar words. Study the following sentences.

Examples:

Kelp and other kinds of seaweed can be made into food.

Some kinds of seaweed, like kelp, can be made into food.

Neither sentence tells you just what kelp is. But both sentences tell you that kelp is one example of seaweed. Now that you have an idea of what kelp is, look at the following sentence.

Marine algae, such as kelp, can be grown in underwater farms.

In this sentence, kelp is mentioned as an example of marine algae. The sentence does not tell you what marine algae means. It does, however, tell you that kelp is one kind of marine algae. From that clue you should be able to figure out that *marine algae* must mean something like "seaweed."

The following key words signal an example (or examples) as a context clue. The key words are in boldface type. The sentences show how they are used to give clues to the meaning of the italicized words.

Elaine has mastered the *half gainer* **and other** difficult dives.

Tony is good at difficult dives **like** the *half gainer*.

Diane can do some difficult dives—the *half gainer*, **for instance.**

Phil is no good at difficult dives **such as** the *half gainer*.

Martha did some difficult dives—**for example,** the *half gainer*.

Kurt is good at all the difficult dives, but **especially** the *half gainer*.

Exercise   Examples

Write a definition for the italicized words in the following sentences. Use context clues alone to write your definitions. Check your definitions in a dictionary.

1. The forest was made up of pine, spruce, fir, and other *conifers*.

2. A good camper knows how to tie a *half hitch*, a *bowline*, a *clove hitch*, and other useful knots.

3. *Perishable* foods, like milk and butter, should be kept refrigerated.

4. I like all kinds of sausage, but I especially like *knockwurst*.

5. In this chapter you will read about such ancient heroes as *Ulysses* and *Hercules*.

6. *Mollusks*, especially clams, oysters, and snails, may be grown on "sea farms" in the future.

7. She's studying *glaucoma* and other diseases of the eye.

8. In this display you'll find *hedgehogs* and other animals that eat insects.

9. We're learning how to make some fancy desserts—*chocolate mousse*—for example.

10. If you're serious about mountain climbing, you'll need *crampons* and other special climbing equipment.

Context Clue 4: Comparison

When you compare things, you look at them to see how they are like each other. You usually compare things that are not much alike in order to point out one important way that they are alike.

Comparisons in writing can give you clues to the meanings of unfamiliar words. Look at the following examples to see if you can get an idea of the meaning of each italicized word.

> Examples:
>
> The hot-air balloon tugged at its *tether* like a dog tugging at its leash.
>
> At last the balloon took off. It was as *buoyant* in the air as a cork is in water.

In the first example, the writer compares a balloon on a tether to a dog on a leash. Both are tugging, trying to get free. The balloon is like a dog. The tether is like a leash. From the comparison you should be able to see that a tether must be something like a leash.

In the second example, the writer compares a balloon in air to a cork in water. You know that a cork floats in water, and that it may bob a bit while it floats. The writer says that a balloon is buoyant in air. The writer says that a cork is buoyant in water. The buoyant balloon is compared to the buoyant cork. From the comparison you should be able to see that something buoyant is something that floats.

Key words that help you spot comparison as a context clue include *like, as,* and *similar to.*

Context Clue 5: Contrast

When you contrast things, you look at them to see how they are different from each other. You often contrast things that are alike in many ways in order to point out one important way that they are different. You don't usually contrast trees and rocks or buses and pickles, because you already know that these things are quite different from each other. Instead, you contrast things that are similar to show an important way in which they are different.

A contrast between two things can give you a clue to the meaning of an unfamiliar word. Look at the following examples to see if you can get an idea of the meaning of the italicized words.

Examples:

Unlike most rats, the *bandicoot* carries its young in a pouch.

Rodents, unlike most animals, have teeth that keep growing throughout their lives.

Tony was *reticent*, but Phyllis spoke right up.

In the first example, the bandicoot is contrasted with "most rats." The writer points out one way in which the bandicoot is different from most rats. Because the writer makes this contrast, you can be reasonably sure that except for this difference the bandicoot is like most rats. A bandicoot, then, must be a kind of rat.

In the second example, the writer contrasts rodents with "most animals." The writer points out one way in which rodents are different from most animals. Because the writer makes this contrast, you can be reasonably sure that rodents are like most animals in other ways. Therefore, rodents must be animals.

In the third example, Tony is contrasted with Phyllis. Tony was reticent. Phyllis spoke right up. This was something that made Tony different from Phyllis. So being reticent must be different from speaking right up. Being reticent must mean something like "not speaking right up."

Key words that signal contrast as a context clue include *unlike, but, on the contrary,* and *on the other hand.*

Exercise   Comparison and Contrast

Write definitions for the italicized words in the following sentences. Use context clues alone to write your definitions. Check your definitions in a dictionary.

1. Anna, unlike most *ailurophobes,* can at least stand to be in the same room with a cat.
2. Like other *marsupials,* a kangaroo carries its young in a pouch.
3. The museum has many examples of early bicycles, such as the *ordinary* and the *high wheeler.*
4. Laura spends her time reading about *griffins, unicorns,* and other imaginary beasts.
5. Some people think he's *irrational,* but he's always seemed reasonable to me.
6. I was *anxious,* but everyone else seemed calm and relaxed.
7. Pull the taffy until it is as *elastic* as a rubber band.
8. When you hit the bar, it will make a *plangent* sound like a bell.
9. Most of us agreed. However, Cheryl *dissented.*
10. *Stalactites* hung down from the roof of the cave like icicles.

Part 2   Gaining Precision in the Use of Words

When you have something to say to someone, you want to say it in such a way that someone will understand it. You don't want people to misunderstand you. Neither do you want them to only *half*-understand you. The only way you can help people to understand you is to use words that make your meaning clear.

If your speaking and writing vocabularies are small, you won't have many words to choose from. You will not be able to say exactly what you mean.

To help people understand exactly what you mean, you must say exactly what you mean. You must choose the best words to express your meaning.

Using Synonyms

In order to be able to say exactly what you mean, you will need to know the synonyms for many words. **Synonyms** are words that have the same, or nearly the same, meanings. However, they do not have exactly the same meanings. When you use a word from a group of synonyms, you must pick the one that is closest in meaning to what you want to say.

Think about the word *run*. It has many synonyms. They include *trot, dash, flee, scamper,* and *sprint*. Each of these synonyms has a slightly different meaning. If you want to describe a squirrel running across a park, you might use *scamper*. However, if you want to describe the finish of the Kentucky Derby, *scamper* would be the wrong word.

If you look at passages of dialogue in stories, you will find many synonyms for the word *said*. You may find some or all of the synonyms shown on the next page.

shouted   bellowed   exclaimed
whispered   declared   muttered

Which of these synonyms would you use for someone speaking in a loud voice? Which would you use for an excited person? You can see that there are important differences among these words.

Exercises   Using Synonyms

A. Following is a list of synonyms for *said* that might be used in sentences 1–10. Choose the word that best fits each sentence.

whispered   chanted
called   cried
announced   muttered
explained   declared
screamed   growled

1. "I am the best violinist in class," _____ Mark.
2. "Don't look now, but someone's watching us," _____ Nancy.
3. "There will be a quiz on Friday," _____ Mr. Hunt.
4. "Wait! You forgot your notebook, hat, and pencil." _____ Madeline.
5. "I can't make this problem work out," _____ Sam.
6. "You have to mulitply, not divide," _____ Mr. Crandall.
7. "Stay in line. Stay in line. Stay in line," _____ Ms. Donovan.
8. "You always get more than I do," _____ Lucy.
9. "If I get any trouble from you, you'll get plenty of trouble from me," _____ Rafferty.
10. "A giant clam has me by the foot," _____ Louise.

B. List as many synonyms as you can for the following words. Use a dictionary for help.

pull   break   hard
funny   fast   angry
dull   intelligent   tired

Using Antonyms

Antonyms are words that are nearly opposite each other in meaning. The words *light* and *dark* are antonyms. So are *old* and *new*. So are *wide* and *narrow*.

Notice that a word may have more than one antonym. The word *old* is an antonym for *new*, but so is *ancient*. The word *new* is an antonym for *old*, but so are *recent* and *modern*.

You can use antonyms to clarify your ideas by making comparisons. If you are comparing two buildings, you could say that one is tall and the other is short. You could say that one is lofty and the other is squat. You could say that one is towering and the other is stumpy. Each comparison creates a different picture. You must decide which words are the best for the picture you want to create.

Exercises   Using Antonyms

A. Write an antonym for each word listed in Exercise B under Synonyms.

B. Use antonyms to compare each of the following:

1. two people
2. two books
3. two television shows
4. two moods
5. two athletes
6. two buildings
7. two metals
8. two seasons
9. two places
10. two cars

Review Exercises   Putting Your Vocabulary
Skills Together

A. Use context clues to decide the meaning of each italicized word in the following sentences. Write a definition for
each word. Then be ready to tell what clue and what keys
helped you decide the meaning.

1. Like all *carnivores*, wolves prefer to eat meat.
2. The design was made of three *concentric* circles; that is,
three circles with the same center.
3. The new government was extremely *fragile*; in other
words, it could easily fall apart.
4. You have to *interlace* the two colors of wool—weave
one over and under the other.
5. For weeks the hunters lived on nothing but *pemmican*,
dried meat pressed into cakes.
6. I gathered my spade, rake, hoe, and other gardening
implements.
7. If you're going to spend the night, you'll have to put
up with the creatures that haunt this castle, including *ghouls*,
poltergeists, and *bogies*.
8. Joan's ideas seemed *incontestable* to me, but Frank
went ahead and argued with her anyway.
9. She used to be a *retiring* type, but now she's the life
of the party.
10. The disease became *pandemic*; that is, it spread through
the entire country.

B. Read each of the following sentences. Try to think of a
more precise synonym for each italicized word. If you need
help, use a dictionary.

1. That was a really *good* dinner.
2. There's a *cold* wind blowing from the north.

3. Elaine *said* that she could beat any of us at ping-pong.
4. I *jumped* over the fence and ran for my life.
5. The quake *moved* the buildings as if they were toys.
6. She *moved* quickly across the floor.
7. Cars *moved* along the highway at rush hour.
8. It was a *bad* place to be.
9. The elephant *walked* slowly down the ramp.
10. The boy *walked* aimlessly down the street.

Chapter 2

Using the Dictionary

How many words are there in the English language? Would you guess 100,000? 200,000? 500,000? A good guess would be more than 500,000, but no one is really sure how many words there are. Old words die out and new ones are born all the time. Some words have short lives. Some live on and on. Some are used often by nearly everyone. Some are not used much at all. No one can know the meanings of so many words. That is why everyone runs into an unfamiliar word now and then. When that happens, a person turns to a dictionary to find out what the word means.

Just what is a dictionary? How can a dictionary help you? A dictionary is a list of words, with information about each word. Some dictionaries list more words than others. A good student dictionary will list about 100,000 words. It will divide the words into syllables and tell you how to pronounce them. It will tell you the meanings of the words. It will tell you what words are related in meaning. Finally, it will tell you the history of each word.

This chapter will show you how to get the most out of a dictionary.

Part 1 Alphabetical Order

The words in a dictionary are listed in alphabetical order. All words that begin with *a* come first. All words that begin with *b* come next. Words that begin with *s* come before words that begin with *t*, and so on. When words begin with the same letter, they are alphabetized according to the second letter. If the second letter is the same, the words are alphabetized according to the third letter, and so on.

The following groups of words are arranged in alphabetical order.

anteater	**a**ardvark	**gra**sshopper
groundhog	**al**batross	**gre**yhound
hedgehog	**an**teater	**gri**ffin
mole	**ar**madillo	**gro**undhog

To find words quickly, learn to open the dictionary at the right spot. Open your dictionary at a spot that seems close to the middle. You should be in the *L's* or the *M's*. If you are looking for a word that begins with a letter from A through L, look in the first half. If the word begins with a letter from M through Z, look in the second half.

If you practice opening your dictionary to a specific letter, you will be able to find words much more quickly.

Alphabetical Order

A. List the following words in alphabetical order.

1	2	3	4
franc	elm	Sun	neck
peso	walnut	Mercury	arm
dollar	beech	Venus	head
rupee	pine	Earth	hand
pound	fir	Mars	heart
mark	oak	Jupiter	foot
drachma	maple	Saturn	finger
lira	redwood	Uranus	toe
yen	mahogany	Neptune	ear
guilder	cedar	Pluto	nose

B. Working with a classmate, practice opening the diction-ary as close as you can to a particular letter. Have your class-mate say a letter. Try to open your dictionary to that letter. Then switch roles and say a letter for your classmate. Con-tinue until you can open the dictionary close to a specific letter most of the time.

Part 2 Guide Words

In most dictionaries you will find **guide words** at the top of each page. These help you find a word more quickly. The guide word on the left tells you the first word on the page. The guide word on the right tells you the last word on the page.

On pages 20 and 21 you will find a reproduction of a dic-tionary page. The guide words for this page are *ridgepole* and *righteous*. Notice that all the other words on the page fall be-tween these two in alphabetical order.

After you have opened to the right section of the dictionary for the word you want to find, you can find the exact page by

ridge·pole (rij′pōl′) *n.* the horizontal timber or beam at the ridge of a roof: also **ridge′piece′**

rid·i·cule (rid′i kyōōl′) *n.* [Fr. < L. *ridiculum*, a jest, ult. < *ridere*, to laugh: for IE. base see VERSE] **1.** the act of making a person or thing seem foolish, as by making fun, mocking, laughing, etc. **2.** words or actions used in doing this —*vt.* -**culed′**, -**cul′ing** to make fun of or make others laugh at; deride; mock

SYN.—**ridicule** implies a making fun of a person or thing by way of showing disapproval [he *ridiculed* her new hat]; **deride** suggests contempt for or a strong dislike of what is being made fun of [to *deride* another's beliefs]; **mock** suggests a ridiculing by the unkind imitation of another's manner-isms or habits [it is cruel to *mock* his lisp]; **taunt** implies insulting ridicule, esp. as shown by jeering at another and harping on something that makes him feel ashamed [they *taunted* him about his failure]

ri·dic·u·lous (ri dik′ya las) *adj.* deserving ridicule; absurd —see SYN. at ABSURD —**ri·dic′u·lous·ly** *adv.* —**ri·dic′u·lous·ness** *n.*

rid·ing[1] (rīd′iŋ) *adj.* **1.** that rides **2.** of or for riders on horseback [jodhpurs and boots are parts of a *riding* habit] ☆**3.** designed to be worked by a rider [a *riding* mower] —*n.* the act of one that rides

rid·ing[2] (rīd′iŋ) *n.* [OE. -*thrithing*, a third part] any of the three administrative divisions of Yorkshire, England

ri·el (rē el′, rēl) *n.* [see RIAL, REAL[2]] *see* MONETARY UNITS, table (Cambodia)

Rif (rif) mountain range along the Mediterranean coast of Morocco: also **Er Rif** (er)

rife (rīf) *adj.* [OE. *ryfe*] **1.** happening frequently or commonly; widespread [gossip was *rife*] **2.** *a*) abundant *b*) abounding; filled [*rife* with error] —see SYN. at PREVAILING —**rife′ness** *n.*

Riff (rif) *same as* RIF —*n., pl.* **Riffs, Riff′i** (-ē) a member of a Ber-ber people living in or near the Rif

☆**riff** (rif) *n.* [prob. altered < REFRAIN[2]] *Jazz* a short musical

to dress; clothe (usually with *out*) [all *rigged* out in a cowboy suit] —*n.* **1.** the arrangement of sails, masts, etc. on a vessel ☆**2.** equipment for a special purpose; gear [a ham radio opera-tor's *rig*] ☆**3.** equipment for drilling an oil well ☆**4.** *a*) a car-riage, etc. with its horse or horses *b*) a tractor-trailer or, sometimes, the tractor alone **5.** [Colloq.] dress or costume, esp. if odd or showy —**rig′ger** *n.*

Ri·ga (rē′ga) capital of the Latvian S.S.R.; seaport on the Baltic Sea: pop. 733,000

rig·a·ma·role (rig′a ma rōl′) *n. var. of* RIGMAROLE

ri·ga·to·ni (rig′a tō′nē; *It.* rē′gä tō′nē) *n.* [It., pl. < pp. of *rigare*, to mark with lines] short, ridged casings of pasta, often stuffed with ground meat, cheese, etc.

Ri·gel (rī′j'l, -g'l) [Ar. *rijl*, foot: in the left foot of Orion] a bright, bluish star, brightest in the constellation Orion

rig·ging (rig′iŋ) *n.* **1.** the chains, ropes, etc. used for support-ing and working the masts, sails, etc. of a vessel ☆**2.** equip-ment; gear

right (rīt) *adj.* [OE. *riht*: for IE. base see REGAL] **1.** orig., straight: now only in mathematics [a *right* line] **2.** *a*) formed by a straight line perpendicular to a base [a *right* angle] *b*) having the axis perpendicular to the base [a *right* cylinder] **3.** in accordance with justice, law, morality, etc.; virtuous [*right* conduct] **4.** in accordance with fact, reason, etc.; correct; true [the *right* answer] **5.** fitting; suitable [the *right* dress for a dance] **6.** designating the side meant to be seen [the *right* side of cloth] **7.** *a*) physically or mentally healthy [he doesn't look *right*] *b*) in a satisfactory condition; in good order [to make things *right* again] **8.** *a*) designating or of that side of one's body which is toward the east when one faces north, the side of the more-used hand in most people *b*) designating or of the corresponding side of anything *c*) closer to the right side of a person facing the thing mentioned [the top *right* drawer] **9.** of the bank of a river on the right of a person facing downstream **10.** of the political right; conservative or reactionary —*n.* **1.** what is right, or just, lawful, proper, etc. [to know *right* from wrong] **2.** *a*) a power, privilege, etc. that a person has or gets by law, nature, tradition, etc. [the *right* of free speech] *b*)

rif·fle (rif′'l) *n.* [< ? or akin to G. *riffel*, a groove: for IE. base see ROW[1]] ☆**1.** *a*) a shoal, reef, etc. in a stream, producing a stretch of ruffled or choppy water *b*) a stretch of such water, or a ripple on it **2.** the act or a method of riffling cards —*vt., vi.* **-fled, -fling 1.** to ruffle or ripple **2.** to leaf rapidly through (a book, etc.) by letting the edges of the pages slip lightly across the thumb **3.** to shuffle (playing cards) in a way like this by holding part of the deck in each hand

riff·raff (rif′raf′) *n.* [< OFr. *rif et raf* < *rifler*, to scrape + *rafle*, a raking in] **1.** those people regarded as worthless, low, coarse, etc.; rabble **2.** [Dial.] trash

ri·fle[1] (rī′f'l) *vt.* **-fled, -fling** [Fr. *rifler*, to scrape < OFr. < MHG. *riffeln*, to scratch] **1.** to cut spiral grooves on the inside of (a gun barrel, etc.) ☆**2.** to hurl or throw with great speed —*n.* ☆**1.** a shoulder gun with spiral grooves cut into the inner surface of the barrel: see RIFLING **2.** [*pl.*] troops armed with rifles

ri·fle[2] (rī′f'l) *vt.* **-fled, -fling** [< OFr. *rifler*, to plunder, orig. to scratch: see prec.] **1.** to ransack in order to rob; pillage; plunder [to *rifle* a safe] **2.** to take as plunder; steal —**ri′fler** *n.*

☆**ri·fle·man** (-mən) *n., pl.* **-men 1.** a soldier armed with a rifle **2.** a man who uses, or is skilled in using, a rifle

rifle range a place for target practice with a rifle

☆**ri·fle·ry** (-rē) *n.* the skill or practice of shooting at targets with rifles

ri·fling (rī′fliŋ) *n.* **1.** the cutting of spiral grooves within a gun barrel, to make the projectile spin when fired **2.** a system of such grooves

rift (rift) *n.* [Dan., a fissure < *rive*, to tear: see RIVE] **1.** an opening caused by splitting; fissure; cleft **2.** an open break in friendly relations —*vt., vi.* to burst open; split

rig (rig) *vt.* **rigged, rig′ging** [< Scand.] **1.** *a*) to fit (a ship, mast, etc.) with sails, shrouds, etc. *b*) to fit (a ship's sails, shrouds, etc.) to the masts, yards, etc. **2.** to fit (*out*); equip **3.** to put together or prepare for use, esp. in a makeshift or hasty way (often with *up*) [to *rig* up a table out of old boxes] **4.** to arrange in a dishonest way; fix [to *rig* an election] **5.** [Colloq.]

or correct report, as of a happening (with *the*) **4.** *a*) the right side [the first door on the *right*] *b*) a turn toward the right side [take a *right* at the corner] **5.** *Boxing a*) the right hand *b*) a blow delivered with the right hand **6.** [*often* **R-**] *Politics* a conservative or reactionary position, party, etc. (often with *the*): from the seating (on the right) of conservatives in some European legislatures —*adv.* **1.** in a straight line; directly [*go right* home] **2.** in a way that is correct, proper, just, favorable, etc.; well [do it *right*] **3.** completely [soaked *right* through his coat] **4.** exactly [*right* here] ☆**5.** immediately [come *right* down] **6.** on or toward the right hand or side **7.** very [he knows *right* well]: colloquial except in certain titles [the *right* reverend] —*interj.* agreed! I understand! —*vt.* **1.** to put in or restore to an upright position [to *right* a capsized boat] **2.** to correct [to *right* an error] **3.** to put in order [she *righted* the room] **4.** to make amends for [to *right* a wrong] —*vi.* to regain an upright position —**by right** (or **rights**) in justice; properly —**in one's own right** through one's own status, ability, etc. —**in the right** on the side supported by truth, justice, etc. —**right away** (or **off**) without delay; at once —**to rights** [Colloq.] in or into proper condition or order —**right′er** *n.* —**right′ness** *n.*

right-a·bout (rīt′ə bout′) *n. same as* RIGHTABOUT-FACE —*adv.,* *adj.* with, in, or by a rightabout-face

right-a·bout-face (-fās′) *n.* **1.** a turning directly about so as to face in the opposite direction **2.** a complete turnabout, as of belief —*interj.* a military command to do a rightabout-face

right angle an angle of 90 degrees, made by the meeting of two straight lines perpendicular to each other

right-an·gled (rīt′aŋ′g'ld) *adj.* having or forming one or more right angles; rectangular: also **right′-an′gle**

RIGHT ANGLE

right·eous (rī′chəs) *adj.* [altered < OE. *rihtwis*: see RIGHT &. -WISE] **1.** acting justly; doing what is right; upright; virtuous [a *righteous* man] **2.** morally right or having a sound moral basis [*righteous* anger] —see SYN. at MORAL —**right′eous·ly** *adv.* —**right′eous·ness** *n.*

following the guide words. Flip pages quickly until the guide words tell you that you are getting close. In your mind, compare the guide words and the word you are looking for. If your word comes before the left-hand guide word in alphabetical order, move farther toward the front of the dictionary. If it comes after the right-hand guide word, look farther toward the back.

Exercises   Using Guide Words

A. Write the numbers 1 through 12 on a sheet of paper. Beside each of the following numerals you will find the guide words for a dictionary page. After the guide words is another word. Decide whether you would find that word on a page *before* the given one, *on* it, or *after* it. Write *before, on,* or *after* on your paper.

1.	**bloodhound**	**blubber**	blowout
2.	**career**	**caribou**	careful
3.	**contact**	**content**	contest
4.	**endive**	**engage**	endow
5.	**frazzle**	**free lance**	freedom
6.	**haze**	**headlight**	haystack
7.	**jubilee**	**jukebox**	juicy
8.	**matted**	**maximum**	mathematics
9.	**Magnolia**	**monopoly**	money
10.	**nonsense**	**northeast**	noodle
11.	**overshot**	**own**	owe
12.	**perilous**	**perk**	period

B. Remember that the purpose of guide words is to help you find words more quickly. See how quickly you can find the following words in your dictionary. Copy the guide words from the page where you find each one.

eggplant	newt	lamprey
iguana	shuffleboard	toad
moose	emu	nautilus
trampoline	anaconda	yak
dolphin	vulture	woodchuck

Part 3 Finding a Word

You may have asked this question before: "How can I look up a word in a dictionary if I'm not sure how to spell it?" You *can* find a word even if you are not sure of the spelling. It will take you more time than it would if you knew the spelling, but you can do it.

On pages 23 and 24 you will find a "Word-Finder Table." This table shows many ways to spell the sounds you may hear at the beginnings of words. To use the table, first find the spellings for the sound you hear. Then check the dictionary under those spellings until you find the word you want.

Word-Finder Table

If the word begins with a sound like . . .	then also try the spellings	as in the words . . .
a in care	ai	air
e in get	a	any
e in here	ea, ee	ear, eerie
f in fine	ph	phrase
g in go	gh, gu	ghoul, guard
h in hat	wh	who
j in jam	g	gym

k in keep	c, ch, q	can, chorus, quick
n in no	gn, kn	gnu, kneel
o in long	a, ou	all, ought
r in red	rh	rhyme
s in sew	c, ps, sc	cent, psychology, scene
sh in ship	s	sure
t in top	th	thyme
u in under	a, o	ago, onion
u in use	you, yu	youth, yule
ur in fur	ear	earn
w in will	wh	wheat
z in zero	x	xylophone

Exercise   Using the Word-Finder Table

Use the Word-Finder Table to find each of the words described below. When you find the word, write its correct spelling beside the number on your paper.

1. the name for a small glass bottle that sounds like *file*
2. the name of an herb that sounds like *time*
3. the name for a wharf or dock that sounds like *key*
4. the name for an African antelope that sounds like *new*
5. a name for a pigtail or a line that sounds like *cue*

Part 4   Word Division

The spelling of a word in the dictionary shows how the word is divided into syllables. Some dictionaries use space to show this. Others use a centered dot.

bub ble   bub·ble

Centered dots are used in the dictionary page shown on pages 20 and 21.

Sometimes, when you are writing or typing a paper, you may find that a long word will not fit at the end of a line. Part of the word will have to run on to the next line. When that happens you should divide the word between syllables. Use a hyphen to show that the word continues on the next line.

Right	Wrong
bub-ble	bu-bble
	bubb-le

Exercises   Word Division

A. Rewrite each of the following words. Show the syllables just as your dictionary does.

jellyfish	bottle	connection
hammer	nameless	parade
helicopter	national	candlestick

B. Use a hyphen to show how you could divide each word at the end of a line. Use a dictionary for help.

gearshift	hacksaw	butterfly
sprocket	chisel	cricket
handlebars	mallet	locust

Part 5   Pronunciation

Sometimes you will use a dictionary to find out how to pronounce a word. Most dictionaries give the pronunciation in parentheses. The pronunciation follows the word itself. As you read the explanation that follows, refer to the dictionary page reproduced on pages 20 and 21.

Accent Marks

In two-syllable words, one syllable gets a stronger emphasis than the other when the word is pronounced. You say **RID**ing and **RI**fle, putting a heavier emphasis on the first syllable in each word. Dictionaries show you where to put this heavier emphasis by using accent marks.

> rid·ing (rīd′iŋ)
> ri·fle (rī′f′l)

The mark (′) following a syllable tells you that the syllable is emphasized, or accented.

In words of more than two syllables, usually two syllables are emphasized. One of the two gets a stronger emphasis than the other. Dictionaries show the two emphasized syllables by using two accent marks. One accent mark is larger and heavier than the other. The syllable with the heavier accent mark gets the heavier emphasis.

> rid·i·cule (rid′i kyo͞ol′)

Respellings

Notice that the respellings of the words on pages 20 and 21 are not exactly the same as the normal spellings. The spelling of the pronunciation is a way of showing the sounds in the word. In the word *right*, the letters *igh* stand for the long *i* sound. The dictionary shows this sound as ī. In the word *ridgepole*, the letters *dge* stand for the same sound as *j* in *jam*. The dictionary shows this sound as *j*.

Most dictionaries use letters of the alphabet in respellings wherever possible. For instance, the letter *b* stands for the first sound in *bat*. Sometimes letters are used in pairs. Many dictionaries use *sh* for the first sound in *sure*.

Some sounds are shown by letters with special marks above them. These marks are called **diacritical marks.** A diacritical mark above a letter shows that it stands for a particular sound. The letter *a* with a short line above it, *ā*, stands for the long *a* sound. This is the sound you hear at the end of the word *pay*. The short line above *a* is a diacritical mark called a **macron.**

A few sounds are shown by special symbols. These symbols are not letters. They are used only to stand for sounds in dictionary respellings.

On pages 27 and 28 is a chart showing respellings that most dictionaries use. After each respelling is a word that shows the sound that the respelling stands for.

Sounds Shown by Letters of the Alphabet

a	ask	b	bat
e	ten	d	dip
i	it	f	fall
u	up	g	get
		h	hat
		j	jump
		k	kick
		l	let
		m	met
		n	not
		p	put
		r	red
		s	sell
		t	top
		v	van
		w	wish
		y	yet
		z	zip

Sounds Shown by Letters in Pairs

oo	look	ch	chip
oi	oil	sh	she
ou	out	th	thin
		th	then
		zh	garage

Sounds Shown by Letters with Diacritical Marks

ā ate
ä hot
ē meet
ī bite
o go
ô law
oo̅ who
yo̅o̅ use

Sounds Shown by Special Symbols

ə ago   ŋ sing

' (shows the sound between *b* and *l* in *bubble*: bub″l)

Not all dictionaries use the same system for respelling words. Your dictionary will have a chart called a **pronunciation key.** This chart will show you the system that your dictionary uses. Most dictionaries print a short version of the pronunciation key at the bottom of every right-hand page. You should study the pronunciation key for your dictionary.

Exercise Pronunciation

Look up each of the following words in your dictionary. Copy the respelling. Be sure to copy the accent marks and diacritical marks and any special symbols that your dictionary uses. Pronounce each of the words.

bucket	difficult	foreign
jewel	masonry	oblique
phonograph	profession	rustle
slight	strawberry	thermometer
turmoil	vacant	weave

Part 6   Definitions

Most often, you will look up a word to find out what it means. Many words in English have more than one meaning. After you find your word, you will have to find the meaning that fits what you are reading.

Try looking up the word *run* in your dictionary. How many definitions are given for it? One dictionary, *Webster's New World Dictionary of the American Language* (Students Edition), gives 45 definitions for this one word!

Look at the definitions for the word *right* on pages 20 and 21. Notice that each different definition has a number. For most of the definitions a phrase or a sentence is given as an example. These examples show how the word is used with a particular definition. The examples may be as much help to you as the definitions themselves.

Exercise   Definitions

Number a sheet of paper from 1–10. Refer to the dictionary entry for *land* on page 30. Write the number of the definition on page 30 that fits each sentence below.

1. Flight 703 will arrive at 6 o'clock and land on runway 24.

2. She hopes to travel to a foreign land.

3. A peninsula is land bordered on three sides by water.

4. I want to leave the city and live out on the land.

5. Ogilvy Construction landed that big urban renewal contract.

6. Munson's second home run landed in the upper deck.

7. The land was too rocky for farming.

8. The package landed right side up.

9. After thirty-seven days at sea, we saw land at last.

10. This land is your land; this land is my land.

Dictionary Entry for <u>Land</u>

land (land) **n.** [OE. < IE. base *lendh-*, heath] **1.** the solid part of the earth's surface not covered by water **2.** *a*) a country, region, etc. [a distant *land*, one's native *land*] *b*) a country's people **3.** ground or soil [rich *land*, high *land*] **4.** ground thought of as property [to invest in *land*] **5.** rural or farming regions [to return to the *land*] **6.** *Econ.* natural resources **—vt. 1.** to put on shore from a ship [the ship *landed* its cargo] **2.** to cause to end up in a particular place or condition [a fight *landed* him in jail] **3.** to set (an aircraft) down on land or water **4.** to catch [to *land* a fish] **5.** [Colloq.] to get or win [to *land* a job] **6.** [Colloq.] to deliver (a blow) **—vi. 1.** to leave a ship and go on shore [the tourists *landed*] **2.** to come to a port or to shore: said of a ship **3.** to arrive at a specified place [he *landed* in Phoenix after a long bus ride] **4.** to alight or come to rest, as after a flight, jump, or fall [the cat *landed* on its feet] **—land on** ☆[Colloq.] to scold or criticize harshly

---

Part 7   Synonyms

As you learned in Chapter 1, **synonyms** are words that have the same meanings. The words *big* and *large* are synonyms. *Happy* and *glad* are also synonyms.

Look at the following dictionary entry for the word *story*. After the definitions you will find the abbreviation SYN. This abbreviation stands for the word *synonym*. A **synonymy** is a list of synonyms for a word.

Dictionary Entry for Story

sto‧ry (stôr‧e) **n.,** *pl.* **-ries** [< OFr. < L. < Gr. *historia:* see HIS-TORY] **1.** the telling of an event or series of events, whether true or made-up; account; narration **2.** an anecdote or joke **3.** a piece of fictional writing shorter than a novel; narrative; tale; specif., *same as* SHORT STORY **4.** the plot of a novel, play, etc. **5.** *a)* a report or rumor *b)* [Colloq.] a falsehood or fib **6.** romantic legend or history ☆**7.** a news event or a report of it, as in the newspapers **—vt. -ried, -ry‧ing** to decorate with paintings, etc. of scenes from history or legend

SYN.—story is a general term for any informative or entertaining account, either oral or written, of something that really happened or that is partly or wholly made-up; **narrative,** a more formal term, is typically a prose account of a happening or series of happenings, either real or fictional; **tale** usually means a simple, leisurely story, more or less loosely organized, esp. one that is made-up or legendary; **anecdote** is a term applied to a short, entertaining, often instructive account of a single incident, usually personal or biographical

Notice that the synonymy for *story* does more than just list synonyms. Three words are given with meanings close to *story.* They are *narrative, tale,* and *anecdote.* The synonymy explains the special meaning and use of each of these words. Sometimes a synonymy will also give sample phrases or sentences to show how each synonym is used.

A synonymy can help you choose the best word for what you want to say. Did that disaster movie *scare, frighten,* or *terrify* the audience? A synonymy will tell you just what the differences among the three words are. Then you can choose the best one.

Exercise   Synonyms

Use your dictionary to find two synonyms for each of the following words. Use each synonym in a sentence to show its specific meaning.

strong	fast	sloppy	support
mystery	praise	impolite	journey
neat	lean	beautiful	obvious

The purpose of this part of the chapter is to see how well you understand how to get information from a dictionary.

A.   Arrange the following words in alphabetical order as they would appear in a dictionary.

shout	say	chatter
whisper	murmur	rave
announce	grumble	growl
cry	mutter	scream
declare	call	mumble

B.   Below are the guide words for ten dictionary pages. Copy the guide words on your paper. Beside each pair, write a word that you would find on that page.

cannon ------------------ cantaloupe
elephant -------------------- ellipse
himself --------------------- hire
mariachi ------------------- market
new------------------------- nice
pasta ----------------------- patent
propel ----------------- proposition
rural ----------------------- Ruth
stance------------------- standoff
try----------------------- tubular

C.   What are two other ways to spell the sound that *s* stands for in *sew*?

D.   Divide each of the following words into syllables.

frisbee	dachshund	mummy	nonresident
salmon	designate	gluttony	specific
calabash	hibachi	pretzel	graphology

E. Write the pronunciation for each of the following words.

mountain	desert	butte
demonstrate	freight	ladle
valley	tundra	mahogany
prevention	semicolon	toboggan

F. Read the sentences below. Each of the italicized words has an unusual meaning. Use your dictionary to find the meanings.

1. He didn't win, but we all admired his *pluck*.
2. Fred's Diner isn't one of my favorite *haunts*.
3. I'd play you a tune, but I can't find my *plectrum*.
4. We'll know how good the day's shooting was when we see the *rushes*.
5. The water for the water cooler is delivered in a *carboy*.
6. The sound of the fire alarm put everyone in a *flap*.
7. The *launch* is sinking!
8. The edges of a quarter are *milled*.
9. No *nostrum* will cure this disease.
10. The cows were *lowing* in the meadow.

Chapter 3

Writing
the
Paragraph

The basic tool for organizing ideas in any kind of writing is the paragraph. If you can write a good paragraph, you have found the key to writing a good composition or report. A paragraph is a group of sentences that *develop* a thought, or idea. In this chapter, you will learn some new ways to organize your ideas within a paragraph and review some of the ways you have already studied.

Part 1 What Is a Paragraph?

A paragraph is *a group of closely related sentences dealing with a single topic or idea.* The main topic or idea is usually stated in the first sentence. The rest of the paragraph contains several more sentences that explain the main idea more fully. Let's look at an example of a well written paragraph.

> The vaquero while working cattle rode hard and was hard on horses, but he never abused them to make a spectacle. The way the vaquero went about taming a horse was not always gentle, but he was not deliberately cruel. He had applied his military riding to the herding of cattle. He never overestimated the intelligence of his mustang, and had studied the degree to which a horse could be taught. He had learned that patience and repetition were the only means to success in teaching the horse. He never asked the animal to do more than could be expected of it.—ARNOLD R. ROJAS

The first sentence tells you that the paragraph is going to be about the treatment of horses. The rest of the sentences give you further information, and they are all related. When all of the sentences in a paragraph are related, and talk about one topic only, we say that the paragraph has **unity.**

Study the following paragraph. Do all the sentences work together to explain the idea that is presented in the first sentence? Do any of the other sentences relate to the first sentence? Does the paragraph have unity? If not, what is wrong with the paragraph?

> Driver's training should be a required course in every high school in the United States. Defensive driving means anticipating what the guy in the next car will do. Millions of people are killed by automobiles every year. Insurance statistics have not proved that teen-agers are unsafe drivers. Many insurance companies offer lower insurance to students who have completed driver's training.

After reading the first sentence, you expect the rest of the paragraph to explain why driver's training should be a required course in high school. However, each of the next three sentences states a completely different idea. The sentences offer no explanation at all. Only the last sentence is related to the idea expressed in the first sentence. Therefore the paragraph does not have unity because it does not develop the topic. It is merely a series of unrelated sentences.

Exercise   Unity in Paragraphs

In each of the following paragraphs, one or more sentences do not relate to the others. In each paragraph, pick out any sentences that do not relate to the others, and thus destroy the unity of the paragraph.

1

There is more to deep-sea diving than putting on a wet suit and an iron mask. There are treasures at the bottom of the Atlantic and Pacific Oceans. A diver must know all there is to know about his equipment and his tools. Working alone 200 feet under water is no job for a bungler.

2

Training is the best break any person can give a dog. Never whip your dog. It takes time and patience to train a dog. Sometimes, in order to train a dog, you will have to pass up an afternoon in the ball field. It's all worth it, though —a thousand times over. Your dog will love you even more for it.

3

Senses are so basic that all animals have them, but not all animals use their senses in the same way. Many people have lost their sense of hearing. A frog's eye, for instance, does not see a fly as we see it—in terms of legs, shape of wings, and number of eyes. In fact, a frog won't spot a fly at all unless the fly moves. Frogs are amphibious animals. Put a frog into a cage with freshly killed insects, and it will starve.

4

My cousin and I learned most of our family's history by playing in Grandmother's attic. Grandmother lived in a little town in Ohio. In one corner stood a brass-bound trunk, filled with forgotten dolls once treasured by aunts and mothers.

Grandfather's World War I uniform hung proudly on a metal rack, along with once-stylish dresses. The clothing now is much more comfortable than it was thirty years ago. When we played with toys our mothers had played with, or dressed up in the old-fashioned clothes, we felt that the past was truly part of our lives.

5

I guess I've been on every kind of diet ever invented or thought of. Many books on diets have been published recently. I remember the time I resolved to eat only fruit and cottage cheese. I gained three pounds, and to this day I hate the sight of cottage cheese. Then there was the B diet: boiled eggs and bananas. I ate so many bananas that I felt like King Kong. The trouble was, I was still shaped like him too.

6

Jeff Daniels is completely deaf, yet he knows when his telephone rings or his alarm clock goes off. His "hearing ear" dog, Rags, tells him. Rags, who was trained by the American Humane Association, alerts his master whenever there is a knock on the door or a phone call, and leads Jeff to the source of the sound. Seeing-eye dogs are used by people who are blind.

7

When the night of the dance arrived, I was in despair. Miserably, I stared into the bathroom mirror. The mirror was large and clear. It was still there—an enormous pimple, like a blossom on my chin. I tried to stay calm as I considered my choices. I could hardly wear a veil. Veils simply weren't in style at Forrest High, especially for boys. I could break my date, but that solution seemed too drastic. Gloria would never speak to me again. She was the most popular girl in school. I would just have to depend on my personality.

8

The word *slothful* has come to mean lazy and careless, but sloths survive in the jungle because of their slowness. Some sloths have two toes; others have three toes. Sloths live high in the trees and have no protection against hawks and eagles, their natural enemies. Sloths sleep most of the day, and when they do move, they travel as slowly as a windup toy with a weak spring. Only the sharpest eyes can detect their movement in the trees. Hawks and eagles can pick up heavy animals in their large claws.

Part 2 The Topic Sentence

To make sure that all the sentences in a paragraph are related to each other, every paragraph should have a topic sentence. The **topic sentence** is usually the first sentence of the paragraph, and it tells what the rest of the paragraph is going to be about. You will find, through your reading and study, that a writer may sometimes put the topic sentence in the middle or at the end of a paragraph. For our present study, however, you will be concerned with the topic sentence at the beginning of a paragraph only.

From the point of view of both a writer and a reader, the topic sentence is important. Because it usually comes at the beginning of the paragraph, and states the main idea, the topic sentence helps you, as a writer, to *focus* on that main idea. That is, it helps you to keep track of your ideas so that you do not bring in ideas that are not related to your main idea. The topic sentence acts as a guide by telling the reader what the rest of the paragraph is going to be about.

To understand more clearly what a topic sentence is, look at the following paragraph.

My husband had very definite opinions about raising children. He believed that parents should provide proper images for their children and should give them guidelines as to what they can and cannot do. Some of his basic aims were to see that our girls are taught to face reality, to accept themselves, to be able to function under supervision, receive some formal training and education, and be made

to realize that it was their spiritual and moral duty to help oppressed people. He believed that children should have a belief in a tradition and that this should come originally from the home. He did not believe in spoiling children.
—BETTY SHABAZZ

In this paragraph, the first sentence is the topic sentence. It states what the rest of the paragraph will be about.

The topic sentence says: "My husband had very definite opinions about raising children." The remainder of the paragraph then explains those opinions. You can see that the topic sentence has stated the main idea of the paragraph. Because all of the sentences that follow are related to the topic sentence, the paragraph is unified.

Exercises   The Topic Sentence

A. In each of the following groups there are several sentences giving specific details that could be used to develop a paragraph, and one sentence giving a general idea that could be used as a topic sentence. Decide which sentence in each group would work best as the topic sentence.

1. a. Living things are organic matter.

 b. Things that were never alive, such as minerals and glass, are inorganic matter.

 c. Lumber, wood, and cotton were once alive, so they are organic matter.

 d. Anything that takes up space in the world is called "matter."

 e. Matter can't be destroyed, but it can be changed into energy.

2. a. Jack drinks so much milk that Dad jokes about buying a cow.

 b. His standard question after school is "What's for dinner?"

c. When Jack packs his school lunch, it looks like a grocery bag.

d. My brother Jack claims that his hobby is eating.

e. Mom is threatening to put a padlock on the refrigerator.

3. a. The trees were outlined in shimmering white garments.

b. The old garage wore a fresh white coat of snow-paint.

c. The bushes in front of the garage were heavy with cotton-ball snow blossoms.

d. Our yard looked magically different after the heavy winter snow.

e. The bird bath by the house had become a comical white gnome.

4. a. Giraffes are the tallest living animals, but sometimes their height can cost them their lives.

b. Every time the giraffe takes a drink of water, he is in peril.

c. The giraffe can't drink easily because he can't kneel down.

d. It takes the giraffe a long time to bend its legs apart.

e. While he is drinking, he is helpless if a lion or tiger attacks.

5. a. When my little brother had the measles, Mrs. Paulson played checkers with him every day.

b. Mrs. Paulson is always baking cookies for us.

c. Mrs. Paulson bandages our scraped knees without scolding us for being careless.

d. Bespectacled Mrs. Paulson is like a grandmother to everyone in the neighborhood.

e. I guess everyone on the block has had her for a babysitter at one time or another.

6. a. Why is it that a boy is dressed when he puts on clothes, but a chicken is dressed by having its feathers plucked?

b. Why do you trim hair by taking some off, but trim a dress by adding something?

c. Anyone who can learn English as a second language is a genius, as far as I'm concerned.

d. The list of examples would confuse the most scholarly Chinese gentlemen.

e. It doesn't seem sensible to spell words like *thumb* and *lamb* by adding a *b* at the end.

7. a. If you are a "litterbug," make up your mind to reform.

b. Put candy wrappers and scrap paper in your pocket if no waste container is handy.

c. Pollution is a big problem that we can all help solve in little ways.

d. When you are camping out, wrap up your garbage and dispose of it properly.

e. Don't bury cans or bottles; take them with you until you can dispose of them properly.

8. a. Generally, a cowboy rode the range for only about seven years before he settled down in town or on his own ranch.

b. A large number of cowboys were Mexican, Indian, or black.

c. Most cowboys were young; the average cowboy was about twenty-four.

d. The real version of the American cowboy was quite different from the John Wayne image seen in movies.

e. Most cowboys had very little "book learning;" many couldn't even write their own names.

B. Select one of the preceding groups of sentences and write a unified paragraph. You may revise the topic sentence and related sentences to help them work together better. You may also add words where necessary to create better unity.

Part 3 Writing Topic Sentences

The topic sentence is usually the first sentence of a paragraph. As you have already seen, it helps the writer to focus on the main idea. However, to be effective, the topic sentence must also do two other jobs:

1. It must be narrow enough so that the topic can be covered easily in one paragraph.

2. It must be interesting enough to catch the reader's attention.

Narrowing the Topic

Sometimes, in writing a topic sentence, a writer may choose an idea that is *too broad* or *too general* to be covered in a single paragraph. Suppose you began a paragraph like this:

> *There are many kinds of dogs.*

This subject is so broad that about all you can do is list the different kinds of dogs. The paragraph would probably be as dull to write as it would be to read.

Suppose you revised the topic sentence like this:

> *The poodle has played a starring role in the history of dog-dom.*

The words *starring role* probably make you curious about just how the poodle figured so importantly in the history of dog-dom. In addition, the writer has narrowed her topic so that the subject may be covered in one paragraph. She goes on to supply more specific information.

The Poodle has played a starring role in the history of dog-dom. It is believed to have originated in Russia, where black standard-sized poodles were used as water retrievers for bird hunters. The Russians called the dog "pudel," which literally means "splashing in water." The breed spread to northern Germany, where the brown color was introduced. German artists as early as the fifteenth century depicted the poodle, and the great Spanish artist, Goya, used this breed in several of his paintings. The first evidence of a toy poodle's existence came from England, where the "White Cuban" breed, said to have originated in Cuba, became an English favorite. Queen Anne had several poodles during her reign in the early eighteenth century.—EVELYN MILLER

The writer has narrowed her topic sufficiently to develop her paragraph in an informative and interesting way.

Writing Interesting Topic Sentences

If a topic sentence is dull and uninteresting, the reader may not want to read the rest of the paragraph. Certainly any writer who puts time and effort into writing wants it to be read.

Look at the following topic sentence:

I'd like to tell you about the use of teaching machines in the schools of the future.

In this sentence, the topic is narrow enough, and it makes clear what the rest of the paragraph is going to be about, but it is dull and unimaginative.

Now, look at this topic sentence:

"In the World of Tomorrow, teaching machines will be designed to work only as fast (or as slowly) as the students using them, taking into account different learning rates."

Your response to that sentence might be, "Gee, that sounds interesting. Tell me more." The writer has caught your attention, and you want to read the rest of the paragraph to find out more about those teaching machines of the future.

In the World of Tomorrow, teaching machines will be designed to work only as fast (or as slowly) as the students using them, taking into account different learning rates. They will offer the child individual attention. They will possibly offer more patience than could be expected from the average teacher. They will offer immediate feedback so that the child knows how well he is doing and can take pride in his progress. More than that, the machines will help make learning fun.

In writing the topic sentence, remember the following:

1. It helps you, the writer, by keeping your ideas in focus.

2. It acts as a guide by letting the reader know what the paragraph is going to be about.

3. It should be narrow enough to cover the ideas easily in one paragraph.

4. It should be interesting enough to catch the reader's attention.

Exercises   Working with Topic Sentences

A. Here is a list of poorly written topic sentences. They are either too broad, too uninteresting, or both. Decide what is wrong with each sentence. Then rewrite the sentence so that it becomes sufficiently narrow to be covered in a paragraph and interesting enough to catch a reader's attention.

1. In this paragraph I am going to explain several ways of conserving energy.
2. Summer is the best time of the year.
3. Mother invited my teacher to dinner.
4. This story about a blind deer made me very sad.
5. There are many ways to raise money when you need it.
6. Younger brothers take advantage of their sisters.
7. My favorite sports are basketball and soccer.

8. This literary masterpiece is going to be about someone I've known for years—me.

9. I like all kinds of music.

10. We had lots of fun at Rhonda's birthday party.

11. It was easy to see that our camp had been visited.

12. America is a land of heroes.

B. In the following paragraphs, the topic sentences have been removed, leaving only the supporting details. Read each of these paragraphs carefully. Then, for each paragraph, write a good topic sentence. Be sure that your sentence is not too broad, and be sure to make it interesting enough to catch the reader's attention.

(1)

Some employers simply refused to hire women except as secretaries or typists. Employers frequently didn't promote women even though they were fully qualified. When workers had to be laid off, women were often the first to be fired. Even now, women are often paid less than men for doing the same work.

(2)

In cities, all deliveries were by horse and wagon. Horses moved urban local passengers, whether by carriage, omnibus, or horse-drawn streetcar. Stagecoaches bore passengers, mail, and baggage across rough and dusty Western roads, negotiating steep grades and fording unbridged streams with utmost unconcern. After 1840, teams of fast trotting horses for light coaches flourished in the East.

3

He was a husky, long-legged chap, to me a perfect physical specimen. I asked him where he'd been, and he replied that he had been climbing the foothills north of town. I asked him why he did it. He told me that his doctor had advised it; that he was trying to correct certain difficulties following an illness. He was climbing the foothills every day to develop his lungs and legs.

4

The dynamite had been frozen and thawed so many times that its paper covering had absorbed the nitroglycerine, making it dangerous no matter how carefully it was handled. In fact, dynamite like that sometimes explodes when two sticks of it are pulled apart, as the ghosts of a good many miners could tell you.

5

There they were—thirty-six whales pulled up on the shore. Every one of them weighed up to 4,000 pounds and measured nearly twenty feet long. They were the true monsters of the deep, the "black-fish" in Melville's famous story of the killer whale, *Moby Dick*.

6

They took him into a room where there were only some boxes and three bananas hanging from the ceiling. They wanted to see how long it would take the chimp to pile up the boxes and climb on them. The chimp did not touch the boxes. He pushed one of the men under the bananas, crawled up on his back, and brought the bananas down in two minutes.

7

The skill of designing silver jewelry is handed down from generation to generation. A boy whose father is a silversmith learned to fashion silver coins into buttons. "Pesh-la-kai" is the Navajo word for silversmith. When a boy or man becomes skillful in making silver jewelry, he can take the name Peshlakai for his last name.

8

In 1970, our daily consumption of petroleum was 14.7 million barrels; in 1973, it was 17.3 million barrels (14 percent more than that of Western Europe, whose population is nearly two-thirds greater than ours). Oil provides nearly half our energy. Five years ago, we were importing 3.4 million barrels a day. Today, though we remain the world's largest oil producer, we import 6.2 million barrels, about 38 percent of what we use.

Chapter 4

Developing the Paragraph

In writing, just as in cooking, you may have all the ingredients for a good product. The trick lies in putting them together. If there is a single basic rule for writing a good paragraph, it is this: *Use only those ingredients that develop the main idea.*

"How long does a paragraph have to be?" is a question asked by many beginning writers. The answer is easier than you might suppose: A *paragraph should be long enough to develop a central idea.* For example, the following paragraph is too short to explain the topic sentence clearly:

Almost all of us boys agreed that Jack was the luckiest boy in town. To our envious eyes, he had everything a boy could ever wish for.

Why was Jack lucky? What did he have? The questions can be answered only by including more details.

Almost all of us boys agreed that Jack was the luckiest boy in town. He had his own minibike, and lots of space to ride it in. When he was tired of that, Fallah, his black mare, stood waiting patiently in the stable. No matter what he asked his Dad for, it miraculously appeared the next day. He even had his own pool table. Furthermore, he didn't have to do chores like the rest of us. The gardener and the stable boy took care of the chores. To our envious eyes, he had everything a boy could ever wish for.

You can see how the detailed information has given you a clearer picture of why Jack was considered the luckiest boy in town.

You already know that a good paragraph is introduced by a topic sentence that catches the reader's attention and tells what the paragraph will be about. What do you do next? How do you support or develop your topic sentence? This chapter will discuss the following ways of developing a topic sentence:

1. By using specific details
2. By using facts or figures
3. By using an example
4. By using a definition

Part 1 Using Specific Details

When you write, you want to share an experience with your reader. No one else in the world sees things in exactly the same way you do. Once you have decided what you want to say, you hope to communicate your ideas clearly so that your reader will, for a moment, see life through your eyes.

Suppose you wrote, "The bird sang in the tree." You have not really painted a clear picture, nor an interesting one. What kind of bird? What kind of tree? You need more specific details to help your reader "see" what you are writing about. If instead you write, "The fat old bluejay chattered angrily in the old pine tree," your picture is much more vivid and will catch your reader's attention.

Suppose you wanted to write about a person. Each person has some special distinction—something in the way he or she looks, or dresses, or acts—which makes that person an individual. These are the specific details you would choose to write about in describing that person. For example, look at the following description written by the early English poet, Geoffrey Chaucer:

> His beard was broader than a shovel, and red
> As a fat sow or fox. A wart stood clear
> Atop his nose, and red as a pig's ear
> A tuft of bristles on it. Black and wide
> His nostrils were.

What a clear picture we have of the person Chaucer is describing, all because of the choice of specific details.

Let's look at another description.

> She was a black child, with huge green eyes that seemed to glow in the dark. From the age of four on she had a look of being full-grown. The look was in her muscular, well-defined limbs that seemed like they could do a woman's work and in her way of seeing everything around her. Most times she was alive and happy. The only thing wrong with her was that she got hurt so easy. The slightest rebuke sent her crying; the least hint of disapproval left her moody and depressed for hours. But on the other side of it was that she had a way of springing back from pain. No matter how hurt she had been, she would be her old self by the next day.—JEAN WHEELER SMITH

Notice the writer's choice of such specific details as "a black child, with huge green eyes," "her muscular, well defined limbs," "alive and happy." These details help us to see the child as a specific individual.

Specific details are also used to describe places or things, as in the following example:

> Our tent was next to the last in a row of several others just like it—a square of brown canvas curtains with a roof sloped like a pyramid, held up by a pole that peeped through a vent at the top. The plank floors of the tents were set up on bricks, the ends of the timbers sticking out in front, making a shelf which we used for a porch. The roof was held down by ropes staked down at the four corners and along the sides. Between the tents there were lean-to's where the women cooked and washed clothes in iron tubs, heating the water over stone fire pits. The swamp came up close in back, and in front spilled into a ditch, making a moat that separated the camp from the tracks just beyond. Over this ditch there was a catwalk of planks leading to the tracks, the main street of the neighborhood.—ERNESTO GALARZA

From these carefully chosen details, the reader gets a clear and interesting picture of what this camp on the outskirts of the village looks like.

Exercise   Developing a Paragraph by Using Specific Details

Following is a list of topic sentences, each one of which may be expanded into a paragraph by using specific details. Choose two of the topic sentences that interest you. Using specific details, develop each of the sentences into a well written paragraph. You will need to use your imagination to complete these paragraphs.

1. Old Rob was certainly a different kind of dog.
2. Not a breath stirred over the free and open prairie.
3. Walking from the marble terrace, we entered the central hall of the mansion.

4. The man from Neptune looked nothing like an earthman.

5. Sam was in his early fifties, and the hair that showed under his hat was iron gray.

6. The old peddler's cart was piled high with fruits and vegetables of every description.

7. It was a furnished room and they had moved enough stuff into it to furnish three rooms its size.

8. The man stood alone, like a bird watcher.

9. It would be dawn soon.

10. Every day I explored a little more of the river.

11. At night I dreamed of nothing but the cat.

12. For the rest of my life, I shall never forget the guest who came to our house that afternoon last September.

13. The house—the largest one in the village—sat on the crest of a low hill.

14. Lencho was an ox of a boy.

15. Above him, high on the cliff, stood the wild stallion.

Part 2 Using Facts or Figures

Sometimes a topic sentence makes a statement that is best developed through the use of specific facts or figures.

> Near the end of the nineteenth century, many American newspapers became filled with abuses and excesses. The type of journalism that became fashionable was called "yellow journalism." It was stimulated in the 1890's by a circulation war between William Randolph Hearst's *New York Journal* and Joseph Pulitzer's *New York World*. In their fight for leadership, the *Journal* and the *World* reached great circulation figures by resorting to techniques of sensationalism. The largest and most prominently featured stories were those concerned with crime, divorce, scandal, and gossip. Large headlines were used as well as "faked" pictures and false interviews.—DAVID J. GOLDMAN

The writer begins his paragraph with a statement: "Near the end of the nineteenth century, many American newspapers became filled with abuses and excesses." He then develops that statement by giving *specific facts*:

1. The abuses were caused by a circulation war.
2. The newspapers resorted to techniques of sensationalism.
3. They prominently featured stories of crime, divorce, scandal, and gossip.
4. They used large headlines, "faked" pictures, and false interviews.

Here is another example:

> Until the 1930's, many Americans believed that anyone who couldn't work was lazy and shouldn't be helped by the government. The experience of the Great Depression (1929–1939) changed that. From 1931 to 1940, the unemployment rate was never less than 14 percent of the total work force. In 1933, the worst year of the Depression, 25 percent (one out of every four persons) couldn't find a job—any job.
> —MARC ROSENBLUM

The writer tells us in his topic sentence that "Until the 1930's, many Americans believed that anyone who couldn't work was lazy. . . ." He then points out that the Great Depression changed that idea. He uses *specific figures* to develop this point.

1. From 1931 to 1940 the unemployment rate was never less than 14 percent.
2. In 1933, the worst year of the Depression, the unemployment rate was 25 percent.

He uses these figures to indicate that there was more than laziness as a reason for a person's not working.

Exercise   Developing a Paragraph by Using Facts or Figures

Following is a list of topic sentences, each one of which may be expanded into a paragraph by using facts or figures. Choose two of the topic sentences that interest you. Using facts or figures, develop each of these topic sentences into a well written paragraph. You may have to do some outside reading in order to complete this assignment. However, make sure the paragraph is your own work. Do not copy the paragraph from some other source.

1. There is proof that the 55 m.p.h. speed limit saves lives.
2. Our wild animals are disappearing too rapidly.
3. Modern highways are killers.
4. It is not too soon to plan for a career.
5. Father penguin helps to "babysit" with his children.
6. The discovery of King Tut's tomb was due to Howard Carter.
7. The Catskill Mountains in New York are a beautiful vacation area.
8. It's easy to spot poison ivy if you know what to look for.
9. The platypus is one of the world's oldest animals.
10. George Washington Carver helped make peanuts big business.
11. The Galapagos Islands are a scientist's treasure trove.
12. *Tyrannosaurus Rex* was the fiercest of all dinosaurs.

Part 3 Using an Example

Sometimes a topic sentence may be a statement that is best developed through the use of a specific example. Using a specific example is not too different from using specific facts or figures. However, by using one specific example, a writer can go into more detail in one paragraph than is possible when using several facts or figures. A specific example can also create a greater emotional impact on the reader than facts or figures.

Poverty can be measured by more than income. There are five people in Cass Tanner's family. They live in a one-bedroom apartment. The building they live in is in violation of at least fifteen city building-code regulations. There is exposed electrical wiring. The plumbing does not work properly. In January, during five days of subfreezing weather, the heat did not go above fifty-five degrees. Cass wakes up each night to make sure that his brothers and sisters are not bothered by rats. Mr. Tanner's take-home pay from a part-time job is $380 per month. The rent is $105 per month. —WILLIAM F. SAALBACH

In this paragraph, the topic sentence, "Poverty can be measured by more than income," becomes understandable and dramatically clear through the specific example of the poverty of the Tanner family.

You may have noticed that the paragraph also contains facts and figures. However, these facts and figures explain the *specific example of the poverty of the Tanners.* If the writer had developed the paragraph by facts or figures as was done in the preceding section, he would have told us that there are many families who live in small apartments, that many families do not have enough heat, that their plumbing does not work properly, or that their homes are infested with rats. By using an example of a specific family, however, the writer gives his reader a feeling of personal involvement with an individual rather than with poor people in general.

Let's look at another paragraph.

Life in this electronic age is tough on kids. Two sixth-graders felt the call of the fishpole one afternoon, and took along their walkie-talkies. Word of this got to the teacher, who borrowed a walkie-talkie from another student. The teacher tuned in and, sure enough, heard the truants, whereupon he promptly cut in to suggest that they appear in the classroom post-haste. They did.—JOHN BROWN

In this paragraph, the writer could have developed his topic sentence by giving several facts about the electronic age being "tough on kids." However, by focusing on the specific example, he gives us a humorous and personal view of how the electronic age is tough on kids.

Exercise **Developing a Paragraph by Using an Example**

Following is a list of topic sentences, each one of which may be developed into a paragraph by using an example. Choose two of the topic sentences that interest you. Using specific examples, develop each topic sentence into a well written paragraph.

1. Daydreams can save your sanity.
2. Not everything that glitters is made of gold.
3. You're never too old to learn to ride a bike.
4. I never believed in ghosts.
6. My dog taught me the meaning of kindness.
7. One today is worth two tomorrows.
8. Running away never solved a problem.
9. You're never too old to cry.
10. Buying a gift for a friend is a pleasurable experience.
11. Just call me "pathfinder."
12. A familiar face in a strange place is a sure cure for loneliness.
13. It's best to let some "fish" get away.
14. People do the craziest things when they think no one is watching.

Part 4 Using a Definition

There are some times when a writer may wish to use a word or an idea that may not be familiar to the reader. To make certain that the word or idea will not confuse the reader, the writer will *define* the word or the idea.

In any definition there are three parts:

1. The word or idea to be defined
2. The general class to which the word or idea belongs
3. The particular characteristic that sets the word or idea apart from the other members of the general class

Study the following examples:

Term To Be Defined	General Class	Particular Characteristics
Hypnotism is	a kind of sleep . . .	induced by motions of the hands or other suggestions.
A tariff is	a tax	placed on certain goods brought into a country.
A pilgrim is	a person	who travels to a sacred place.
A quarterback is . .	a football player . .	who directs the team.
Sorrow is	a feeling of grief . .	that comes from suffering, loss, or regret.
Geography is	a science	dealing with the earth and its life.
A granary is	a building	in which grain is stored.

In writing definitions, a writer must be careful not to make the following errors:

1. Defining the word by using *where* or *when.* For example:

"Sorrow is when a person feels grief," or "A granary is where grain is stored." *Sorrow* is not a "when"; it is a feeling. A *granary* is not a "where"; it is a building.

2. Defining a word with the same word or a variation of the same word. For example:

"Hypnotism is the process of hypnotizing."

3. Putting the word into too large a general class. For example:

> "A granary is a *place* where grain is stored."

A good definition is most useful to the reader when it is accompanied with explanation and illustration. Therefore, the definition is often expanded into a paragraph, as in the following examples:

1

Water that is fit to drink is called *potable water*. It must be clear and colorless, pleasant-tasting, free of harmful bacteria, and fairly free of dissolved solids. Although distilled water is pure, it does not make the best drinking water. Small amounts of mineral matter and air in the water make it taste better, unlike distilled water which has a "flat" taste.—TRACY, TROPP, AND FRIEDL

2

Empathy is a feeling of positive regard for others—being able to sense how the other person is feeling and the emotion taking place. It also takes in the ability to communicate the feeling back to that person in the receiver's own words. It means "the ability to walk in another person's moccasins." —GWEN MOJADO

3

Genuineness is a feeling of being authentic. It is the ability to be yourself and share your feelings with others. Some people feel they have to create some distance between themselves and others. They find it somewhat threatening or risky to reveal themselves totally as a "real" person. Hence, they hold up a facade as a protective curtain to shield themselves from being hurt. To be genuine means to be able to share the "real" you.—GWEN MOJADO

In these paragraphs, the definitions function as the topic sentences. Each definition contains the three necessary parts.

Term To Be Defined	General Class	Particular Characteristic
Potable water is ...	water	that is fit to drink.
Empathy is	a feeling	of positive regard for others.
Genuineness is ...	a feeling	of being authentic.

The other sentences in each paragraph give additional details about the word being defined, so that the reader has a clear understanding of what the word means.

Exercises Developing a Paragraph by Using a Definition

A. Before writing a paragraph developed by definition, you need to make certain that you can tell what a good definition is. In the following sentences, parts of the definition are missing. The general class may be too large, the particular characteristic may be missing, the word may have been defined as where or when, or the word may have been defined with the same word. Correct each of the definitions. You may wish to divide your paper into three columns, each with its specific heading.

1. A good friend is a person who is honest with you.
2. Play is activity.
3. A novel is written in prose.
4. Studying is when you read and think.
5. A dog is an animal that eats flesh.
6. A fly has two wings.
7. C.O.D. is a commercial term.
8. A bicycle is a machine with two wheels.
9. A friend is a person who can be trusted.
10. Quarantine is where you're isolated because you're sick.
11. Law is a rule of action.

12. The sun is something that gives off light and heat.

13. Anthropology is all about people.

14. A lyric is a song.

15. Graduation is the act of being graduated.

16. R.S.V.P. is when you answer somebody's invitation.

17. A hat is a thing people wear on their heads.

18. Passing a course is where you get above a certain grade.

19. A carrot is something to eat.

20. A laboratory is where scientific studies are made.

B. Following is a list of topics that may be expanded into paragraphs by using definitions. Choose two of the topics that interest you. Write a topic sentence containing a three-part definition for each of your topics. Expand your topic sentences into well written paragraphs.

motorcycle	snob
sorceress	elevator
honor	energy
rectangle	conservation
minnow	equality
loyalty	fad
carburetor	helicopter
friend	nitrogen
leaf	love

Chapter 5

Kinds of Paragraphs

If you have ever baked a cake, you know that some cakes are blended together differently from others, and contain different ingredients. When you write a paragraph, you are using words and sentences as ingredients. You must decide what kind of paragraph you want to write, just as you must decide what kind of cake you are going to make before you begin.

What is the main idea of your paragraph? Do you want it to tell a story? Do you want to describe something? Do you want to explain something to your reader? When you decide on the purpose of your paragraph, there are some things you can do that will make your blending easier and more successful.

There are three major kinds of paragraphs, and each is put together in a slightly different way.

1. The narrative paragraph
2. The descriptive paragraph
3. The explanatory paragraph

Part 1   The Narrative Paragraph

In its simplest form, the narrative paragraph tells a story. When you tell a friend what happened on the way to school, or about the program you saw on TV, or about your friend's experience at camp, you probably tell what happened in the order the events took place. This is called **chronological order.** It is an easy, natural way of writing, just as it is a natural way of speaking.

The First-Person Narrative Paragraph

Your first reaction to writing about events might be, "What events? What can I write about?" Things happen to you every day—funny things, serious things, exciting things. Your problem as a beginning writer is to turn these events into an interesting paragraph. When you write about something that happened to you yourself, you are writing a **first-person narrative** paragraph.

Suppose you decide to write a paragraph about your first ride on a motorcycle. Your first thought may be, "Gee, my first motorcycle ride really was exciting, but how can I write a paragraph about it?"

Take a few minutes to plan your paragraph before you begin to write. How did you feel about riding on a motorcycle? Were you enthusiastic or frightened? Whose motorcycle was it? These are the details that can give your paragraph a logical beginning.

Next, think of how you felt when you were actually on the motorcycle. Was it like riding a roller coaster? a fast bicycle? Can you develop your paragraph by using an incident or anecdote? The ride itself will probably form the middle of your paragraph. Can you round off your paragraph by using a final sentence that brings it to a satisfactory conclusion?

Following is an example of how your paragraph might look when you have finished writing and revising it:

> I was torn between panic and pleasure when Pete offered to drive me to school on his new motorcycle. Suppose I fell off? My hands felt clammy-cold at the thought. Bravely, I managed a weak smile. With fingers shaking, I buckled on the helmet Pete offered and hoisted myself behind him. With a roar like a jet, we took off down the street. Gradually, I relaxed my knuckle-white grip and looked around. It was like skimming over the streets on a sleek, two-wheeled space ship. By the time we reached school, all my fears had been blown away by the force of the wind around us. The motorcycle seemed like an old friend, and I had been the first girl in school to ride on it.

The paragraph begins with a topic sentence, then tells what happened in chronological order. The specific details are interesting and expressed with imagination. The experience has created a vivid impression on the reader.

Exercise   Writing a First-Person Narrative Paragraph

Following is a list of topic sentences that may be developed into first-person narrative paragraphs. Choose one of these sentences, or one of your own, and develop it into a well written paragraph.

1. Sometimes, exciting things happen when you least expect them.

2. I still blush when I think of my most embarrassing experience.

3. It was the funniest April Fool trick I had ever played.

4. I knew something was going to happen the moment I woke up.

5. It was a baby-sitting job I'll never forget.

6. It was my first speech, and I tried not to show how nervous I felt.

7. It's hard being the ＿＿＿＿＿＿ child in the family.

8. Last summer, I did something I've never done before.

9. I was determined to succeed at ＿＿＿＿＿＿.

10. The day I broke my arm began like any other day.

The Third-Person Narrative Paragraph

Thus far, you have written paragraphs about your own personal experience. However, you may also wish to write about something that happened to someone else. To do this well, you must put yourself in the other person's place. You must use your imagination to decide how you would feel if you were actually in the situation you are writing about. In a first-person narrative, you are telling what you yourself did. In a **third-person narrative,** you are telling what someone else did.

Here is an example of a third-person narrative paragraph:

The cobra's head hit Grace's hand, but he did not bite. He struck with his mouth closed. As rapidly as an expert boxer drumming on a punching bag, the snake struck three times against Grace's palm, always for some incredible reason with his mouth shut. Then Grace slid her open hand over his head and stroked his hood. The snake hissed again and struggled violently under her touch. Grace continued to caress him. Suddenly the snake went limp and his hood began to close. Grace slipped her other hand under the snake's body and lifted him out of the cage. She held the reptile in her arms as though he were a baby. The cobra raised his head to look Grace in the face; his dancing tongue was less than a foot from her mouth. Grace braced her hand against the curve of his body and talked calmly to him until he folded his hood. He curled up in her arms quietly.—DANIEL P. MANNIX

After beginning the paragraph with a topic sentence, the writer tells what happened in the order that it happened. Because the story tells what Grace did, it is a third-person narrative.

Exercise   Writing a Third-Person Narrative Paragraph

Write a third-person narrative paragraph from your own imagination. You may use one of the topic sentences suggested below, or a topic sentence of your own.

1. When Jack awoke, he found that he had become invisible.

2. Gloria tried to run, but her legs had turned to water.

3. The two boys had been marooned on the island for a month.

4. Jenny was determined to win first prize.

5. Steve was in the bank when the robbers entered.

6. The bicycle lay upside down, its wheels still turning.

7. The search for the lost child continued through the night.

8. When Tom learned that his uncle had left him a million dollars, he began to make plans.

9. Jean had always wanted to be an actress.

10. Darlene's childhood had been filled with hardships.

Part 2   The Descriptive Paragraph

When you write a descriptive paragraph, you are trying to communicate a picture or feeling in words. You may wish to tell your reader how something looks, or how it sounds, smells, feels, or tastes.

If you say that the new girl in class is "pretty," your listener's next question will almost certainly be, "What does she look like?" However, if you say that the new girl has curly jet-black hair, creamy skin, and clear blue eyes with long black lashes, anyone listening would probably be able to pick her out in a crowd. Specific details help to create a vivid picture or impression in your reader's mind.

Choosing Words and Details Carefully

Word pictures of sight and sound are the most familiar forms of description because sight and sound are usually the most highly developed of our senses. The best sight pictures are created when a color is named or when movement is suggested. Most writers can create a sight picture more easily than they can a sound picture, because the eye is better trained than the ear.

Read the following descriptive paragraph.

By the time the boy had got to the house, the walking man was only halfway down the road, a lean man, very straight in the shoulders. Jody could tell he was old only because his heels struck the ground with hard jerks. As he approached nearer, Jody saw that he was dressed in blue jeans and in a coat of the same material. He wore clodhopper shoes and an old flat-brimmed Stetson hat. Over his shoulder he carried a gunny sack, lumpy and full. In a few minutes he had trudged close enough so that his face could be seen. And his face was as dark as dried beef. A mustache, blue-white against the dark skin, hovered over his mouth, and his hair was white, too, where it showed at his neck. The skin of his face had shrunk back against the skull until it defined bone, not flesh, and made the nose and chin seem sharp and fragile. The eyes were large and deep and dark, with eyelids stretched tightly over them. Irises and pupils were one, and very black, but the eyeballs were brown. There were no wrinkles in the face at all.—JOHN STEINBECK

This paragraph is a vivid and interesting word picture of the old man. Suppose, however, the writer had written his description like this:

> By the time the boy had got to the house, the walking man was only halfway down the road. Jody could tell he was old; and, as he approached nearer, Jody saw that he was dressed in old jeans and a coat. He wore old shoes and an old hat. Over his shoulder he carried a sack. In a few minutes he had walked close enough so that his face could be seen. His face was very dark. He had a white mustache and white hair, dark eyes, and thin nose. There were no wrinkles in the face at all.

The picture is now dull and lifeless.

The reason the word picture is so clear in the first example is that the writer has been careful to choose specific details with which to paint that picture. He has used details such as "heels struck the ground with hard jerks," "dressed in blue jeans and in a coat of the same material," "clodhopper shoes and an old flat-brimmed Stetson hat," "a gunny sack, lumpy and full," and "his face was as dark as dried beef."

By choosing different specific details, the writer can change his picture completely. Here is a different word picture.

> By the time the boy had got to the house, the walking man was only halfway down the road, a short, fat man, very round-shouldered. Jody could tell he was young only because his heels struck the ground with short, quick jerks. As he approached nearer, Jody saw that he was dressed in white duck pants and a coat of the same material. He wore dusty white shoes and a new black derby hat. In his right hand he clutched a bright red and black carpetbag, plump and full. In a few minutes he had walked close enough so that his face could be seen. And his face was as white as blackboard chalk. A thin mustache, black against the white skin, drooped over his mouth, and his hair was black, too, where it showed at his neck. The skin of his face was puffed out until it was difficult to define bone, and the nose and chin seemed lost in rolls of flesh. The eyes were small and pale blue, with thin

black eyebrows arched above them. There were no wrinkles in the face at all.

Now, rather than creating a picture of a lean, hard old man, we have created a picture of a small, fat young man merely by changing the details.

At the beginning of this section, we said that the two most common kinds of descriptive paragraphs are those concerned with sight and sound. The preceding examples are definitely concerned with sight. Let's look at two more examples, the first one concerned with sight and the second one with sound, to see how the writers used specific details to create their word pictures.

1

I never watched the sun when it was overhead, dragging the day after it. I saw it twice each day. I saw it in the morning outside the kitchen window, up the hill and behind the elevated subway, so close to the pillars they seemed crisp and flimsy like burnt match sticks. I saw it again later when it had hopped to the other side of the sky, when, as big as a saucer and the color of orange sherbet, it slid behind the stiff old monuments in Woodlawn Cemetery. I should have watched it glide overhead, for surely that was the way Indians told time, and I was an Indian most Saturdays.
—WILLIAM MELVIN KELLEY

2

The sound of a strange song floated in the air and seemed to be coming right out of the tree's trunk. I stopped short. My feet were inclined to run away, but I could not move from the spot. I stood there, turning my ears around in search of the source. The voice was light and unstrained, like some bird, and with a melancholy, human note. Only the sounds of the frantic children screaming for me to hurry with the ball moved me from the spot. My heart drummed fiercely, and a heaviness was in my feet as I ran back to my team. I dared not look back, for I felt some unknown force close behind me.—J. E. FRANKLIN

Most of the descriptive paragraphs you have read thus far have appealed mainly to the sense of sight. Because you use your sight more often than any of your other senses, it is probably your strongest sense. Good descriptive paragraphs may appeal to other senses as well, but they are more difficult to write. When you write a descriptive paragraph, you want the reader to share a personal experience with you. Since no one else in the world hears things exactly as you do, nor has quite the same sense of touch, taste, or smell, it is very important to use exact words in your description.

In the following paragraph, all of the senses have been used together to create a word picture that makes you feel you are actually in the kitchen the writer is describing.

I close my eyes and remember my mother's kitchen. The cocoa steamed fragrantly in the saucepan. Geraniums bloomed on the window sills, and a bouquet of tiny yellow chrysanthemums glowed in the center of the table. The curtains, red with a blue and green geometrical pattern, were drawn, and seemed to reflect their cheerfulness throughout the room. The furnace purred like a great sleepy animal; the lights glowed with steady radiance. Outside, alone in the dark, the wind still battered against the house, but the angry power was subdued by the familiar comfort of the kitchen.

Following a Logical Order

Like the narrative paragraph, the ideas in a descriptive paragraph must also be arranged in some kind of order. The order usually used in the descriptive paragraph is *arrangement according to space relationship*. Because you are describing a person, a place, or a thing in the descriptive paragraph, it is not usually possible to use chronological order. Therefore, a writer usually describes something by showing how it is situated in relation to something else in the same area or space.

To understand this idea more clearly, look at the following description.

> The river ran smooth and shallow at our feet, and beyond it a wide sandy beach sloped upward gently to the edge of the forest, against which the rocks shone as white as weathered bones. The red soil bank on our side of the river, the silver sheet of water in front of us, the wet browns and greys of the sandbars, the whitewashed ramp of rocks on the opposite shore, the green forest front and the pale purple of the Sierra Madre were like stripes of water colors. Across them strings of mules and donkeys moved with their loads, fording the river with their bellies awash. The drivers followed, their white *calzones* rolled above their thighs and the water up to their waists, carrying their belongings in bundles on top of their heads to keep them dry.
> —ERNESTO GALARZA

In this description, the writer has shown the relationship of one thing to another through the use of specific relation words, or direction words, such as "at our feet," "beyond it," "sloped upward," "to the edge," "on our side," "in front," "on the opposite shore," "across," and "on top of their heads." These direction words help the reader to see where the things the writer is describing are situated in relation to each other.

In writing the descriptive paragraph, you must choose specific details carefully. You must also place these details in a space relationship through the use of direction words, so that the reader understands the word-picture you are creating.

Exercises Writing Descriptive Paragraphs

A. In each of the following groups of sentences, choose the sentence that creates a more vivid image in your mind.

1. a. The branch clicked against the window like the sound of snapping fingers.

     b. The branch made little noises as it was blown against the window.

2. a. My mother baked a delicious dessert last night.
     b. My mother baked a juicy apple pie last night.

3. a. Tom's sunburn felt as though his back were on fire.
     b. Tom's sunburn was painful.

4. a. Dad gave mother some beautiful flowers for her birthday.
     b. Dad gave mother a dozen long-stemmed red roses for her birthday.

5. a. The steak was as tough as shoe leather.
     b. The steak was not as good as I had expected.

6. a. She had a voice that sounded like chalk squeaking against a blackboard.
     b. She had an unpleasant voice.

7. a. The night was like black velvet.
     b. The night was extremely dark.

8. a. The cute little girl was adorable when she smiled.
     b. The dimpled little blonde girl lit the room with her smile.

9. a. The sandwich filling tasted like old library paste.
     b. The sandwich filling tasted awful.

10. a. My sister teetered down the stairs in her new high heels.
     b. My sister walked down the stairs in her new high heels.

B. Following is a list of topic sentences. Choose two that interest you—one describing sight, and one describing sound. Using either your personal experience or your imagination (or both), develop the two sentences into descriptive paragraphs. Use specific details and a clear space relationship. If none of these topic sentences interests you, you may write one of your own.

1. Sometimes on Sundays, I hear the sound of church bells.

2. My window was on the second story above the garage.

3. After the storm, a rainbow appeared.

4. From the sound of her voice, I knew she was scared.

5. Late in the evening, I heard the distant rumbling of cars over the bridge.

6. My aunt gave me a lovely Japanese doll for my birthday.

7. My favorite painting is _____.

8. Immediately at sunup, construction on the building across the street began again.

9. I hear the sound I love, the sound of the human voice.

10. The Golden Gate Bridge is beautiful at sunset.

11. He heard the lonely sound of the geese flying south for the winter.

12. The rock group seemed more concerned with quantity of sound rather than with quality of sound.

13. He was the oldest man I had ever seen.

14. I awoke at midnight to the sound of a fire siren.

15. Nefertiti was a gorgeous Siamese cat.

C. Using as many senses as you can, write a one-paragraph description of at least six sentences. You may choose one of the ideas below, or an idea of your own. Remember to begin with a good topic sentence.

1. A lazy summer day in a garden
2. The kitchen at home just before dinner
3. The laundry room or laundromat
4. A barbecue or picnic
5. Your street at night
6. A hospital room
7. Cows grazing in a pasture
8. A circus or carnival
9. A gas station or machine shop
10. A busy shopping center

Part 3 The Explanatory Paragraph

The explanatory paragraph is one of the most important kinds of paragraphs that you must learn to write. You will probably do more explanatory writing throughout your life than any other kind. The explanatory paragraph *explains*. In as clear a language as possible, it tells *how, what,* or *why.*

The "How" Paragraph

Of the three kinds of explanatory paragraphs, the "how" paragraph is the easiest to write. It simply explains, in *chronological order,* how something is done. As clearly as possible, you explain what to do first, what to do next, and so on.

Suppose, for example, you are standing on a street corner and a stranger asks you for directions to a certain place. To make sure that he or she can follow your directions, you must make them as clear as possible.

> We're on the corner of 5th South and State Street. Fifth South isn't a through street, so to get to the VA Hospital the easiest way, you'll first have to go south one block to 6th South. At 6th South, turn to your left and go east. Go straight east until you reach 13th East, then turn north. Go north on 13th East for one block until you reach Foothill Drive. Turn east on Foothill Drive and continue going east for about a mile. There you'll see the VA Hospital on the south side of the street.

Suppose you have been invited to a Chinese banquet, where you know you will be expected to eat with chopsticks. A note from a friend who is experienced in using chopsticks gives you the following directions:

> Learning to eat with chopsticks adds an extra something to any Chinese meal. Learning to use them properly is not hard;

after all, even a Chinese toddler can do it. First, hold the sticks in your right hand, about a third of the way from the ends. Next, place the lower stick at the base of your thumb, resting it also on the tip of your fourth (or ring) finger. Then, place the second stick between the tip of your thumb and the tips of your index and middle finger. Hold the lower stick steady, but move the upper stick so that together they act like "tongs." Remember to keep your hand relaxed; hold the chopsticks lightly but firmly.

If after practive you can make your chopsticks work for you at the banquet, your friend's instructions have been clear and well organized.

Exercise   Writing the "How" Paragraph

You have learned how to do thousands of things since you were a baby, ranging from tying your own shoelaces to being an expert cook, a dependable baby-sitter, or a skillful model rocket builder. Following is a list of topic sentences, each of which may be developed into a "how" paragraph. Choose one of the sentences and expand it into a well written paragraph. Remember, you are explaining *how something is done.* If none of these sentences interests you, you may make up one of your own.

1. One of the first things you have to learn in archery is how to string the bow.
2. My grandmother taught me how to crochet.
3. Changing a bike tire is easy.
4. I taught my little sister how to finger paint.
5. I can make ice cream the old-fashioned way—in a crank freezer.
6. It's not too hard to housebreak a pup.
7. To pass a test, you first have to learn how to study.
8. Let's conserve our water resources.

9. Hiking is fun—if you know how to do it right.
10. Do you know the easiest way to learn to play the guitar?
11. Taking good photographs is fun.
12. You can teach your parakeet to talk.
13. Part of the fun of swimming is learning how to dive.
14. My brother taught me how to dance the ＿＿＿＿＿＿＿.
15. To be good citizens, we need to know how to become involved in our community.

The "What" Paragraph

Having already studied and written paragraphs that were developed by definition, you should have no difficulty in writing a "what" paragraph. A "what" paragraph *defines.* It explains what something is and what it does.

As a review, let's go over the process of definition. Remember, we said that the topic sentence of a paragraph developed by definition—that is, a "what" paragraph—contains three parts. It contains the term to be defined, the general class to which the term belongs, and the particular characteristics that set the term apart from the other members of the general class. Look at these examples:

Terms To Be Defined	General Class	Particular Characteristics
A zebra is	an animal like a horse	with wide black-and-white stripes
A snorkel is	a breathing tube	that can be used only on the surface of the water
A hurricane is	a strong, swirling storm	that usually measures several hundred miles in diameter.

The remainder of the paragraph is made up of supporting details that further explain the definition.

> A *hurricane is a strong, swirling storm that usually measures several hundred miles in diameter.* Winds blow at 75 miles an hour or more. Death and destruction, unfortunately, are too often part of the hurricane's story. The eye of the hurricane, often measuring 20 miles wide, is usually calm and has no clouds.

Exercise Writing "What" Paragraphs

Following is a list of topics that may be expanded into "what" paragraphs by using definitions. Choose one of the topics that interest you. Write a topic sentence containing a three-part definition for the topic you choose. Then, expand the topic sentence into a well written paragraph.

1. hang-glider	6. celebrity	11. hockey
2. gossip	7. hamburger	12. civil war
3. rose	8. popularity	13. loneliness
4. tadpole	9. battery	14. lizard
5. courage	10. giraffe	15. circle

The "Why" Paragraph

The "why" paragraph explains *why the writer believes something is so or why something has happened.* The topic sentence states a fact or an opinion. Then, through additional facts or opinions, the writer gives the reasons why he or she thinks the fact or opinion stated in the topic sentence is true. Therefore, this kind of paragraph is an answer to a "why" question. "Why didn't you do your homework?" "Why did the United States fight the Civil War?" "Why are we running out of energy?" All these questions require reasons—either fact or opinion—for answers.

Quite often, when such questions are asked, the typical answer is something like "I didn't feel like it"; "The North and the South couldn't agree on slavery"; "We're wasteful." The person feels that the answer to the question is satisfactory. Unfortunately, this is not true. In order to be satisfactory, the answer must give adequate supporting details.

I didn't do my homework last night because I didn't feel like it. Right after school, I had softball practice; and we practiced for about two hours. Just before we finished the last inning, I was playing catcher. John threw a fast ball. I tried to jump aside, but the ball hit me in the stomach and knocked all the wind out of me. When I got home, I was so tired and so sick to the stomach, I just didn't feel like doing my lesson.

The supporting details have now made the reason clear—and much more satisfactory.

To write a convincing "why" paragraph, you need good supporting details—strong facts or strong reasons. Let's look at another example of a good "why" paragraph.

Beavers do a lot of good when they build their dams in the right places. Beaver dams hold water back so that it does not run away so fast. Brooks that would dry up in the summer will flow all year 'round if a beaver dam holds the water. Wells that go dry in summer hold water all year when beavers are put on streams near them. Trees and bushes grow and hold the soil so that it will not be washed away.—THOMAS E. STIMSON, JR.

The topic sentence raises the question, "Why do you believe beavers do a lot of good when they build their dams in the right places?" The writer then gives his reasons, arranging them from the least important to the most important.

1. The dams keep the water in the streams from running too fast.

2. They keep brooks from drying up (*because the water doesn't run so fast*).

3. They keep wells from drying up (*because the slow-moving waters, and the water kept behind the dam, have a better chance to seep into the ground and fill the wells; then, people will have more water to use.*)

4. They keep trees and bushes alive (*and this is very important because trees and bushes help to hold back the water; they help to control soil erosion; and they help to stop flooding*).

With this kind of arrangement of the supporting facts or opinions, the reader of the "why" paragraph can easily follow the writer's reasoning.

Exercises   Writing "Why" Paragraphs

Following is a list of topic sentences that can be developed into "why" paragraphs. Some may be developed by the use of facts; others, by the use of opinions. Choose one topic sentence of each kind; then write two well written paragraphs, one developed with facts, the other with opinions.

1. Physical training is more important than mental training.
2. Boys should learn cooking in school.
3. Young people should be given a regular allowance.
4. Our country has a great need for more vocational schools.
5. Baby-sitting is a job that requires training.
6. The cost of electrical energy in our country is growing.
7. Our school needs a better heating and air-conditioning system.
8. Everyone should learn how to dance.
9. Horse racing is known as "the sport of kings."
10. Every citizen should read a newspaper regularly.
11. There are too many automobiles in America today.

12. Mouth-to-mouth resuscitation saves lives.

13. Students should occupy alternate seats during a test.

14. I think _____ should be made captain of our _____ team.

15. Japan is the fastest growing industrial nation in the world.

Chapter 6

Writing the Composition

Don't let the word *composition* frighten you. A composition is simply a group of closely related paragraphs that develop a single topic or idea, just as a paragraph is a group of closely related sentences that develop a single topic or idea. If you can write a good paragraph, you can also write a good composition.

Part 1 Parts of the Composition

You already know that a well written paragraph has a logical beginning, middle, and end. The composition has the same parts. Usually, a composition begins with an *introduction* that tells the reader what the composition will be about, in the same way that a paragraph begins with a topic sentence. Because you are developing your ideas more fully in a composition, you will need a whole paragraph to introduce your reader to your topic instead of just a single sentence.

The *middle*, or *body*, of the composition develops the idea you have written about in your introductory paragraph. For example, if you decided to write a composition about what animals do when winter comes, you might include a paragraph on animals that hibernate, another on birds that fly south for the winter, and a third paragraph about animals like deer and rabbits, that must struggle to stay alive when cold weather comes. Each paragraph in the body of the composition should begin with a topic sentence that tells what the paragraph is going to be about.

The *conclusion*, or final paragraph, of your composition should summarize what you have written. Since the final paragraph is the last idea your reader will take away, you will want to tie everything together in a way that contains the main idea of the composition.

Part 2   Finding a Subject

When you talk with your friends, you probably have no problems about what to say. Words almost trip over one another in your haste to communicate your ideas. However, when you are faced with a blank sheet of paper and told to write a composition, you may feel that you have absolutely nothing to say.

Try using yourself as a subject. Imagine that your best friend has been away for several months, and asks you what has been happening lately. What would you tell him or her? Maybe you would tell about the spaghetti dinner that your class sponsored, or about a trip you have taken. Perhaps you would share a funny or frightening experience you have had.

You can't write well unless you have something to say. That means that you must write about topics you are familiar with —things you have done, or studied, or learned from others. No matter what you are writing about, in some way or other you are always writing about yourself. Whenever you can, try to give your writing a personal touch; that is, a fresh way of writing about the topic you have chosen.

In the following composition, the writer has used a personal approach to describe his experience with housekeeping.

GOOD HOUSEKEEPING

My Mom is a super-saleswoman, so Dad and I weren't surprised when she won a trip to Bermuda for selling more mailing machines than anyone else in her division. At first, she was a little uneasy about leaving Dad and me to manage on our own for ten days. But we finally convinced her that we could sail along smoothly on the sea of housekeeping without her at the helm.

Since Mom is also super-organized, she left us a list of the things that should be done in her absence. The list included such simple operations as how to run the dishwasher, the laundry equipment, and the new microwave oven. On the way back from driving Mom to the airport, Dad announced that he would be the Captain in her absence, and I would be the First Mate.

As Captain, Dad announced that he would be in charge of the cooking, and I would run the cleanup detail. The first night didn't go too badly. Mom had left us a casserole, and Dad mixed up a salad. The casserole was delicious. Unfortunately, we had to throw the salad out because Dad got mixed up and used corn syrup instead of vinegar for the dressing. After that, we stayed pretty much with TV dinners. They really cook fast in a microwave oven. We cremated two chicken dinners before we got the knack to it.

It was almost a week before disaster really struck. The dishwasher was crammed with plates and glasses, and, as First Mate, it was my job to keep the kitchen shipshape. Unfortunately, we were out of dishwasher soap, so I used laundry detergent instead. Since the dishes were so sticky, I used a heaping cup of Clens. Suds poured over the kitchen floor like a frothy tidal wave. But, as Dad pointed out, at least we got the floor mopped. Only he said that we'd "swabbed down the deck." I think he was trying to protect his "Captain" image.

By the time Mom was due to return, our little household ship was sinking rapidly. Both Dad and I were wearing pink undershirts because we hadn't bothered to sort the wash before we tossed it into the washing machine. We had become experts on the different varieties of TV dinners. Dad liked the roast beef best, while I preferred chicken.

We spent a frantic morning cleaning house before we drove to the airport to meet Mom. As we got into the car, Dad gave me a tired pat on the back. "I think, son," he said, "that we should keep the details of the past ten days just between us men."

In this composition, the writer has used a humorous point of view to describe his experience. The first paragraph introduces you to the main idea of the composition, "sail along smoothly on the sea of housekeeping." The body of the composition develops that idea by using details, incidents, and anecdotes. The last paragraph ties up the composition by telling you that the mother will not be told about the rough sailing on the sea of housekeeping while she was away. You can use your own experience and imagination as subjects for an interesting composition, too.

Exercise   Finding a Subject

The following list of topics includes some subjects you may know about from your own experience, and others you may have learned about from other sources. After you have studied the list, make a list of five topics of your own that would interest your classmates. Write *P* after the topics you know about from personal experience, and *S* after those you have learned about from other sources. If any of the following topics interest you, you may add them to your list. *Keep your list for future reference.* Later, you will be asked to write a composition on one of the subjects you have selected.

1. My Idea of a Perfect Day
2. How Bats Use Radar To Find Their Way
3. How To Budget Your Allowance—Sort of
4. Jonas Salk's Discovery of the Polio Vaccine
5. My Pet Peeves
6. When My Mother/Father Went to School
7. The Night I Told My Little Brother/Sister a Ghost Story
8. How My Dog Trained Me
9. What Scientists Have Discovered About the Planet Mars
10. The Social Life of a Beehive
11. My Collection of _____.
12. My Least Favorite Chore at Home and Ways To Avoid It
13. The Legend of St. Valentine
14. Teen-Age Blues
15. How To Sail a Boat
16. Walking Alone at Sunrise/Sunset
17. Smart Answers Are Not Always "Smart"
18. Scouting
19. The Dream Nobody Wanted To Hear
20. Don't Be Afraid of Your Feelings

Part 3 Planning the Composition

A good composition does not come into your mind full-grown. At first, it may be merely a vague idea of something you wish to write about. Beginning writers often treat this idea as the completed idea, without giving it enough thought. They begin to write rapidly as soon as they get the idea. Then, after a few sentences, they find that they have nothing more to write about. All they have done is waste time.

You know that in order to write well, you must first think over very carefully what you want to write about. Then you must make a simple, but logical, plan for your composition. This all takes time. A good composition is not written in a hurry.

Narrowing the Topic

One of the first things you must do in making a plan for a composition is to decide on a *general* topic. Then you must decide how far to *narrow* the topic so that the material can be covered easily in your composition. If the topic is not narrow enough, you will have to use so much general information that your reader really won't know very much about your subject.

Study the following topics:

1. *The Ape That "Talks" with People*
2. *The Geography of Latin America*

In the first example, the writer has decided to write about an ape that "talks" with people. Because the topic is about one specific ape rather than about all apes, the writer can easily cover his material in a well organized, well written composition. The topic is narrow enough as it is.

In the second example, however, the writer has a problem. Latin America, which covers all the countries from Mexico to the tip of South America, is a huge area. There are so many different kinds of geography that the writer could give only the briefest and most general points of information to the reader.

In order to give more specific information, the topic "The Geography of Latin America" must be narrowed. The easiest way to do this is to choose one specific area or one specific country in Latin America. For example, if the topic were narrowed to "The Geography of Mexico," it could be covered in an interesting and meaningful way.

Narrowing the Topic

From the list of topics you made in the preceding exercise, choose the one topic you would like to write about. Study it carefully. Decide if it is narrow enough to be covered in a composition of five or six paragraphs. If it is too general, narrow it so that you can write a clear and interesting composition on it. You may wish to check your final topic with your teacher.

Putting Down Ideas

After you have decided on your general topic, then narrowed it to the point where it can be easily covered in a composition, the next step in your planning is to write down brief notes and ideas about what you want to write about. Simply jot down the ideas as they occur to you. Later, you will rearrange them according to a logical order. The important thing at the moment is to get all your ideas down while they are fresh in your mind. If you write each idea on a separate note card, you will have a much easier time arranging your ideas later.

Once you have put down all the ideas you can think of, the next thing you will want to do is *check your facts*. This is not much of a problem if you are writing about something from personal experience. However, if you are writing something from personal knowledge, it is a good idea to check your information to make certain that what you are writing is accurate—and complete.

Suppose, for example, you have decided to write about "The Geography of Mexico" because you are familiar with that very interesting country. There are, however, a few facts you may wish to check to make sure that you have them correct. You may also wish to make sure you have included all the important facts. For example, does Mexico have four seasons as the United States does? What are the important crops grown in Mexico? These are just two of the facts you would want to check.

As you check your information, it is a good idea to write the facts down with the rest of your notes. Then you will not have to look them up again when you begin writing your composition.

Exercise   Putting Down Ideas

Having decided on the topic for your composition, and narrowed it so that you can cover the information easily, you should now begin to put down ideas of what you are going to write about. Be sure to check any facts you are not quite sure of.

Grouping Ideas

Once you have completed your list of ideas and checked your facts, your next step is to group your ideas together. Put into one group those ideas that are most closely related to each other because they have to do with one part of your subject. Put into another group those ideas which have to do with another part, and so on. You may now see that some of your ideas are not related to any part of your subject, so those ideas should be put aside. As an example, let's continue with the subject "The Geography of Mexico."

Our list of ideas may look something like this:

> Mexico is a long triangle pointing to Eouth America.
> Cold mountain roads; warm, humid valleys
> The mountains are breathtakingly steep and high
> Mexico is wide at the top and narrow at the bottom
> Mountains produce gold, silver, and other minerals
> Paricutin volcano
> The people of Mexico love to sing and dance
> Mexico is a place of ups and downs
> Some peaks are wild and rugged
> Wet season in summer; dry season in winter

In the dry months, no rain falls

In the wet months, the rain is so heavy it carries the soil from the mountains

The first white explorers in Mexico were the Spaniards

One village now lies at the bottom of a lake

Some mountains are planted in orderly plots

Coastal lands produce oil

Mexico is a land of flowers and color, but it is also a land of the unexpected

Crops: maguey
       sugar cane
       corn
       cotton
       bananas
       mangoes

As you can easily see, these ideas are not related to each other, but as you study the list you can begin to see that certain ideas fit together.

The first idea we have listed is "Mexico is a long triangle pointing to South America." Let's put all the ideas about *shape* together.

1. Mexico is a long triangle pointing to South America.
2. Mexico is wide at the top and narrow at the bottom.

If we study our list carefully, we see that our ideas can now be grouped according to *climate*, to *crops and products*, to *ups and downs*, and to the *unexpected*. Therefore, our arrangement might now look something like this.

Shape

1. Mexico is a long triangle pointing to South America
2. Mexico is wide at the top and narrow at the bottom

Climate

1. Cold mountain roads; warm, humid valleys
2. Wet season in summer; dry season in winter

3. In the dry months, no rain falls
4. In the wet months, the rain is so heavy it carries the soil from the mountains

Crops and Products

1. Mountains produce gold, silver, and other minerals
2. Coastal lands produce oil
3. Crops: maguey
   sugar cane
   corn
   cotton
   bananas
   mangoes

Ups and Downs

1. Mexico is a place of ups and downs
2. The mountains are breathtakingly steep and high
3. Some peaks are wild and rugged
4. Some mountains are planted in orderly plots

The Unexpected

1. Mexico is a land of flowers and color, but it is also a land of the unexpected
2. Paricutin volcano
3. One village now lies at the bottom of a lake

Having grouped all our ideas together, we can now see that two of our original ideas do not belong in our composition. "The people of Mexico love to dance and sing," and "The first white explorers in Mexico were the Spaniards" have nothing to do with the geography of Mexico, so those two ideas we will put aside.

Exercise   Grouping Ideas

Put your own list of ideas into related groups.

Organizing Ideas

Once your ideas have been grouped, your final step in planning is to organize your ideas into some kind of logical order. Because you want to build your reader's interest, you will want to organize your ideas so that they build to a *climax* wherever possible. Therefore, the general order of the ideas will be from the less important to the most important. Because the most interesting part of our composition is about Mexico's being a land of the unexpected, we will organize our ideas so that idea is last. The final organization of our ideas might look like this:

Shape

1. Mexico is a long triangle pointing to South America
2. Mexico is wide at the top and narrow at the bottom

Ups and Downs

1. Mexico is a place of ups and downs
2. The mountains are breathtakingly steep and high
3. Some peaks are wild and rugged
4. Some mountains are planted in orderly plots

Climate

1. Cold mountain roads; warm, humid valleys
2. Wet season in summer; dry season in winter
3. In the dry months, no rain falls
4. In the wet months, the rain is so heavy it carries the soil from the mountains

Crops and Products

1. Mountains produce gold, silver, and other minerals
2. Coastal lands produce oil
3. Crops: maguey
   sugar cane
   corn
   cotton
   bananas
   mangoes

The Unexpected

1. Mexico is a land of flowers and color; but it is also a land of the unexpected.
2. Paricutin volcano
3. One village now lies at the bottom of a lake

By organizing your ideas in this manner, you should now have little difficulty in filling in the final, specific details.

Exercises   Organizing Ideas

A. Following are three lists of ideas. Rearrange each of the lists into a logical order.

1

The Values of Reading a Good Novel

1. It sharpens our understanding of human character.
2. It affords relaxation and entertainment.
3. It gives us information about different kinds of societies.
4. It sometimes leads to changes in law, education, politics, etc.
5. It is a valuable aid to the study of history and geography.

2

Every Boy Should Learn How To Cook

1. It will be useful when he camps out.
2. It will teach him to be helpful at home.
3. Good cooking is necessary to good health.
4. He may have a special talent for it.

3

How To Make Yourself Popular

1. Don't take offense easily.
2. Avoid arguing over differences.

3. Don't attack the beliefs and opinions of others.
4. Don't expose the weaknesses of others needlessly.
5. Follow the golden rule.
6. Don't betray secrets.

B. Organize your own list of ideas into a logical order.

Part 4 Writing the Composition

The plan for your composition is now finished. You have chosen your topic, listed and checked your information, grouped your ideas, and put the groups of ideas into a logical order. You are now ready to begin writing the first draft of your composition.

In our discussion of the composition at the beginning of this chapter, we noted that a good composition has a beginning, a middle, and an end. The first step in writing your composition, therefore, is to write the beginning.

Writing the Introduction

As you learned earlier, the beginning of the composition is the introductory paragraph that tells what the composition is going to be about. The introductory paragraph must do more than that, however. It must also be interesting enough to catch your reader's attention. If your introduction is boring, your reader may not want to finish reading what you have written. You will certainly want to avoid such dull, uninteresting paragraphs as these:

> When my father was in the Army, we lived in Germany. Germany is a pretty neat place to live. In my composition, I will try to tell you what it's like to live in Germany, and why I think it's so neat.

I'd like to tell you about the geography of Mexico. Mexico is a very interesting country. Its geography is very interesting, too, because it's so different.

Both of these introductions tell us what the compositions are going to be about, but both of them are so dull that no one would want to read further.

Now, look at the following example:

Mexico is a long triangle, pointing to South America. In the North it is a wide land, with many miles of cactus country between the Gulf of Mexico and the Pacific Ocean. In the South the country narrows as it meets the Central American states.

This is an interesting, well written introductory paragraph based on the first section of the notes on "The Geography of Mexico"—*shape*. If, like many people, you are unfamiliar with the geography of Mexico, you probably have never thought of Mexico as being shaped like a long triangle. You probably never thought of Mexico as a country with many miles of cactus, either. Because of these facts, the writer has caught your attention and has told you, in an interesting way, what the composition is going to be about.

Exercises   Writing Introductory Paragraphs

A. Following are eight introductory paragraphs. Read them carefully and decide which ones are good because they are interesting and tell what the composition is going to be about. Be prepared to explain in class why you think the other paragraphs are not good.

1

The first English arrived in India about the same time that the English arrived at Plymouth Rock and at Jamestown, in what is now the United States. Those long-ago settlements were very interesting, and I would like to tell you more about them.

2

There's something about Halloween night that always frightens me, even though I'm too old to believe in ghosts and goblins. The black always seems blacker, and the shadows more eerie. Even the familiar howl of the neighbor's cat sounds different, somehow.

3

I think that we ought to make every citizen vote. If I were President, I would make it a law that every citizen had to cast a ballot in every election. Voting is important, so everyone ought to vote. When I grow old enough, I am going to vote in every election. Everyone else should vote, too.

4

Many of us open our ears to compliments, yet close them to any criticism. Yet, often criticism can teach us more than the most well meant compliment. It is from criticism that we learn our mistakes, and how to do better next time.

5

There are many different kinds of pollution. There is noise pollution, water pollution, and air pollution. There are probably even more kinds than that. Anyhow, pollution is a problem that we should all try to solve.

6

New York is the largest city in the United States. Chicago is a big city, too, and so is San Francisco. Last summer, my uncle and I visited New York. So far, I haven't been to Chicago or San Francisco.

7

Hector was a small dog, but he thought he was a Great Dane. Whenever he spied an intruder in our yard, his tail stood up stiffly, and he growled as loudly as his small stature allowed. Imagine our surprise when one day he actually trapped a burglar.

8

My friend took a trip to Yellowstone Park. She had a lot

of fun because she likes the West, and likes living outdoors. Her name is Debbie Jennings, and she lives across the street from me. Her father is a lawyer, and her mother works in the hardware store.

B. Write the introductory paragraph to your composition.

The Middle

The middle, or body, is the most important part of a composition. It is here, through the use of specific information, that the topic presented in the introductory paragraph is developed or explained. As you learned earlier, these paragraphs may be developed in several different ways. They may use specific details, specific facts and figures, or specific examples.

To see how the body of the composition develops or explains the introductory paragraph, let's continue with our composition on "The Geography of Mexico." The introductory paragraph said the following:

> Mexico is a long triangle, pointing to South America. In the North it is a wide land, with many miles of cactus country between the Gulf of Mexico and the Pacific Ocean. In the South the country narrows as it meets the Central American states.

This paragraph says that the composition is going to tell us what the country of Mexico is like—not its people, or its customs—but its geography. In organizing the ideas of our composition, we decided that we would write about the geography of Mexico in the following order:

1. Shape
2. Ups and Downs
3. Climate
4. Crops and Products
5. The Unexpected

Our introductory paragraph includes the information on shape, so the body of our composition will begin with "ups and downs" and follow through according to our plan.

MEXICO: AN UP AND DOWN LAND

Mexico is a long triangle, pointing to South America. In the North it is a wide land, with many miles of cactus country between the Gulf of Mexico and the Pacific Ocean. In the South the country narrows as it meets the Central American States.

Mexico is a place of ups and downs. The mountains are breathtakingly steep and high. Some of the great peaks are wild and rugged, and others are planted in orderly plots so far up that they look like patchwork patterns against the sky.

The climate is up and down, too. From a cold mountain road, where pines recall Canadian forests, one may look down on warm and humid banana groves and on thatched roofs of huts made of sticks. Mexico has a wet season in summer and a dry season in winter. In the dry months no rain falls, and the steep slopes become brown and gray. When the rains come, water pounds the roofs of mud huts like drumbeats and washes down the mountainsides through deep ravines in a rushing roar. The slopes grow green and flowers spring out all over them. The rains carry away soil from the mountains, however, and run so fast through the ravines that they do the earth of the lower slopes little good.

The mountains of Mexico contain gold and silver and other minerals. The coastal lands on the Gulf produce oil. The earth grows strange plants and fruits. The cactus appears as round as a barrel, as pointed as a lance and in great, fierce hedges. Maguey is a century plant, ancient and useful, for it gives a drink called pulque, as well as rope and food for pigs. It grows only in high altitudes. Sugar cane and corn and cotton grow farther down. The fruits of Mexico are many—bananas, guavas, mangoes, cactus, and soft mameys and sapotes, sweet and sticky.

Mexico is a land of flowers and color. It is a land of song and brilliant birds. Snow-topped volcanoes glitter against a

sky of vivid blue. Mexico is serene and beautiful, but it can also be unexpected and violent. Only a few years ago a volcano, called Paricutin, thrust abruptly up through a farmer's field while he was ploughing. It quickly buried a village under lava and ashes. A lake once covered a town, and the church spire may be seen by looking straight down into the water from a boat. Mexico is a land where anything can happen.
—MAY MCNEER

In addition to showing you how the body of the composition develops an introductory paragraph, this example also illustrates two other important points concerning the body of the composition.

1. The composition is always divided into paragraphs. The division of the composition into paragraphs relieves the monotony of the page and makes the composition easier to read. Suppose, for example, that the sports page in the newspaper ran all its paragraphs in one long, continuous column. For one thing, you wouldn't want to read that mass of black type; and even if you did decide to read it, it might take you hours just to find out who won the baseball game.

Because each paragraph is a new idea, the indentation at the beginning of each paragraph shows when the composition is moving from one idea to another. It becomes something like a rest stop on a road you are traveling. It tells you where you are going, and it gives you a chance to relax for a moment.

2. Each paragraph of the composition usually begins with a topic sentence. As you have already seen from the examples you have studied, each topic sentence tells what the paragraph will be about.

The supporting details in each paragraph are related to the topic sentence, just as each paragraph is related to the introductory paragraph. Thus, the whole composition, like each individual paragraph, will have *unity*.

Complete the body of your composition, making sure that you follow your plan of organization. When you have finished your writing, reread your composition. Revise where necessary.

The Conclusion

You have almost reached the end. Only one step remains in writing the first draft of your composition—the conclusion.

Like the introductory paragraph, the conclusion of the composition is important. Because the conclusion is the last idea the reader will take from your composition, you want it to be as clear and interesting as your first idea. You also want to tie everything together, so that it clearly indicates "The End" to your reader.

In our composition on Mexico, we have already taken care of our conclusion. We have followed through our list of ideas from "a land of ups and downs" to our most important idea, "Mexico is a land of the unexpected." The last paragraph of our composition ends with the sentence *"Mexico is a land where anything can happen."* That sentence effectively summarizes all the other ideas that have gone before, and it clearly indicates "The End."

The conclusion might be a short, interesting *sentence* that summarizes our idea, like "Mexico is a land where anything can happen." It might also be a short, interesting *paragraph* that summarizes our ideas:

> Mexico is truly a land of contrasts. It is a land of ups and downs, a land of hots and colds. It is a land of bright green mountains and grey-brown deserts. Above all else, Mexico is a land where one learns to expect the unexpected.

Exercise   **Writing the Conclusion**

Write the ending of your composition.

Chapter 7

Kinds of Compositions

You will find that writing a composition is easier if you remember two important rules. First, you must have something to say. Second, you must decide on how you want to say it. Suppose, for example, that you know a great deal about gerbils, and you decide to write a composition on the subject. First, you must decide what you want to say. Do you want to tell a story about an experience you had with your own gerbils? Do you want to describe them? Do you want to explain how to care for gerbils?

If you want to tell a story about the time your gerbils were lost in the classroom, you will write a narrative composition that tells what happened. If you want your reader to be able to "see" your pet gerbils, you will write a descriptive composition. If you want to write about how to care for gerbils, you will write an explanatory composition giving step-by-step instructions.

You have already learned how to write narrative, descriptive, and explanatory paragraphs, so you know there are several kinds of paragraphs. In this chapter you will learn how to expand those paragraphs, as you did in the preceding chapter, so that you can also write longer narrative, descriptive, and explanatory compositions.

The thing to remember about writing these kinds of compositions is that they follow the same steps you used in the preceding chapter. In writing these kinds of compositions, you must do the following:

1. Choose a topic you are familiar with—one from your own experience or knowledge.
2. Narrow your topic so that it can be covered easily in the composition.
3. List the ideas you want to cover, and check your information.
4. Put your ideas into related groups.
5. Arrange your ideas in a logical order.
6. Write an interesting introductory paragraph that catches the reader's attention and tells what the composition is going to be about.
7. Write the body of your composition, making sure that each paragraph has a topic sentence, and that all ideas are related to the introductory paragraph.
8. Write an interesting ending to your composition.
9. Reread your composition, and revise where necessary.

Part 1　The Narrative Composition

A narrative composition is a piece of writing that tells a story. Think of a few of your own favorite stories. They probably had several things in common. Chances are that all of them were told in chronological order; that is, the time sequence in which the events took place. All of them had a logical beginning, middle, and ending. As a rule, the beginning led up to the main event or events in the story, the middle told of the main happening or happenings, and the end told you what happened as a result of the events.

When you write a narrative composition, your purpose is to interest and entertain your reader. Specific details and dialogue help your reader feel that the events you write about are really happening, either to you or to someone else. Let's look at some examples.

First-Person Narrative

I WASHED THE DISHES

When my brother enlisted in the Navy, I inherited his record player, his lower bunk on the bed we shared—and his job of doing the dishes. Now, I don't mind taking out the trash or raking leaves, but I hate doing dishes. A gloomy future of dishpan hands stretched before me unless I could convince Mom that I was a real menace in the kitchen.

The day after Will left for boot camp, Mom handed me a bottle of detergent and pointed to the dirty dishes waiting on the side of the sink. "Get busy," she ordered.

"But Mom," I moaned, "I'd rather mow the lawn or something like that." (I was pretty safe in saying that because there was snow on the ground and the walks had already been shoveled.) "Besides, I've got tons of homework that I should be doing."

Mom eyed me coldly. "It will only take you a few minutes," she said. "Then you can buckle down to your homework."

I realized that I was getting nowhere fast, so I decided to try a new angle. I filled the sink with cold water, squirted in a splash of detergent, and began to wash dishes.

I put all the plates, glasses, silverware, and utensils into the sink at the same time. I didn't bother to scrape the plates beforehand, and bones, scraps, and soggy bread crusts floated to the top of the water like survivors of a miniature shipwreck. I rescued a few plates from the murky water and set them on the drainboard. Small flecks of food still clung to them. Then I took a misfit glass that wasn't too important, and dropped it on the floor. It broke with a crash that brought Mom directly to the kitchen. "What was that noise?" she asked. Then she noticed the dishes on the drainboard and the mess in the sink. From the look on her face, I could tell my scheme was working.

"On second thought," she said, "I think you'd better run along and do your homework."

"Why, thanks, Mom," I said naively. As I left the room I commented, "I'm sure glad you'd rather have a scholarly son than a dumb one with dishpan hands."—ALLAN SMART

The first paragraph of the composition introduces you to the problem: how to avoid doing the dishes. Then the writer relates, in chronological order, the steps he took to convince his mother that he was a menace in the kitchen:

1. He filled the sink with cold water.
2. He put all the plates, glasses, silverware, and utensils into the sink together.
3. He didn't bother to scrape the dishes.
4. He dropped a glass on the floor.

As a conclusion, the writer tells us the "clever" thing he said to his mother after winning his battle.

Third-Person Narrative

THE WISE KING

Once there ruled in the distant city of Wirani a king who was both mighty and wise. He was feared for his might and loved for his wisdom.

Now, in the heart of that city was a well, whose water was cool and crystalline, from which all the inhabitants drank. Even the king and his courtiers drank from this well, for there was no other.

One night when all were asleep, a witch entered the city, and poured seven drops of strange liquid into the well, and said, "From this hour he who drinks this water shall become mad."

Next morning all the inhabitants, save the king and his lord chamberlain, drank from the well and became mad, even as the witch had foretold. And during that day the people in the narrow streets and in the market place did naught but whisper to one another, "The king is mad. Our king and his lord chamberlain have lost their reason. Surely we cannot be ruled by a mad king. We must dethrone him."

That evening the king ordered a golden goblet to be filled from the well. And when it was brought to him he drank deeply, and gave it to his lord chamberlain to drink. And there was great rejoicing in that distant city of Wirani, because its king and its lord chamberlain had regained their reason.—KAHLIL GIBRAN

In this composition the writer says his story is about a wise and mighty king, but he waits until the second paragraph to catch our attention. This he does by telling us there is only one well in the city, and that everyone, including the king, drinks from the well. We begin to wonder what the well has to do with the king. We want to find out what is going to happen. The writer then tells us, in chronological order, what happened.

1. A witch put a strange liquid into the well that would make people go mad.
2. All the people except the king and the lord chamberlain drank from the well.
3. The people went mad, and decided that the king and the lord chamberlain should be dethroned because *they* were mad.
4. The king and the lord chamberlain drank water from the well and became mad.

The writer, in his concluding paragraph, creates an interesting ending by telling us that because the king and the lord chamberlain were also mad, the people were happy because they "had regained their reason."

Exercise   Writing the Narrative Composition

Following are two lists of topics for narrative composi-tions. Choose one, or one of your own, and write either a first-person or third-person narrative composition. If you feel, from previous study, that you are already familiar with the first-person narrative, you would do well to practice writing a third-person narrative.

In writing the composition, be sure to follow all the neces-sary steps in narrowing your topic, organizing your ideas, and writing your composition. Use dialogue wherever pos-sible. Be sure to reread your composition, and revise where necessary.

First-Person Narrative

1. The Day I Broke the Neighbor's Window
2. My New Job
3. Teen-age Responsibilities
4. The Experiment That Failed
5. My Shopping Spree
6. The Day I Would Like To Forget
7. The Time I Lost My Temper
8. I Turn Over a New Leaf
9. Resolutions I Have Made and Broken
10. My Secret Ambition

Third-Person Narrative

1. When My Mother Went to School
2. My Father Made the Breakfast
3. Some People Were Born To Make Trouble
4. My Kind of Crazy, Wonderful Person
5. My Dog Loves Everybody
6. She Didn't See the "Wet Paint" Sign
7. My Sister Loves Cats
8. The Clown Looked So Sad
9. The Creature Appeared Unexpectedly
10. He Knew He Had Taken the Wrong Road

Part 2 The Descriptive Composition

No two people see things in exactly the same way. When you write a descriptive composition, you are sharing a little of your own personality with your reader. For a short time, your reader sees the world through your eyes, and shares your sense of sound, touch, taste, and smell. Like the descriptive paragraph, the descriptive composition uses specific details organized in a space relationship so that the reader clearly sees or hears what is being described.

Read the following example.

BY DAWN'S EARLY LIGHT

The dawn is the freshest, most beautiful part of the day. The traffic has just started. One car at a time goes by, the tires humming almost like the sound of the brook behind the hill. The sound carries not because it is loud, but because everything else is still.

It isn't exactly a mist that hangs over the thickets, but more nearly the ghost of a mist. It will be gone three minutes after the sun comes over the treetops. The lawns shine with a dew not exactly dew. There is a rabbit bobbing about on the lawn. If it were truly a dew, his tracks would shine black on the grass, and he leaves no visible track. Yet there is something on the grass that makes it glow a depth of green it will not show again all day. Or is it something in the dawn air?

There is a mountain laurel on the island of the driveway turnaround. From somewhere on the wind, a white morning glory rooted near it and climbed it. The laurel is woven full of white bells tinged with the first rays through the not-quite mist. Only in the earliest morning can the morning glories be seen.

And now the sun is shining in full. The leaves of the Japanese red maple seem a transparent red-bronze when the tree is between me and the light. This is the only tree I know

109

whose leaves let the sun through in this way—except when the fall colors start. Green takes sunlight and holds it; red and yellow let it through.

I hear a brake squeak and know that the newspaper has arrived. I sit on the patio and read until the sun grows too bright on the page. Suddenly a hummingbird the color of green crushed-velvet hovers in the throat of my favorite lily, a lovely high-bloomer. The lily is a crest of white horns with red dots and red-velvet tongues along the inside of the petals and with a fragrance that drowns the patio. The hummingbird darts in and out of each horn, then hovers an instant and disappears.

Even without the sun's glare, I have had enough of the paper. I'll take the hummingbird as my news for this dawn. It is over now. It's time to call it a day.—JOHN CIARDI

Notice how the writer has appealed not just to your sense of sight, but to your other senses as well. For example, "Tires humming almost like the sound of the brook", "the color of green crushed-velvet", "a fragrance that drowns the patio." The careful choice of words and details helps you experience the writer's feelings. For a short time, he has succeeded in sharing his favorite time of day with you.

Exercise Writing a Descriptive Composition

Have you ever seen storm clouds forming, or a cat teaching her kittens how to hunt? Perhaps you remember an especially beautiful sunset, or your back yard after the first snowfall. Maybe you know an interesting person. Choose a topic from your own experience that you think you can describe for your classmates. Write a descriptive composition of at least five paragraphs. Use comparisons and sensory impressions to help your reader "see" what you are describing. Also, organize your details in a clear space relationship. When you have finished your first draft, reread it, and make any changes you think are necessary before you turn it in.

Part 3 The Explanatory Composition

The explanatory composition, like the explanatory paragraph, explains something to your reader. It may explain *how* something is done, *what* something is, or *why* something is so.

The "How" Composition

The "how" composition usually explains how something is done. It is usually written in chronological order, telling you what is done first, what is done next, and so on.

However, there are times when an explanation cannot be given in chronological order because the "how to do it" does not follow one step after another. When this happens, the organization of the ideas is usually from the least important to the most important, as in the following example:

READING THE WATER

If you want to catch more fish, learn how to read the water. Your favorite lake, pond, or stream is full of clues that point to fish. If you look for the clues before you start casting, your chances of catching fish are sure to improve.

Anglers who like to wade streams for bass or trout read the water carefully. Riffles where water bubbles over the rocks and flows into a quiet pool are good fishing places. Especially during the mornings and evenings, fish gather around riffles to feed. They lie pointed upstream, waiting for the current to carry food to them. Cast a bait or lure above the riffles, and let the current carry it into the pool with the natural foods. Do this carefully at the right time of day, with the right bait, and you'll learn that reading the water means more fish.

In the warmer, brighter times of day the fish, especially the bigger ones, may be hiding in deep holes. Fish like to rest in shady places. This may be beside a rock or beneath a half-sunken log. It may be along a rocky ledge dropping off into the stream or lake. It may even be a hole so deep that the light is dim near the bottom. Also, watch for weedy places. Fish may be resting under submerged weeds, and a spinner or plastic worm worked along the edge of a weed bed can bring them out. Find where the smaller streams feed into a river, and you have located another fishing spot worth exploring.

Lakes, like fishing streams, can also be read by the fisherman who knows what to look for. Every lake has some fishing spots that are better than others. You can learn a lot just by looking at the surface of the lake. Are logs lying partly submerged on the edge of the lake? These are good hiding places for bass and other fish. Look around for other signs. The mouths of streams emptying into the lake, rocky ledges reaching into the water, old roads buried when the lake was filled, and fields of stumps sticking from the water are all good places to fish.

The more you study a lake or stream, the more fish you are going to catch. That is the best reason for learning to read the water.—GEORGE LAYCOCK

Fishing is a sport that many people enjoy. In the opening paragraph, the writer tells you that you can "read" clues in the water that will help you catch more fish. The body of the composition tells you in a clear, interesting way what signs to look for. The last paragraph summarizes the topic in a way that lets you know that the writer has finished what he had to say.

Exercise   Writing a "How" Composition

You learn how to do something new almost every day. Sometimes you learn from reading, sometimes from another person's explanation or example. Think of something you know how to do well, something your classmates might enjoy learning about. Then write a composition of at least five paragraphs that clearly explain how to do it. Revise your composition, and copy it in ink before you hand it in. You may choose one of the topics listed below, or an idea of your own.

1. How to play a certain game
2. How to build a birdhouse or anything else
3. How to budget your time
4. How to paint a bicycle
5. How to make bread
6. How to drive a minibike
7. How to stretch your money
8. How to put up a tent
9. How to plan a party
10. How insects are helpful to us

The "What" Composition

The "What" composition, like the "what" paragraph, defines. The definition in the composition has the same three parts: (1) the term to be defined, (2) the general class to which the term belongs, and (3) the particular characteristics that set the term apart from the other members of the general class.

The remainder of the composition is made up of supporting details, usually arranged from the least to the most important, that further explain the definition. Read the following example:

THE FEAST OF LIGHTS

For most Americans, the big winter festival is Christmas, but for Americans of Jewish faith, this season is the time for another important winter festival called Hanukkah. Hanukkah is also called the Feast of Lights because it is observed by lighting a new candle for each of the eight days it includes. On the eighth day, all the candles are lit. Hanukkah also is observed by religious services in the temple, by parties at home, and by giving gifts. It usually occurs in December. Like Christmas, Hanukkah is a joyful family holiday.

Hanukkah celebrates an event that took place more than 2,100 years ago. At that time, the land that is now Israel was ruled by the Seleucid Empire. The Seleucids worshipped the Gods of ancient Greece, and insisted that the Jews worship their gods too. For nearly twenty years, the Maccabees, or Jewish soldiers, fought for their freedom and independence. The decisive battle occurred in 165 B. C. when the Maccabees returned to Jerusalem and destroyed the Greek statues. Then they repurified the temple and dedicated it to their God. In Hebrew "Hanukkah" means dedication, and the feast takes its name from the rededication of the temple in Jerusalem.

There is a legend that when the Maccabees were ready to light the oil lamps in the temple, they found enough oil for only one day. By a miracle, however, the lamps burned for eight days. That legend is the reason that Hanukkah lasts for eight days.

In Jewish homes today, the main feature of the Hanukkah celebration is the lighting of a candle each evening. On the first night, the candle at the far right of the candelabrum is lit. On the second night, the one next to it is lit. This continues each night until all eight candles are lighted. A special blessing is said before each lighting.

In most Jewish homes, children receive gifts during Hanukkah. In some homes, gifts are given each night. In others, there are gifts only on the first and last nights. However it is celebrated, Hanukkah is a time of joy for every Jew.

In the first paragraph, you learn that Hanukkah is a Jewish holiday similar in many ways to Christmas. The body of the composition explains what the Hanukkah celebration is, and why it is celebrated. The conclusion ties the subject together by saying that Hanukkah is "a time of joy."

Exercise Writing a "What" Composition

Suppose that an amazing time machine has taken you back to the days before the Revolutionary War, when there were no automobiles or airplanes, no telephones or electrical appliances. There were, in fact, none of the conveniences that you take for granted today. Write a "what" composition of at least five paragraphs, explaining a modern-day invention for a man or woman living in the days of George Washington. Remember that your explanation should include the general class of things to which your subject belongs, and what special qualities it has, or what it is used for.

The "Why" Composition

Like the "why" paragraph, the "why" composition explains why something is so, why something has happened, or why something should be done. It begins with a statement of fact or opinion. Then the body of the composition gives additional facts or opinions to explain why the writer feels the fact or opinion stated in the introductory paragraph is true.

In writing the "why" composition, you must make certain that you know the difference between your facts and your opinions so that you do not confuse yourself *and* your reader. In writing the "why" composition, as in writing the "why" paragraph, you need good supporting details—strong facts or strong reasons.

Study the following example:

WHY WE SHOULD ALL WORK TO
CONSERVE ENERGY

Last night after dinner I told my family the bad news. I had had a class assignment to monitor our use of energy at home for a week. Our family got an F.

Tuesday night my brother watched the same two-hour movie on his TV set that the rest of the family was watching in the living room. That was a wasteful duplication of energy. Thursday, Mom ran an entire dishwashing cycle for three cups, two plates, a knife and three little spoons. That's a lot of electricity and hot water down the drain.

Dad drives twenty-eight miles back and forth to work. He drives alone even though two men he works with live nearby. They could carpool and save about a thousand gallons of gas a year. I myself am guilty of wasting energy, too. I went out and left the radio blaring in my room all Saturday morning. I certainly felt guilty when I realized how careless I had been.

Last night at the dinner table we discussed the problem. We all agreed to do everything we could to conserve energy. We decided to take faster showers, lower the thermostat, and drive fuller cars. It is a fact that this country is using up energy faster than we produce it. I read that we may run out of oil—forever—in thirty years. That's scary. Unless every person on every block does his part, the future looks pretty dim.

I am getting more and more concerned about the future. Very shortly, that is where I am going to be.

The title tells you what the composition is going to be about, and the introductory paragraph catches your interest because the writer uses a personal approach to back up her statements.

In the body of the composition, she uses factual examples of how her family has wasted energy. She makes her composition even more effective by suggesting solutions to the problems. The conclusion is an important statement, emphasizing the need for a satisfactory solution to the energy problem.

Exercise Writing a "Why" Composition

From your own experience or knowledge, choose a problem that you feel strongly about. Following the necessary steps, write a "why" composition in which you explain the "why" of the problem. If possible, include a solution to the problem.

Reread, and revise where necessary.

Chapter 8

Writing Social and Business Letters

Writing letters is a good way to keep friendships alive. It is also a good way to obtain information, to order products, and to express your opinions. If you are like most people, you enjoy receiving letters. In order to receive them, however, you must also write them yourself.

There are three basic types of letters: friendly letters, social notes, and business letters. Each type has its own form. Having a form to follow can make letter writing a much easier and more pleasant task, because each form is a kind of guideline for what to say.

Part 1   Writing Friendly Letters

In a friendly letter, your writing can be casual, just as if you were talking. The purpose of a friendly letter is to let your friend know what you have been doing and your feelings about what has been happening. Letter writing is an enjoyable sharing experience between friends, but even casual letters need a standard form to keep them organized and easy to read. The following example of the form for a friendly letter will help you review the five parts of a friendly letter.

The Form for a Friendly Letter

Heading   *267 Palm Drive*
           Cruz, California 95063
           July 18, 1978

Salutation

Dear Terry,

                    Body

Love, Closing

Beth Signature

The **heading** is written in the top right-hand corner. It consists of three lines. The first line is your street address. The second line is your city, state, and zip code. The third line is the date of the letter. In the heading, pay particular attention to punctuation and do not abbreviate, especially on the date line.

The **salutation,** or greeting, is the way you say "hello" to your friend. It can be as casual or personal as you wish. Here are some examples:

Dear Todd,   *Greetings Pal,*
Hi Manuel,   *Hello Good Buddy,*

The salutation begins at the left margin. The first word and all other nouns are capitalized, and the last word in the salutation is followed by a comma.

The **body** of a friendly letter is where you communicate your message. Since you are writing to someone you know well, your writing can be conversational, just as if you were talking. In this way, your personality will show through and your writing will be more interesting. In the body, remember to indent each paragraph.

The **closing** is a simple way of saying "good-bye" to your friend. Capitalize only the first word of the closing and use a comma at the end of the closing. Usually the closing lines up with the first word in the heading. Some closings are common and some are more personal. Here are some suggestions for closings:

Love,   *Your friend,*   *Missing you,*
Sincerely,   *Still waiting,*   *Confused,*

The **signature** in a friendly letter is written below the closing. Only your first name is needed. Keep your letter personal by always writing your signature by hand, even if you have typed the rest of the letter.

Guidelines for Writing Friendly Letters

What you do every day may not seem particularly interesting to you, but remember that a friend enjoys just keeping in touch. A friendly letter gives you the chance to write about events and feelings that are meaningful to you and interesting to your friend. The following guidelines will help you to write an interesting, lively letter, a letter that your friend will want to answer.

1. In the first paragraph, make comments about the last letter you received from your friend.

2. Write one or more paragraphs about people and events that interest both you and the person to whom you are writing.

3. Use specific words for detailed descriptions and action.

4. Ask questions so that your friend has something to write back about.

5. Make your handwriting neat and legible.

6. Use the proper letter form.

Read the sample of a friendly letter on page 123. See how each part is developed.

Exercises Writing Friendly Letters

A. Choose one of the following paragraphs and rewrite it. Develop each situation more specifically, and describe the incidents more vividly to make the paragraph more interesting for a friendly letter.

1. We bought a puppy last week. It's really cute but it's always getting into trouble and it's very hard to train.

2. When my brother left for college he said I could use his CB. I have it set up in my room. It's a lot of fun.

318 Laurel Road
Bexley, Ohio 43209
October 28, 1978

Dear Julie,

I was so glad to get your letter at last. I guess I just couldn't wait to see the pictures. Boy, are they fantastic! I especially like the one of you and Andy in the sailboat. Of course, Jim's favorite is the one where we're all standing there like drowned rats holding up our fish. That's just like a brother, especially since he caught the biggest fish. Anyway, it was a great family reunion, and already I can't wait until the next one.

You'll never guess what I'm doing in school. I actually tried out for the girl's basketball team and made it! Our first game is next week so I'll be writing again soon to let you know how it went. I'm really excited.

I really have to get to my homework now. Say "hi" to your family for me and write soon.

Miss you,
Suzanne

3. Last weekend I babysat for a family of six kids. You wouldn't believe how busy they kept me. What a mess!

B. Write a friendly letter to one of your best friends. You may write about events that have actually happened to you, or you may want to use some of those suggested in the following list. Follow the guidelines listed on page 122. Include all five parts of a friendly letter and use your best handwriting.

> Student Council elections at school
> How your cat destroyed your science project
> What happened at the school dance
> The movie you saw last weekend
> How you redecorated your bedroom
> The break-in at your neighbor's house
> How your brother dented the family car
> Your friend's surprise birthday party
> Your recent camping trip

Part 2 Social Notes

Social notes are written for a specific purpose, such as an invitation, a thank-you note, or the acceptance of an invitation. Social notes have the same form as a friendly letter except that they are much shorter. Sometimes only the date is used in the heading instead of your whole address.

Writing social notes is a form of courtesy that people appreciate. The following kinds of social notes are the ones you will write most often.

The Thank-You Note

Usually a thank-you note is written after you have received a gift. Even if you don't particularly like the gift, it is still important to thank the person for thinking of you.

Another form of thank-you note is called a "bread-and-butter" note. You write this note when you have stayed overnight at someone's house.

Both forms of thank-you notes express your appreciation for someone else's thoughtfulness toward you. The following are samples of the two types of thank-you note.

A Thank-You Note

2217 Massachusetts Avenue
Lawrence, Kansas 66044
December 28, 1978

Dear Aunt Alice,

The sweater you sent me for Christmas is beautiful. It is so soft and warm that I'm sure it will become my favorite. It matches perfectly the skirt Mother made for me, but what I appreciate the most is that you knitted it yourself. It must have taken many hours of work. Thank you so much.

Our family had a very close and generous Christmas together. I hope your holidays were just as good.

Love,
Cindy

4950 North Marine Drive
Chicago, Illinois 60640
April 14, 1978

Dear Mr. and Mrs. Pacini,

Thank you very much for letting me spend last weekend at your house while my parents were out of town. I had a great time at the baseball game and I had never played marathon Monopoly before.

I really enjoyed myself and I hope that Tom can spend a weekend with me soon.

Sincerely,
Matt Brendan

Notes of Invitation, Acceptance, and Regret

Invitations have to be written carefully to make sure that all the necessary details are included. Use the following checklist when you write an invitation:

1. Type of activity
2. Purpose of activity
3. Where the activity will be held
4. The day, date, and time of the activity
5. How the person should reply to the invitation

If you are inviting out-of-town guests, be sure to include directions or transportation suggestions.

An Invitation

417 Monroe Avenue
Mapleton, Iowa 51034
June 1, 1978

Dear Juanita,

You are invited to attend a graduation party at my house on Friday, June 14. The party will start immediately following our graduation ceremony, at approximately 10:00. Your parents are welcome to stay and visit with my parents upstairs during the party.

I sure hope you can be there.

Sincerely,
Carla

R.S.V.P.

The abbreviation R.S.V.P. stands for a French phrase that means "please respond." The person sending the invitation would like to know how many people are going to attend the party. Sometimes there will be a phone number next to the R.S.V.P. so that all you have to do is call. Usually, however, you should send a note of acceptance or regret. Always answer an invitation as soon as possible. The following examples will help guide you in writing either a note of acceptance or regret.

A Note of Acceptance

June, 5, 1978

Dear Carla,
    After graduation is a great time to have a party. Being at your house is always lots of fun. My parents will be coming, too.
    Thanks for the invitation.

Your friend,
Juanita

June 5, 1978

Dear Carla,

I wish I could attend your graduation party. I know it will be
lots of fun. Unfortunately my
parents have already invited several
of our relatives over for a celebration.

Ask if you can spend the night
on Saturday so you can tell me all
about the party.

Your friend,
Juanita

Exercise   Writing Social Notes

Choose two of the following situations and write the appropriate notes on plain paper.

1. Write a note to your uncle for helping you with a project. You select the project.

2. Write an invitation to a surprise birthday party.

3. Write a note thanking a friend's parents for taking you on vacation with them.

4. Write a note to a neighbor apologizing for crushing her flowers. You decide how it happened.

5. Write a note accepting an invitation to join a club of some kind.

6. Write a note thanking your grandmother for a present you didn't particularly like.

7. Write a note of regret for a barbecue you are unable to attend.

8. Write a note congratulating a friend for being elected president of the student council.

Part 3   Writing Business Letters

When you need to request information, or order a product, or even complain about a product, you will need to write a business letter. A business letter is written for a specific purpose and requires a different kind of writing from that of a friendly letter. A business letter should be brief, clear, and to the point. It should also follow the required form.

Business Letter Form

When writing a business letter, always use 8½″ × 11″ unruled white paper. If possible, type your letter. If you do not type well, write your letter with blue or black ink. Leave equal margins on both sides, and at the top and bottom of the paper, and use only one side of the paper.

The form for a business letter is similar in many ways to the form for a friendly letter. There are two types of business letter forms: **block form** and **modified block form.** They are illustrated on pages 131 and 132.

The block form for a business letter is to be used only when the letter is typewritten. Notice that all parts of the letter begin at the left margin. There is a double space between paragraphs, and the paragraphs are not indented.

Block Form

Heading
920 South Lake Avenue
Greenville, South Carolina   29602
November 23, 1978

Inside Address
The Danbury Mint
47 Richards Avenue
Norwalk, Connecticut   06856

Dear Sir or Madam: Salutation

Body
_____

_____

_____

_____

_____

_____

_____

_____

_____

_____

Sincerely,   Closing

Valerie Hayward   Signature
Valerie Hayward

Modified Block Form

Heading
920 South Lake Avenue
Greenville, South Carolina   29602
November 23, 1978

Inside Address

The Danbury Mint
47 Richards Avenue
Norwalk, Connecticut   06856

Dear Sir or Madam: Salutation

Body

_____

_____

_____

_____

_____

_____

_____

_____

_____

_____

_____

Yours truly, Closing

Valerie Hayward   Signature
Valerie Hayward

The modified block form is always used when the letter is handwritten. In this form, the heading remains in the upper right-hand corner, as in a friendly letter. Notice that in this form the paragraphs are indented and the closing and signature line up with the heading.

Parts of a Business Letter

The parts of a business letter are similar to the parts of a friendly letter except that they are written more formally. Follow these suggestions for writing the parts of a business letter:

1. **Heading.** The heading of a business letter is the same as the heading for a friendly letter. Check capitalization and punctuation and do not abbreviate.

2. **Inside Address.** The inside address consists of the name and address of the firm or organization to which you are writing. This address follows the same capitalization and punctuation rules as the heading. The inside address always begins at the left margin.

3. **Salutation.** The salutation begins two lines after the inside address and ends with a colon (:). If you are writing to a specific person, use *Dear* and then the person's name such as *Dear Mr. Reed:*. If you do not know the name of the person to whom you are writing, use a general greeting such as *Dear Sir or Madam:* or *Ladies and Gentlemen:*

4. **Body.** The body of a business letter is brief, courteous, and to the point. State clearly the purpose of your letter.

5. **Closing.** The closing appears on the first line below the body. The most common closings for a business letter are these:
   Sincerely yours,   Yours truly,
   Very truly yours,   Respectfully yours,
   Notice that *only* the first word of the closing is capitalized and that the closing is followed by a comma.

6. **Signature.** Type or print your name four spaces below the closing; then write your signature in the space between. In this way, your name can be clearly read.

It is best to make a copy of your business letters so you will have a record of what you wrote and when you wrote it. You can do this easily by using carbon paper. Always mail the original.

Part 4   Types of Business Letters

There are three basic types of business letters, each with its own specific purpose: the letter of request, the order letter, and the letter of complaint or adjustment. Each of these business letters follows the same basic business letter form and includes the same parts of a letter. The only difference is the information you include in the body of the letter.

The Letter of Request

This type of business letter is particularly useful for getting first-hand information for reports, for receiving catalogs and pamphlets, and for researching a product before you buy it. In a letter of request, be sure to include the following information:

1. Identify yourself.
2. Tell why you are contacting that particular person or company.
3. Tell what specific information you need.
4. Tell why you need that information.

Notice how these guidelines are followed in the letter of request on page 135.

58 Eagle Road
La Crosse, Wisconsin 54601
February 10, 1978

Action for Children's Television
46 Austin Street
Newtonville, Massachusetts

Dear Sir or Madam:

Our language arts class at Winston Junior High School is studying television and advertising Our teacher listed your organization as a good resource for information on this subject. My particular report concerns advertising for Saturday morning papers. I would appreciate your sending me any information you have on this subject. It is necessary that I receive this information by March 1 for my report.

Yours truly,
David Stewart

Write a letter of request dealing with one of the following situations. Include all of the necessary information and use correct business letter form. (Do not send the letter.)

1. You have just started backpacking as a hobby and would like to join a group or club. Write to International Backpackers Association, P.O. Box 85, Lincoln Center, ME 04458.

2. Your uncle has given you his stamp collection. You would like to continue this collection, but you need more information about your stamps. Write to *National Stamp News*, P.O. Box 4066, Anderson, SC 29622.

3. Your family is moving to Texas and you want to learn all you can about the state. Write to Texas Tourist Development agency, Box 12008, Dept. MW, Austin, TX 78711.

The Order Letter

In the order letter, you must include many specific details to make sure you receive the exact merchandise you want to buy. Include the following information in an order letter:

1. The name of the product and how many you want
2. The name of the publication in which you saw the ad
3. The catalog number, size, and/or color
4. The price of the item(s)
5. The cost of the postage and handling
6. Compute the price of your total order in your letter, especially if you are ordering several items.
7. State any item you are enclosing, such as a check or money order, a picture, etc.
8. Restate any particular terms that are a part of the ad, such as delivery time.

The following is a sample of an order letter that you can use as a guide:

An Order Letter

163 Poinsetta Drive
Tampa, Florida 33684
October 14, 1978

Masterwork
1708 17th Street
Santa Monica, California 90404

Dear Sir or Madam:

Please send me the photo belt buckle advertised in the September issue of Better Homes and Gardens. I am enclosing $7.95, plus $1.00 postage.

I am enclosing the black and white photo to be used. I understand that my photo will be returned and that delivery will take four to six weeks.

Yours truly,
Robert Takamoto

Exercise   Writing Order Letters

Choose two of the following situations. Write an order letter for each. Include all of the necessary information and use the correct business letter form. (Do not send the letter.)

1. Order one sports equipment caddy, Style Q–56, $8.50 ppd., from Spear Engineering Company, Dept. 3053, Box 7025, Colorado Springs, CO 80933, as seen in the September issue of *Better Homes and Gardens*.

2. Order two sets of 14 personalized pencils, each with your full name. $1.00 per set with 25¢ handling per set, from Atlas Pencil Co., Dept. BHG, Hallandale, Florida 33009, as seen in the July issue of *Boys' Life*.

3. Order the following plans as seen in *Popular Mechanics*: PL–1715, $5.95; PL–1406, $14.95; PL–1401, $6.95; PM Catalog, 50¢; ppd. from Popular Mechanics Plans Library, Box 1014, Radio City Station, New York, NY 10019. Allow 4–6 weeks delivery.

4. Order a jigsaw photo puzzle 8″ × 10″ B/W or color, $3.95 plus 50¢ postage, from Cadlyn's, Dept. BH9, 10250 N. 19th Ave., Phoenix AZ 85021, as seen in the August issue of *Camping Journal*.

The Letter of Complaint or Adjustment

When you have spent both time and money ordering or buying a product, you naturally want to be a satisfied customer. The manufacturer of that product usually wants you to be a satisfied customer. If you are not totally satisfied, write directly to the company and courteously state your problem. When writing a letter of complaint, include the following information:

1. The specific name of the product
2. When and where the item was purchased
3. The specific nature of the problem

4. Instructions as to how to have the problem corrected or a statement that you are returning the merchandise either to be fixed or for a refund.

A Letter of Complaint or Adjustment

557 Lindal Avenue
Seattle, Washington 98124
August 18, 1978

Holiday Gifts
Department 409-8H
Rock Ridge, Colorado 80034

Dear Sir or Madam:

When I received my personalized sweat-shirt in the mail, I noticed that my name was misspelled.

I have already waited four weeks and I am very disappointed.

I am returning the sweatshirt to you and would like to have the mistake corrected as soon as possible. If delivery will take another four weeks, please refund the $4.95 that I have already paid.

Respectfully,
Frank Steiner

Choose one of the following situations and write an appropriate letter of complaint. Use correct business letter form. Use your local telephone directory or a product you own as a resource for an appropriate address.

1. Write to a candy company complaining about the freshness of a candy bar you bought.

2. The magazine subscription you ordered cost $8.00 for a year's subscription. When you received the bill, it read $80.00.

3. The catalog you ordered still has not arrived. The ad stated 3–4 weeks' delivery. It has now been 6 weeks and you have already paid $3.00 for the catalog.

4. The new 10-speed bike you bought is missing a part. The store can't replace it so you must write to the company.

5. Write to your local city or village government complaining about a particularly dangerous intersection.

Part 5   Preparing Your Letter for the Mail

Once you have taken the time to write either a friendly letter or a business letter, it is important to fold the letter correctly so it can be read easily. It is also important to address the envelope carefully so that the letter will reach its destination.

Folding Your Letter

If your friendly letter is written on writing tablet paper, which is generally 6″ x 8″, you should first fold the paper in half. If the letter is still too large for the envelope, fold it in thirds beginning from each side, as shown in the following diagram.

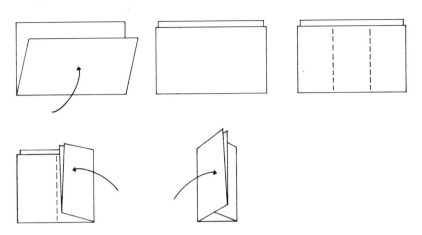

A business letter that is written on standard 8½″ x 11″ paper should be folded into thirds. First, fold from the bottom up and then fold the top third down, as shown in the following diagram.

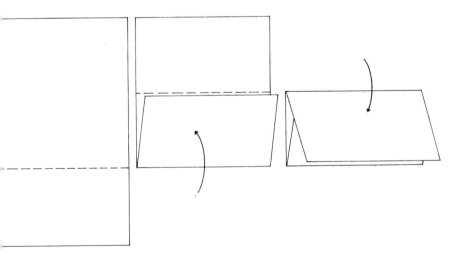

Addressing the Envelope

A simple mistake, such as reversed numbers, the wrong state abbreviation, or the wrong zip code could send your letter to the Dead Letter Office in Washington, D.C. Your telephone book or a call to the local post office will give you the correct zip code.

The following steps should be taken when addressing your envelope:

1. Make sure the envelope is right-side up.
2. Always put your return address on the envelope.
3. Double-check all numbers to make sure they are in the proper order.
4. Include the correct zip code.

Addressing Envelopes for Friendly Letters

Envelopes for friendly letters are usually small, such as 6½″ x 3½″ or 5″ x 5″.

Miss Annette Johnson
7562 North Hoyne
Chicago, Illinois 60645

Mr. James Speare
2013 St. James Street
Philadelphia, Pennsylvania 19111

When you write out the name of the state, you must place a comma between the city and the state. However, when you use the two-letter abbreviation for the state, capitalize both letters in the abbreviation and do not include a comma.

Addressing Envelopes for Business Letters

When addressing a business envelope, follow the same procedure you did for a friendly letter but always include your return address on the front of the 9½″ x 4″ envelope that is used for business letters. In addressing a business envelope, you may need an additional line if you are writing to a particular person in the company or if you want the letter to go to a specific department in the company.

Mrs. Joan Caedmon
856 Burke Avenue
Mission KS 66202

Mr. Lawrence Laski, Sales Manager
Heraldica Imports, Inc.
21 West 46th Street
New York NY 10036

Exercise   Addressing Envelopes

Address an envelope for each of the following addresses. Use your own address as the return address. Draw a 9½″ × 4″ space on your paper for a business envelope and a 5″ × 5″ space for a friendly letter or invitation.

1. Ms. Maria Talbot, Personnel Director, Ventura Industries, Inc. 1700 4th Ave., Portland, Oregon 97201

2. Mr. W. L. Young, 2600 Vista Blvd., Fresno CA 93717

3. Casual Designs, 325 S. Washington, Dept. BHG 9, Royal Oak MI 48067

4. Ms. Caroline Bexley, 2308 Algonquin Rd., Bay Minette, Alabama 36507

Chapter 9

Thinking Clearly

Clear writing begins with clear thinking. If you have thought your ideas through, and are sure that they are clear and that they make sense, you are already well on the way to making yourself understood.

You will also find that if you learn to recognize faulty thinking in yourself, you can recognize it in what others say and write. You will be better able to read and listen critically.

In this chapter you will study examples of clear and faulty thinking. You will learn to correct faulty thinking in your own writing and to spot it in the writing of others.

Part 1 Separating Fact from Opinion

A fact is a piece of information that can be shown to be true. If you write that the population of Kansas is over one million people, you are stating a fact. Your reader can check to see if what you have said is true. The reader could count the people in Kansas or find the report of a recent census. If you say that paper burns, you are stating a fact. This statement can be checked, too. Someone can try burning a piece of paper.

Only statements that can be checked to see if they are true are statements of fact. A fact can be true in one of two ways. It can be true by definition. It can be true by observation.

Suppose you wrote the following sentence.

Frogs are amphibians.

That sentence is a statement of fact. It can be checked. The best way to check it would be to look in a dictionary. "Frog" is the name given to one kind of amphibian. The statement "Frogs are amphibians" is true by definition. Now suppose you have written the following sentence.

Frogs will eat only live food.

Again, you have written a statement of fact. It can be checked. A person could get some frogs and observe them to see whether what you've said is true. Scientists have already made this observation, so your statement can be checked more easily. Your reader can find out whether frogs eat only live food by looking in an encyclopedia or in a book about frogs. These books report observations made by other people. Your reader doesn't have to make the observation. Someone else has already done it. Your statement is still true by observation.

Now consider the following statement.

Frogs are ugly.

That statement is not a statement of fact. You may agree with it. You may not. If you ask each of the three million-or-so people in Kansas to look at some frogs and tell you whether they are ugly or not, some of them will say they are, and some will say they are not. The statement cannot be proven. It cannot be checked, either by definition or by observation. It is a statement of opinion, someone's judgment of frogs, someone's personal belief about frogs.

Following are three sets of statements. In each set the first two statements are statements of fact. The third is a statement of opinion.

> More than 70 million families own TV sets in the United States.
> Television is one kind of electronic communication.
> There is too much violence on television.
>
> Apples are fruit.
> Apples can be eaten raw or cooked.
> Apples are delicious.
>
> Photography can be an expensive hobby.
> Millions of people in America own cameras.
> Americans are wasting their money on photography.

There is nothing wrong with opinions. We all have them. Some of us like spinach. Some don't. Some of us think frogs are cute. Some think they are ugly. The opinions we hold are part of our individual personalities. We are entitled to them. But we are not entitled to present them to a reader as if they were facts.

Exercise   Separating Fact from Opinion

Read each of the following pairs of statements. Identify each statement as *fact* or *opinion*.

1. Sixty per cent of prime-time television shows are situation comedies.

There is not enough variety in prime-time television.

2. Mayor Franklin has done an excellent job.

Mayor Franklin has proposed construction of six new neighborhood parks.

3. Yesterday was a holiday.

The weather was miserable.

4. Dr. Rivers told me to get plenty of rest and avoid heavy work.

She's the first sensible doctor I've found.

5. Mr. Hanover shouted at Ken for not paying attention.

Mr. Hanover has a short temper.

6. My neighbor hasn't said a word to me for six months.

This is an unfriendly city.

7. The Celtics are the greatest basketball team in history.

The Celtics won the NBA championship eight years in a row.

8. Sandy seldom gets her homework done on time.

Sandy is lazy.

9. It's time for a change in our city government.

Eliot Burger has served three terms as mayor.

10. In this city the law requires that dogs be leashed at all times.

Unleashed dogs are a menace to people and property.

Judgment Words

Judgment words are words with built-in opinions. Often they are adjectives, as in the following examples.

a foolish idea
a beautiful voice
a worthless suggestion

The words *foolish, beautiful,* and *worthless* are all judgment words. They do not tell us facts about the idea, the voice, or the suggestion. They give us someone's opinion of these things.

Take a careful look at the adjectives in anything you write. Ask yourself whether they state facts that can be checked. Following is a list of judgment words. Be especially careful of these words and their synonyms.

sensible	foolish
beautiful	ugly
valuable	worthless
good	bad

Exercise   Judgment words

Find the judgment word in each of the following statements.

1. McKinley is an outstanding pitcher.
2. The great novelist Stephen Crane was born in 1871.
3. He wasted six years trying to perfect the invention.
4. The nation faces a serious energy shortage.
5. The committee reported some frightening statistics.
6. Some council members still have the mistaken idea that a dam on the Baxter River is unnecessary.
7. Are we going to waste thousands of dollars on another study of this problem?
8. Watching television is a useless way to spend your time.
9. I have a better idea.
10. This is an example of a good five-paragraph composition.

Connotations of Words

Many words have two kinds of meanings. One kind is specific and direct. This kind of meaning is given in a dictionary. It is called a word's **denotation** or **denotative meaning.** The other kind of meaning is not as specific and is only suggested. This kind of meaning comes from the ideas a word brings to a person's mind. This suggested meaning is called a word's **connotation** or **connotative meaning.** The following pairs of examples show how connotation may change the meaning of a phrase.

> an inexpensive pair of shoes
> a cheap pair of shoes
>
> living in the country
> living in the sticks
>
> recyclable container with resealable top
> glass jar

The connotations of words can make them work like judgment words. Both *inexpensive* and *cheap* mean "low in price." But *cheap* has the connotation "low quality." Both *the country* and *the sticks* mean "a rural area." But *the sticks* has the connotation "dull, unexciting." A glass jar is a recyclable container with a resealable top. The term *glass jar* has no strong connotations. The phrase *recyclable container with resealable top* has good connotations for many people. It sounds like something specially designed to be convenient and to conserve resources.

Exercises   Connotations of Words

A. Automobiles are often named for animals. Following are the names of ten animals. Think about the connotations of each name. Explain why the connotations of each make it a good or a bad choice as a name for a car.

rabbit	flounder	crow	shark
skunk	colt	panther	
hawk	lamb	elephant	

B. Each of the following statements contains a word or phrase with strong connotations. The strong connotations make it resemble a judgment word. Find the word or phrase. Replace it with a word or phrase that does not have strong connotations.

1. The manufacturer confessed that some parts had been defective.
2. Johnson's speech dragged on for twenty minutes.
3. Carl demanded that we listen to his plan before deciding.
4. In the fall hunters take to the woods to slaughter ducks and deer.
5. The Cougar defense limped off the field.
6. At five o'clock the expressway is choked with cars.
7. Hobson and others hatched a plot to gain control of the company.
8. Are we going to throw away more money on this project?
9. Opponents of the bill are using television advertising to lure voters to their side.
10. In the runoff election, Eleanor Dawson trounced all other candidates.

Slanting

When a writer uses the power of connotation and judgment words to influence a reader's opinions, we say the writing is **slanted.** The term **slanting** comes from the idea that the writer "leans" toward one interpretation of the facts or one side of an issue. The following sentences show how statements can be slanted in different directions.

1

Enormous increases in spending on sports and other frills have made the school budget skyrocket.

2

Spending for necessary improvements in the fitness and enrichment programs has caused an increase in the school budget.

If you come across such statements in reading—or if you write them yourself—ask yourself which words are judgment words and which words have been chosen for their connotations. In the examples, *enormous, frills, skyrocket,* and *necessary* are all judgment words. And *frills, fitness,* and *enrichment* have all been chosen for their connotations.

Exercise Slanting

Following are three reports. Two are slanted. One is neutral. It is not slanted; it is just a report of facts. Find every example of slanting in the two slanted reports. Explain how each is an attempt to influence the reader.

1

Representative Phillips has jumped on the airport expansion bandwagon. She claimed to have letters from residents supporting this needless project. She quoted a statement from one pressure group that described the airport as "inadequate and unsafe." She admitted that the latest study shows that noise levels would increase dramatically. A careful study conducted by the city concluded that a larger airport would bring little new income to the area.

2

Representative Phillips spoke in favor of expanding the airport. She said that most of the letters she has received from residents supported the project. According to Phillips, a group of pilots who use the airport has submitted a statement describing the facility as "inadequate and unsafe." The latest study indicates that noise levels in nearby areas would increase by 10%, she added. The city's own study concluded that a larger airport would bring half a million dollars in new yearly income to the area.

3

Representative Phillips has endorsed the plan for a truly modern airport. She announced that her mail showed broad support from residents. A concerned group of professional pilots submitted a statement warning that the airport is now "inadequate and unsafe." The latest study indicates that there would be only a slight increase in noise levels. The city's own study shows that a large modern airport would bring significant new yearly income to the area.

Part 2 Checking Your Facts

In the first part of this chapter, we said that facts are pieces of information that can be true or false. They can be checked. Since they can be checked, you owe it to yourself and to your reader to check them before you present them as true.

You owe it to yourself because an incorrect fact can embarrass you as a writer. You don't want to build an argument on a key fact only to have someone point out to you that your information is wrong.

You owe it to your reader because your reader is likely to be willing to give you the benefit of the doubt. Your reader is likely to take your information as you present it—as true information. The honest writer makes certain that it *is* true.

Someone once said that a good motto for a careful writer is, "Assume nothing." Let's say that you have thought for some time that the population of your city is about 100,000 people. Where did you get that information? Did someone mention it in a conversation? Did you read it somewhere? Can you remember where? Don't assume that it is correct. If you plan to use it as a fact, check it.

We get our information in two ways. Some of it we get at first hand, directly from personal experience. Some of it we get at second hand, from other people. Second-hand information may come from conversation, from television, from reading, or from any of several other sources.

Suppose you have some information from your own experience. Perhaps you've made some observations or conducted an experiment. Can you repeat the observations to check the information? Can you repeat the experiment to check the results? Can you describe your observations or experiment so that your reader could repeat to check you? If you or your reader cannot repeat your experience, your information cannot be checked. It may still be true, but you can only report it as the experience of one person at one time. That information is only as reliable as you are as an observer and a reporter. Factual information that can be checked is much stronger.

We get much more information at second hand than we do at first hand. How do you know that George Washington ever lived? How do you know what the far side of the moon looks like? You have no direct personal information about these things. You have learned them at second hand, from someone else.

Before accepting second-hand information as true, ask yourself the following questions.

> What is the source of this information?
> Is the source reliable?

If you cannot remember the source for some information, don't think of it as a fact.

A reliable source is one that is widely recognized, qualified, and unbiased.

A source will be *widely recognized* only if many people have used its information and found it to be correct. A source is *qualified* if an attempt has been made to get as close as possible to first-hand information and to check the facts in advance. A source is *unbiased* if it has nothing to gain from presenting inaccurate facts. Which source is likely to be less biased in a report on toothpaste, researchers at a dental college or a toothpaste company?

Reliable sources for a wealth of information can be found in the reference section of your library. There you will find encyclopedias, almanacs, atlases, and dictionaries that will answer many of your needs in checking facts.

Exercise Checking your facts

Following are twenty sentences. Some are correct. Some are not. Check the facts in each statement. Use reliable sources. Tell what source you used to check each. Correct the statements that are incorrect.

1. The population of Cincinnati in 1970 was under 500,000.
2. Madagascar is an island in the Pacific Ocean.
3. When it is 10:00 A.M. Eastern Standard Time, it is 8:00 A.M. Pacific Time.
4. All of Florida is in one time zone.
5. The capital of Florida is Miami.
6. Miami is also the name of an Algonquian tribe.
7. The Miamis did not live in the part of the United States that is now Florida.
8. Hernando Cortez claimed Florida for Portugal.
9. Cortez was born in 1444.
10. Today the population of Portugal is over nine million.
11. An earthquake struck Lisbon, Portugal on November 1, 1755, killing 60,000 people.
12. Samuel Johnson published his dictionary of English in 1755.
13. Samuel Johnson was born in Scotland.
14. Glasgow is the capital of Scotland.
15. Edinburgh is the largest city in Scotland.
16. Scotland is part of The United Kingdom of Great Britain.
17. Bermuda is also part of the United Kingdom.
18. Bermuda is an island in the Pacific Ocean.
19. The population of Bermuda is under 50,000.
20. Bermuda is south of Miami.

Part 3   Making the Facts Clear

If your reader can't understand the facts you've written, it won't matter how carefully you've checked them. To make them clear, you must choose the most specific words you can. You must also be careful not to choose words that say more than you can prove.

Be Specific

Words refer to, or name, things. A **general word** is a word that refers to a great number of things. A **specific word** is a word that refers to a small number of things. The more general a word is, the more things it names. The more specific a word is, the fewer things it names. Think about the following pairs of sentences.

> All morning I've been thinking about food.
> All morning I've been thinking about a pepperoni pizza.
>
> Headease has more pain reliever than Brand X.
> Headease has more aspirin than Brand X.
>
> We have a plan to reduce pollution.
> We have a plan to make West River clean enough for swimming.

In each pair of statements, the second is more specific than the first. The word *food* refers to an enormous number of things. *Pepperoni pizza* names one kind of food. The term *aspirin* is one kind of *pain reliever*. There are many kinds of *pollution*. There are many areas in any community that suffer from pollution. A plan may *reduce* pollution by a large or small amount. The phrase *reduce pollution* is so general that it does not tell us much. However, *make West River clean enough for swimming* specifically states where pollution would be reduced and how much.

Often a more general statement tends toward a judgment. Look at the following sentences.

Downtown there are many tall buildings.
Downtown there are twelve buildings ten stories tall, or taller.

Ten-story buildings may be tall in the opinion of the writer, but they are not likely to seem tall to any reader who lives in a large city.

When you report information in specific terms, your reader will know just what you mean. You will be able to make certain that you can prove what you say. Look at the following four statements.

Nat likes sports.
Nat is a football fan.
Nat is a Panther fan.
Nat watches all the Panther games on TV.

Think about the ways that the first three statements could be challenged.

Is Nat a Panther fan? Does he go to their games? Does he have the players' autographs? Does he collect Panther souvenirs? Can he name all their players?

Is he a football fan? Does he watch games that the Panthers are not in? Does he follow the standings in other leagues? Can he name all the pro teams?

Does he like sports? How many sports has he seen? How many does he play?

The first of the statements is very general. It covers a wide area. The word *sports* can mean anything from gymnastics to wrist wrestling. The word *likes* can mean anything from the way Nat feels about ice cream to the way he feels about geometry. This statement would be hard to prove.

The second statement is more specific than the first because it names a single sport. The third statement is still more specific. It narrows the sport down to a single team. The last statement is the most specific. It tells us one thing that Nat does. It can be proven.

Give Your Source

Tell your reader where your information comes from. You will show that you've gone to the trouble of checking it. You will show that your information is from a reliable source. Your reader will know that your facts can be checked.

> Nat's father says that Nat watches all the Panther games on TV.

> The Hargrove Chamber of Commerce reports that there are twelve buildings in Hargrove ten stories tall or taller.

Exercise   Making the Facts Clear

Choose the more specific statement from each pair.

1. Nick moved to Utah.
   Nick moved to Salt Lake City.

2. We caught clams, mussels, and oysters.
   We caught three kinds of shellfish.

3. I'm involved with the entertainment industry.
   I'm in TV.

4. I'm in TV.
   I'm a television actor.

5. I act in television commercials.
   I'm a television actor.

6. I act in television commercials.
   I was the talking potato in the Fresh Fries ad.

7. They're rich.
   They have a new car.

8. Old MacDonald had a farm, and on his farm he had a pig.
   Old MacDonald had a farm and some livestock.

9. Public services in this city are unreliable.

Our garbage wasn't picked up yesterday.

10. This is a low-mileage car loaded with options.

This car has 55,000 miles on the odometer, and it has a radio and an automatic transmission.

Part 4 Logical Reasoning

Logical reasoning is reasoning that makes sense. Illogical reasoning is reasoning that does not make sense. (The prefix *il-*, of course, means "not.") In this part you will look at several kinds of reasoning. Some are clear, logical, and sensible. Some are illogical.

Unfortunately, illogical reasoning is not always easy to spot. Some illogical reasoning seems to make sense at first. It takes a close look to find what is wrong. In this part you will learn what to look for and how to spot errors in reasoning.

Generalizing

Generalizing is one of the ways we learn. It is also called induction or inductive thinking. When we see something happen many times, we may find a pattern. Once we spot the pattern, we have made a generalization.

Some people have jobs that depend on generalizing. A football scout, for example, is paid by one team to watch its opponents' games. The scout is expected to find patterns in the way the other teams play. The scout may report something like, "The Cougars like to call a draw play on third down with short yardage." The scout has seen the Cougars do this many times. From these many times, the scout makes a generalization.

A storekeeper may have noticed that in the summer of 1974

people didn't buy many chocolate bars. The same was true in the summer of 1975. It was also true in the summers of 1976 and 1977. In the summer of 1978 the storekeeper doesn't order many chocolate bars. "People don't buy chocolate bars in the summer," she says. She has made a generalization.

Errors in Generalizing

Mistakes in generalizing usually occur in one of two ways: (1) There may not have been enough cases for a true pattern to show up. (2) The generalization may be too broad. It may try to take in more occurrences than the facts will support.

Suppose the football scout had watched only one quarter of a game. Would that have been enough for him to make a generalization about the Cougars? Probably not.

Think about each of the following generalizations.

> The Sharks always pass on first down.

> Everybody likes apple pie.

> Sandra Weatherbee was arrested for robbing a bank, and Don Weatherbee was arrested for forgery. That Weatherbee family is no good.

> Tony had a violin lesson last Wednesday, and he has another one this Wednesday. Tony has violin lessons on Wednesdays.

The first three generalizations are too broad. The Sharks don't *always* pass on first down. Any team that thinks they do will be in trouble. There are people who don't like apple pie. We don't know anything about the rest of the Weatherbee family.

The fourth generalization comes from too few cases. (Suppose Tony's lessons are supposed to be on Tuesdays, but his teacher wasn't available on Tuesday this week or last week?)

Qualifying Generalizations

Generalizations become too broad when you try to make them cover *all* cases. Words like the following can push your generalizations too far.

always	never	everybody
everyone	every	no one
nobody	all the time	

Even if you don't use words like *always* and *never*, your generalizations can be too broad if you fail to qualify them. Qualifying a generalization means telling how many cases it applies to. You might qualify a generalization with words like the following.

sometimes	often	most
rarely	frequently	many
some	infrequently	a few

If you don't use a qualifying word, your generalization may seem too broad even if you don't mean it to be. Look at the following sentences. Compare the sentences in each pair. Which one is an accurate generalization?

The Sharks call a draw play on third down and short yardage.
The Sharks often call a draw play on third down and short yardage.

People like apple pie.
Many people like apple pie.

Tony has violin lessons on Wednesdays.
Tony sometimes has violin lessons on Wednesdays.

Giving Evidence for a Generalization

Generalizations are useful. Without them we couldn't "see the forest for the trees." We'd always be looking at details, and we wouldn't see the patterns in life and in the way people behave. But the danger of generalizations is that we think of them as rules or as true statements that apply to every case. You can avoid this danger by telling your reader how you made your generalization. Consider the following example.

> Most people do not talk to the people they sit next to on buses. I have ridden on city buses to and from school for the last four months. On each trip I've watched the people on the seat ahead of me. Out of the 150 pairs of people I observed, only 22 said anything to each other.

This is a generalization that the reader can accept. The writer tells how the generalization came about. The reader can see that the facts support the generalization.

Exercises   Generalizing

A. Read each pair of statements below. Decide which of the two statements is better. Explain what is wrong with the other.

1. The American child sees more than 6,000 violent deaths on television before he or she reaches eighteen.

According to a survey conducted by the Center for Children's Television, the average child in America sees more than 6,000 violent deaths on the screen before he or she reaches eighteen.

2. We tested six laboratory rats in a maze with twelve turns. They learned the correct path in an average of just over four tries. Based on this evidence, we would say that a rat can learn to find its way through a complicated maze in about four tries.

A rat can learn to find its way through a complicated maze in about four tries.

3. Americans are wasting energy.

I heard on last night's news that half the new housing in America does not have enough insulation.

4. Wars are fought to gain territory.

Some wars have been fought to gain territory.

5. In last week's game, Phillips completed only three out of fifteen passes.

Phillips can't pass.

6. Most voters are in favor of the plan to extend rapid transit beyond the city limits.

A poll of 1000 voters showed that most support the plan to extend rapid transit beyond the city limits.

7. A survey in six major cities showed that half the students did not get enough protein from the lunches they ate.

Students don't eat the right foods.

8. People like movies with happy endings.

The five movies with the highest attendance last year all had happy endings.

9. American writers use everyday speech in dialogue.

Mark Twain, Stephen Crane, and Bret Harte used everyday speech in dialogue.

10. This exercise program will work for anyone.

This exercise program will work for anyone who is healthy enough for strenuous activity.

B. One hundred students in a school were given a list of ten kinds of stories. They were asked to tell which kinds they liked and which kinds they didn't. The results are shown in this chart.

Kind of Story	"Like"	"Don't Like"
mystery	64	36
adventure	59	41

ghost story	58	42
science fiction	52	48
animal fantasy	50	50
humor	50	50
true animal story	48	52
sports	47	53
sea story	44	56
fable	32	68

Which of the following are good generalizations, according to the chart?

1. Most students like mystery stories.
2. Most students in this school like mystery stories.
3. Most of the students who were asked like mystery stories.
4. Some students in the survey like fables.
5. Students like animal fantasy stories about as much as humorous stories.
6. Many students in the group don't like mystery stories.
7. Many students in the group don't like science fiction.
8. Students would rather read mystery stories than sea stories.
9. Everybody likes a good mystery.
10. Sports stories are popular with the students in this group.

Cause and Effect

We can see cause and effect at work every day. One thing makes another thing happen. Something causes something else to happen. You push a button and a doorbell rings. Your pushing the button is the cause. The ringing of the doorbell is the effect. You put a pan of water on a hot stove. The water boils. The heat of the stove is the cause. The boiling of the water is the effect.

We often use the words *if* and *then,* or the word *because,* to show cause and effect. The following sentences are examples of cause-and-effect statements. Notice that the word *then* is not included in the fourth sentence, but is assumed to be understood.

> The doorbell rang because I pushed the button.
> If I push the button, then the doorbell will ring.
> You flunked that test because you didn't study.
> If you don't study, you'll flunk the test.

Fallacies

Fallacies are mistakes in thinking. Two fallacies that can occur in cause-and-effect thinking are the Wrong-Cause Fallacy and the One-Cause Fallacy. We can find these fallacies in the thinking of many people.

The Wrong-Cause Fallacy

Many superstitions and prejudices get their start from the Wrong-Cause Fallacy. Following are two examples.

> I wore my red socks on Monday and Wednesday, and we won. I forgot to wear them on Tuesday and we lost. I'd better wear them from now on.

> For ten years there has never been an accident in this neighborhood. Then that family moved in next door. Since they moved in, there have been three accidents. They're a jinx.

What we know about the world ought to tell us that wearing red socks does not cause a team to win a game. There are certainly many causes for a team's winning a game, but the color of their socks is not one of them.

Accidents also have many causes, and certainly people can cause accidents. But the writer of the second example does not show that anyone from the new family caused an accident through clumsiness or carelessness. The writer suggests that the new family caused accidents just by moving into the neighborhood. Again, what we know about the world should tell us that this can't be so.

The One-Cause Fallacy

> We switched to Tasty Paste last year. We haven't had a cavity since then. We owe it all to Tasty Paste.
>
> We would have won the game if Cunningham had been able to play.

What is wrong with these two sentences? Many things affect tooth decay. What a person eats, how often a person brushes and flosses his or her teeth, and illness are all involved. Tasty Paste may be one cause of healthier teeth. But it is not the only one.

There are many causes for a team's winning or losing a game. Every player is involved. No one player is the cause of a team's winning or losing.

The One-Cause Fallacy ignores all causes but one. It does not give a true picture of what causes something to happen.

Making Cause and Effect Clear

To make certain that your reader understands your cause-and-effect reasoning, use words that show cause and effect. Following is a list of such words.

caused	was caused by
made	because
created	resulted
produced	if . . . then

Watch out for a common error in the use of the word *because*. Many student writers write sentences like the following.

We had a flat tire, because it was making a thumping noise.

Herb must have lost his match because he seemed unhappy.

Expanding the airport is unpopular because a poll showed that most people are against it.

Remember that a cause-and-effect statement is supposed to show that something makes something else happen. But the fact that the tire made a thumping noise did not make it flat. The fact that Herb seemed unhappy did not make him lose his match. The fact that a poll showed that most people are against expanding the airport did not make it unpopular. What is wrong with each of the examples? The writer has tried to show what made him or her know that the tire was flat, know that Herb lost his match, and know that expanding the airport is unpopular. These revisions would make the reasoning clear.

We had a flat tire because we ran over a nail. We knew it was flat because it was making a thumping noise.

Herb lost his match because he was out of practice, he was playing with a borrowed racket, his arm was sore, and his opponent was better. I could tell that he had lost because he seemed unhappy.

Expanding the airport is unpopular because it will mean more noise and air pollution. I know that it is unpopular because a poll showed that most people are against it.

Exercise   Cause and Effect

Tell what is wrong with each of the following cause-and-effect statements.

1. If Gilmore doesn't pass more often, we'll never win this game.

2. If I could get into Ms. Johnson's class, I'd do better in math.

3. The committee didn't use my idea because I'm from out of town.

4. I'd be a much better player if I had a new racket.

5. Unemployment is high because this month's government report says that 7 percent of the labor force is out of work.

6. We should do a lot better this year because we have a new coach.

7. My parents say they were never any good at spelling; no wonder I have so much trouble.

8. Spring is here because I saw a robin.

9. The drama club failed because people stopped coming to meetings.

10. Lou must be in trouble again. There was a police car outside his place this morning.

11. Elaine is sure to win the essay contest because her mother is a writer.

12. If you would just pay attention, you'd understand what I'm saying.

13. Practice makes perfect.

14. If it rains at night, the next day will be bright.

15. Early to bed and early to rise makes a person healthy, wealthy, and wise.

Either-Or Thinking

How many times have you heard someone say, "There are two sides to every question"? How many times have you said it yourself? That statement is a generalization. Like most generalizations, it is not true all the time. Many questions have more than two sides. Many occurrences have more than one cause. Many problems have more than one solution. The following statements show incorrect either-or thinking.

> Either you're with us or against us.
> Support Cogsworthy or watch the city go to the dogs.
> If you're not behind Cogsworthy you're behind the times.
> Buy it or watch it go by. (from a sports car advertisment)

A person who isn't with us isn't necessarily against us. The person could be neutral. The person could be waiting to hear all the arguments before taking sides. The person could think that taking sides is a bad idea. A compromise might be better.

If you don't support Cogsworthy, you don't have to watch the city decay. The opponent may be better. The city may decay with or without Cogsworthy. And you're not necessarily old-fashioned if you don't agree with Cogsworthy. You may have ideas that haven't even occurred to Cogsworthy.

And if you don't buy the expensive sports car, you don't have to watch it go by and wish you had one. You can ignore it. You can laugh at it while you save fuel and money in your economy car.

Either-or thinking forces a person to choose between two sides when there are really more choices available.

There are some true either-or situations. Right now you are either whistling or not whistling. A radio is either on or off. In baseball a base runner is either safe or out. Each of the preceding statements could be rewritten to make it true.

> Either you're with us or you're not.
> Support Cogsworthy or don't support Cogsworthy.
> You're behind Cogsworthy or you're not.
> Buy it or don't buy it.

Exercise   Either-Or Thinking

Each of the following is an example of either-or thinking. Tell what is wrong with each.

1. The choice is yours: rust or Rustnomore.

2. We'll see who comes to tonight's meeting. Then we'll know who cares about our schools and who doesn't.

3. Some people are good at math, and some aren't. That's all there is to it.

4. Do you think you'll go to college or to a trade school?

5. Why didn't you come to the meeting? Don't you support us?

6. If new school taxes aren't approved, we'll have to eliminate sports.

7. If you can't say something good about someone, don't say anything at all.

8. Which would you rather do, spend ten dollars on an oil change or a few hundred dollars on an engine overhaul?

9. You didn't touch your dinner. I guess you don't like fish.

10. Half the group wants to go to the science museum, and the other half wants to go to the aquarium. It's hopeless.

11. If I can't find my ticket, I'll have to skip the concert.

12. There are two kinds of people: winners and losers.

Review Exercises   Putting Your Thinking Skills Together

A. Tell which of the following are statements of fact and which are opinions. Tell how you would check each fact to see if it is correct.

1. There are too many commercials on television.

2. Public television has no commercials.

3. We should have only public television stations.

4. Out of every hour of television broadcasting, twelve minutes are filled by commercials.

5. These commercials are annoying.

6. They interrupt the programs.

7. Only 5% of the stations in the United States are public.

8. Most of these are in large cities east of the Mississippi.

9. We have to find a way to get public television to the areas that do not have it.

10. Programs are more interesting when they are not interrupted by commercials.

B. Following are examples of faulty cause-and-effect reasoning and either-or thinking. Tell what is wrong with each example.

1. If we had had more time to practice, we would have won the band contest.

2. Andy is going to be late because I saw him stop at the corner store.

3. Would you rather live in the city or in the country?

4. Winter is early this year because we already have the heat on.

5. He's a good actor because he won an Academy award.

6. You're not voting for Smith? Don't tell me you want Jones for president.

7. She won't make the basketball team because she's too short.

8. If you liked the book, you'll love the movie.

9. It's the high cost of welfare that makes our taxes so high.

10. Smith would have been elected if he had spent more on advertising.

C. Following are examples of faulty generalizing. Use a qualifying word or phrase to make each generalization accurate.

1. People won't go out of their way to help others.

2. Popular people serve Crunchy Bits.

3. Californians play a lot of tennis.

4. People don't buy things they don't need.

5. Two people can get a job done in half the time of one.

6. Americans would rather watch the news on television than read newspapers.

7. Left-handed people are clumsy.

8. Students aren't interested in politics.

9. People don't want to work after age 65.

10. Traveling by train is not as comfortable as traveling by plane.

Chapter 10

The Library and How To Use It

Each year that you are in school, the building, your teachers, and your friends may change, but the uses of a library and the organization of a library will not. That is why each year you will be expected to be able to work more independently in the library.

Fortunately, the books in every library are organized by the same basic system. Of course, not all libraries have exactly the same books. For that reason it is important for you to become familiar with all of the materials offered in the particular library that you use.

Just how well do you know the library that you use? This chapter will help you to review what you already know about the library. The chapter will also help you make better use of the library than ever before.

Part 1   The Classification and Arrangement of Books

Books are classified into two major groups: **fiction** and **nonfiction** books. Each group is classified in a different way for your convenience in finding individual books.

The Classification of Books

Fiction

Fiction books contain stories that the author has imagined or invented. These books are arranged on the shelves alphabetically by the author's last name and are usually marked with an F for fiction on the spine.

Nonfiction

Nonfiction books are books that are true and factual. They can help you to learn about any subject you can possibly think of. Nonfiction books are classified according to the Dewey Decimal System. This system was originated by the famed American librarian, Melvil Dewey. The Dewey Decimal System classifies all books by an assigned number in one of ten major categories:

000–099	**General Works** (encyclopedias, almanacs, etc.)	
100–199	**Philosophy** (conduct, personality, psychology, etc.)	
200–299	**Religion** (the Bible, mythology, theology)	
300–399	**Social Science** (economics, law, education, government, folklore)	
400–499	**Language** (languages, grammars, dictionaries)	
500–599	**Science** (mathematics, chemistry, physics, biology, astronomy)	

600–699	**Useful Arts** (farming, cooking, sewing, nursing, radio, television, business, gardening)
700–799	**Fine Arts** (music, painting, drawing, acting, photography, games, sports, amusements)
800–899	**Literature** (poetry, plays, essays)—not fiction
900–999	**History** (biography, travel, geography)

The Dewey Decimal System is a highly organized system for classifying books. By taking an even closer look below, you can see that each major section is divided into even smaller, more detailed categories. The 900–999 History section, for example, is further divided as follows:

900 **History**
- 910   Geography, travel, description
- 920   Biography
- 930   Ancient history
- 940   Europe
- 950   Asia
- 960   Africa
- 970   North America
- 980   South America
- 990   Other parts of the world

Each of the preceding divisions within the 900 History category is then subdivided to become even more detailed as in the following example:

970 **North America**
- 971   Canada
- 972   Middle America
- 983   United States
- 974   Northeastern states
- 975   Southeastern states
- 976   South central states
- 977   North central states
- 978   Western states
- 979   States of the Great Basin and Pacific Slope

These divisions and subdivisions of the Dewey Decimal System make it possible for all of the books on one particular subject to be put on the library shelves together so it will be easier for you to find them.

Call Numbers

The **call number** is an organized sequence of numbers and letters printed on the spine of a book that helps you to identify that book. Books are arranged on the shelves by the details included in their call number. This arrangement makes it easier for you to find the book you need. The following example will help you to understand the parts of a call number:

Book: *Bicycling*
Author: Nancy Neiman Baranet

Call number: **796.6**
              B 225 b

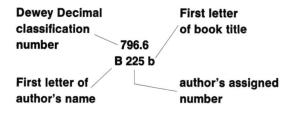

Books are first arranged by the Dewey Decimal number on the top line. Then, within each classification number, the books are arranged by the first letter of the author's last name.

Both the Dewey Decimal number and the call number identify books as precisely as possible in order to make it easier for you to find them. Within this system, there are three sections that deserve special mention:

Biography. Biographies and autobiographies are nonfiction books classified together and shelved in a special section of the library. The class numbers reserved for biography are 920 and 921.

920 This class number is reserved for collective biographies. These are books that contain the life story of more than one person. The call number for a collective biography is 920, plus the initial of the author's or editor's last name.

For example:
Five Artists of the Old West by Clide Hollmann

Call number: 920
                       H

921   This class number is used for individual biographies and autobiographies. These books are arranged differently on the shelves. They are arranged alphabetically by the last name of the *person written about*. For this reason, the call number is composed of 921 and the initial of the last name of the person the book is about. For example, the call number for a biography about Benjamin Franklin would be: 921
                                                                       F

Reference Books. Reference books of particular types or on specific subjects are also shelved together, with the letter R above the classification number: R
                                                          423.1
                                                          D56

Fiction. Fiction books are arranged on the shelves alphabetically by the author's last name. For this reason, fiction books are labeled with an *F* on the top line and with the first initial of the author's last name on the second line along with the author number and the initial of the first word of the title. This is especially important when the author has written more than one book.

The Outsiders   F
by S. E. Hinton   H666

Short Story Collections. Most libraries keep the fiction books that contain several short stories in a separate section. They are usually marked with *SC* which stands for "Story Collection." The initial of the author's or editor's last name is placed below the SC. The books are arranged alphabetically by the author's or editor's last name. Here is an example:

SC   *Journey to Another Star and Other Stories*
E   by Roger Elwood

Exercises   **The Classification and Arrangement of Books**

A. Using the Dewey Decimal System outlined on pages 174 and 175, assign the correct classification number for each of the following.

1. _____ *Skylab, Pioneer Space Station,* Wm. G. Helder

2. _____ *You and Your Feelings,* Eda J. LeShan

3. _____ *Inside Jazz,* James Lincoln Collier

4. _____ *The Right To Remain Silent,* Milton Meltzer

5. _____ *Understanding Photography,* George Sullivan

6. _____ *Plays for Great Occasions,* Graham DuBois

7. _____ *Hieroglyphs for Fun,* Joseph and Lenore Scott

8. _____ *Insects as Pets,* Paul Villiard

9. _____ *Dictionary of Mis-information,* Tom Beunaur

10. _____ *We, the Chinese,* Deirdre Hunter

11. _____ *Myths and Legends of the Greeks,* Nicola Ann Sissons

12. _____ *Bicycle Repair,* Irene Cumming Kleeburg

B. Each of the following books belongs in one of the special categories of *biography, collective biography,* or *short story collection.* After reading the title carefully, assign the proper call number code to each special category.

_____ *Record-Breakers of the Major Leagues,*
Lou Sabin

_____ *Carly Simon,* Charles and Ann Morse

_____ *Masters of Modern Music,* Melvin Berger

_____ *The Phantom Cyclist and Other Short Stories,* Ruth Ainsworth

_____ *Driven to Win: A. J. Foyt,* Mike Kupper

_____ *Americans in Space,* Ross Olvey

_____ *Annie Sullivan, A Portrait,* Terry Dunnahoo

_____ *Men and Machines; Ten Stories of Science Fiction,* Robert Silverberg

C. Go to your school library and complete the following survey. List these headings on your paper: *Fiction, Nonfiction, Biography, Reference, Magazines,* and *Audio-Visual Materials.* Under each heading, list three titles and authors of books and materials that you would be interested in using.

Part 2   Using the Card Catalog

The **card catalog** is a cabinet of small drawers in which a card for each book is filed alphabetically in the library. There are usually three cards for the same book in the card catalog: the *author card,* the *title card,* and the *subject card.* Each of these cards has the same information. However, each would be found in a different section of the card catalog. Look carefully at the following examples for the book A *Special Kind of Courage* by Geraldo Rivera.

The Author Card

If you happen to know only the name of the author and not the title of the book, you should use the card catalog to look up the name of the author. The author card will tell you the call number of the book you want to read. Also, the titles of all of the other books that the author has written and that are in that library will be listed on a separate card and filed alphabetically by the first word in each title. Cards for books *about* the author are filed *behind* his or her author cards. Here is an example of an author card for the book A *Special Kind of Courage*:

```
920     Rivera, Geraldo
R621

            A special kind of courage; profiles
            of young Americans.
            Illus. by Edith Vonnegut.
            Simon 1976.
                 319p., illus.
            1. Courage    2. Youth—Case Studies
                            ○
```

The Title Card

When looking up the title of a book in the card catalog, remember that A, *An*, and *The* do not count as first words in a title. Here is the title card for A *Special Kind of Courage*:

```
920          A special kind of courage
R621
          Rivera, Geraldo
               A special kind of courage;
               profiles of young Americans.
               Illus. by Edith Vonnegut.
               Simon 1976.
                    319p., illus.
               1. Courage    2. Youth—Case Studies
                            ○
```

The Subject Card

When you want to find resources on a particular subject, the best approach is to look up the subject in the card catalog. A subject card for the book *A Special Kind of Courage* would be found under the heading *Courage,* as in the following example:

```
920      COURAGE
R621
              Rivera, Geraldo
                      A special kind of courage;
              profiles of young Americans.
              Illus. by Edith Vonnegut.
              Simon 1976.
                      319p., illus.
              1. Courage    2. Youth—Case Studies
                              O
```

Notice that all three types of catalog cards (author, title, subject) give the same information. This information includes the following:

1. The call number.

2. The titles, author, publisher, and date of publication.

3. The number of pages and a listing of special features such as illustrations, index, maps, etc.

Often the card will also provide a brief description of the material in the book and a listing of other catalog cards for the book. Pay particular attention to the use of capitalization on the catalog cards. Only proper names and the first word of the title are capitalized. To find the title, look at the entry immediately following the author's name.

Cross Reference Cards

When you look up a subject you will sometimes find a card that reads *See* or *See also*. The "See" card refers you to another subject heading in the catalog which will give you the information you want. For example, if you want a book on commercials, you might find a card that reads:

```
Cars
   see
Transportation




                    ◯
```

This "See" card tells you that the library catalogs all books on cars under the subject heading of *transportation*.

```
       COOKING
          see also
  Appetizers
  Barbecue cookery
  Casserole cookery
  Food as gifts
  Frying
  Microwave cookery
  Salads
  Sandwiches
  Soups
  also names of individual foods, e.g., Rice
                    ◯
```

The "See also" card refers you to other subjects closely related to the one you are interested in. This card will help you to find a variety of information on the topic. A "See also" card is shown at the bottom of page 182.

Guide Cards

Guide cards are placed in the card catalog to help guide you to the correct place in the alphabet for the word you are looking for. These cards extend above the other cards, and they have letters, complete words, or general headings on them. For example, if you were looking under the subject of *housing* in the following catalog drawer, you would look between the guide cards *Hos* and *How*.

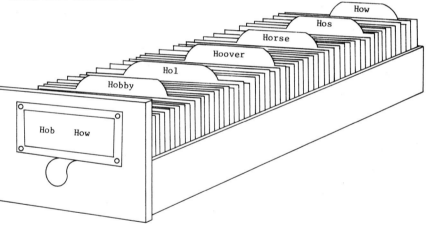

Exercises   Using the card catalog

A. What subject cards would give you information about the following topics? Discuss your answers in class.

1. How to make a film
2. Backpacking in Maine
3. Records of the
    Superbowl

4. Careers in medicine
5. How to improve your
     tennis game
6. Designing stained glass
7. The founder of soccer
8. How to refinish
     furniture
9. Building a greenhouse
10. Vacationing in national
     parks

B. Use the card catalog to find the title, author, call number, and publication date of the following books.

1. A book about rock music
2. A book of detective stories
3. A book about Pelé
4. A book about astronomy
5. A book on flags
6. A book of Christmas plays
7. A book about aquariums
8. A book about the Boston Tea Party
9. A book about World War II planes
10. A book about newspapers

C. Using the card catalog, list the title, author, call number, and publication date of all resources about two of the following:

1. Babe Didrikson
2. A career as a cartoonist
3. Hank Aaron
4. Franklin D. Roosevelt
5. General Douglas MacArthur
6. Space exploration
7. A career as a dentist

8. CB radios
9. Martin Luther King, Jr.
10. Olga Korbut

Part 3 Using Reference Materials

Every library has either a reference room or a reference section. It is here that you will find a variety of reference materials which include the following: dictionaries; encyclopedias; pamphlets, handbooks, and catalogs; almanacs and yearbooks; atlases; biographical reference books; and magazines. Each of these reference books is used for a certain purpose and each has its own particular organization. Some offer you very general information about a topic while others are very specific and detailed.

Learning to use the many different reference books that are available will provide you with the detailed, up-to-date information you need for a thorough report on any subject you may choose.

Dictionaries

General Dictionaries. The dictionary is one of the best and most convenient general references you can use. A dictionary gives you the spelling, pronunciation, and meanings of a word, as well as brief information about many subjects, such as people, places, abbreviations, and foreign terms.

There are three major types of dictionaries:

> **Unabridged Dictionaries.** These are the largest and most complete dictionaries. They contain well over 250,000 words, and give the complete history of each word and every definition and use for that word.

> **Abridged Dictionaries.** These dictionaries are often called

"desk" or "collegiate" dictionaries. They contain about 130,000 to 150,000 words. They contain the information you would normally need about spellings, pronunciations, definitions, and matters of usage. In addition, they usually provide special sections that contain information such as biographical and geographical references.

Here is a list of frequently used abridged dictionaries:

General Dictionaries

The American Heritage Dictionary of the English Language
The Macmillan Dictionary
The Random House Dictionary of the English Language
Thorndike-Barnhart Dictionary
Webster's New World Dictionary of the American Language
Webster's New Collegiate Dictionary

Pocket Dictionaries. These dictionaries are very limited in the number of words they contain. They should be use mainly to check the spelling of ordinary words or to give you a quick definition of an unfamiliar word you may come across in your reading.

Dictionaries About Your Language. Another group of dictionaries contains information about specific aspects of the English language, such as synonyms, antonyms, rhymes, and slang. These dictionaries have a limited but specific use.

Dictionaries About Your Language

Abbreviations Dictionary
Brewer's Dictionary of Phrase and Fable
A Dictionary of Slang and Unconventional English
A Dictionary of Word and Phrase Origins (3 volumes)
Mathew's Dictionary of Americanisms
The New Roget's Thesaurus in Dictionary Form
The Oxford Dictionary of English Etymology
Roget's International Thesaurus
Wood's Unabridged Rhyming Dictionary

The *thesauruses* that are included in the language dictionary list have a special purpose to you as a writer. A **thesaurus** is a dictionary of words that have similar meanings. It is sometimes called a dictionary of synonyms. By using a thesaurus when you write, you will be able to use words that convey the exact meaning you need, and you will avoid repeating already overused words.

Here is an entry from a thesaurus. You can see how helpful a thesaurus can be when you are looking for a word that fits a particular meaning.

An Entry from *Roget's International Thesaurus*

TRAVEL: 1. n. locomotion, course, journeying, globetrotting, parade, caravan
2. n. wandering, roving, nomadism, vagabondism, wanderlust, tourism.
3. n. migration, passage, trek, emigration, immigration.
4. n. walking, ramble, hike, march, tramp, stroll, promenade, jaunt, hitchhiking (slang, U.S.)
5. v. journey, tour, hit the trail (slang), globetrot, flit, wander, roam, rove, traipse, prowl, stray, straggle, meander, jaunt, stroll, saunter, tramp.
6. v. step, stride, shuffle, hobble, stagger, toddle, scuttle, prance, flounce, stalk, strut, amble, swagger, tiptoe, march, run.

Dictionaries on Specific Subjects. There are also many dictionaries that deal with specific subjects such as music, geography, medicine, and science. The following list includes the names of many of these dictionaries. There are far too many to name, so check to see how many different kinds your library offers.

Special-Subject Dictionaries

Compton's Illustrated Science Dictionary
Dictionary of Economics
Dictionary of American History (5 volumes)

Dictionary of Literary Terms
Dictionary of Sports
Grove's Dictionary of Music and Musicians (10 volumes)
Harvard Dictionary of Music
An Illustrated Dictionary of Art and Archaeology
Mathematical Dictionary
Webster's Biographical Dictionary
Webster's Geographical Dictionary
Webster's Dictionary of Proper Names

Encyclopedias

General Encyclopedias. An encyclopedia contains general articles on nearly every known subject. This information is organized alphabetically into volumes. There are guide words at the top of each page to help you find information. Each set of encyclopedias also has an index, which you should check before looking for your information. The index is usually in the last volume of the encyclopedia or in a separate volume. The following encyclopedias are used frequently by people of your age:

General Encyclopedias

Collier's Encyclopedia (24 volumes)
Compton's Encyclopedia (26 volumes)
Encyclopaedia Britannica (29 volumes)
Encyclopedia Americana (30 volumes)
World Book Encyclopedia (22 volumes)

The library also has many encyclopedias that deal with specific subjects. Here are some of them:

Encyclopedias on Specific Subjects

The Baseball Encyclopedia
Better Homes and Gardens Encyclopedia of Cooking
The Encyclopedia of American Facts and Dates
Encyclopedia of Animal Care
Encyclopedia of Careers and Vocational Guidance

The Encyclopedia of Folk, Country, & Western Music
Encyclopedia of World Art (15 volumes)
Family Life and Health Encyclopedia (22 volumes)
The Illustrated Encyclopedia of Aviation and Space
The Illustrated Encyclopedia of World Coins
La Rousse Encyclopedia of Mythology
McGraw-Hill Encyclopedia of World Biography
    (12 volumes)
The Mammals of America
The Negro Heritage Library (9 volumes)
The Ocean World of Jacques Cousteau (19 volumes)
Popular Mechanics Do-It-Yourself Encyclopedia
    (16 volumes)
Rock Encyclopedia
Universal Encyclopedia of Mathematics

This list is by no means complete. You should check your library to see the many kinds of encyclopedias that are available.

Exercises   Using the Dictionary and the Encyclopedia

A. To answer the following questions, first determine whether you should use a dictionary or an encyclopedia. Then answer each question, and list the title of the reference book used.

1. How many different kinds of rhinoceroses are there?

2. Where are these three colleges: *Monmouth, Hollins, Simpson?* Which is the oldest?

3. How many different methods of gold mining are there?

4. When was the French painter Henri Matisse born?

5. Where exactly is the Mason-Dixon line?

6. How are diamonds mined?

7. What are the chief facts in the life of Neil Armstrong?

8. What are four synonyms for the word *meagre?*

9. How do you draw the alphabet symbol for the Greek word *delta?*

10. Who discovered the Hawaiian Islands?

11. For what is the Medal of Honor given?

12. Are these words singular or plural: *dice, Magi, bacteria, datum, genus?*

B. Study the thesaurus entry for *travel* shown on page 187. Find a precise synonym to complete the following sentences. You may need to add *s* or *ed* to the end of the word.

1. The thief —————— around the room in the dark.

2. The lone sheep was bleating because it had —————— from the flock.

3. The Boy Scouts were tired from their seven-mile ——————.

4. His —————— took him around the world.

5. Suzanne —————— down the street in her new clothes.

6. After being wounded, he —————— and then fell.

C. Using either your dictionary or thesaurus, answer the following questions. Write the name of the resource you used after each answer.

1. Would you use a *serigraph* to cook dinner or to hang on your wall?

2. Name five synonyms for the word *serious?*

3. From what language is the word *aardvark* derived? What does the translation of the word mean?

4. List four synonyms for the word *wet,* and choose an appropriate noun for each synonym to describe.

5. Do you have a *palaestra* at your school?

6. Name five antonyms for the word *noisy.*

7. If you were a *plebe,* what would you be?

8. Does *quay* rhyme with *day, me,* or *buoy?*

9. What is the monetary value of a *krone?*

10. Rewrite the following sentence by replacing the underlined words to make it more interesting:

He put on his <u>hat</u> and walked away <u>quickly</u>.

Almanacs and Yearbooks

Almanacs and yearbooks are published annually. They are most useful sources of information, facts, and statistics on current events and historical records of government, sports, entertainment, population, and many other subjects. The information in an almanac is not arranged in any one particular order, so you will have to consult the index and the table of contents to find the location of the information you need. Here is a partial list of the most widely used almanacs and yearbooks:

Guinness Book of World Records
Information Please Almanac, Atlas, and Yearbook
World Almanac and Book of Facts
World Book Science Yearbook
World Book Yearbook of Events

Atlases

An atlas is a reference book that contains many large, detailed maps of the world. It also contains other sources of geographical information such as statistics about population, temperatures, oceans, and other specific areas. Some atlases publish different information, so it is a good idea to study the table of contents and any directions given to the reader before you try to use it. The following is a list of reliable atlases:

Atlas of World History
The Britannica Atlas
Collier's World Atlas and Gazetteer
Goode's World Atlas
Grossett World Atlas
The International Atlas from Rand McNally
National Geographic Atlas of the World
The Times Atlas of the World
Webster's Atlas with Zip Code Directory

Biographical References

Both a dictionary and an encyclopedia will give you information about people. However, the best references to use when you need detailed information about a particular person are biographical references. They are specific subject books that deal only with information about people. Some of the most commonly biographical references used are these:

> *Contemporary Authors*
> *Current Biography*
> *Dictionary of American Biography*
> *Dictionary of National Biography*
> *The Interational Who's Who*
> *Twentieth Century Authors*
> *Who's Who*
> *Who's Who in America*
> *Who's Who in the East (and Eastern Canada)*
> *Who's Who in the Midwest*
> *Who's Who in the South and Southeast*
> *Who's Who in the West*
> *Who's Who in American Women*

Exercises Using Almanacs, Atlases, and Biographical References

A. Use both an almanac and an atlas to answer the following questions. List the reference you used after your answer.

1. What is the largest lake in the world?
2. What were the first words sent over the telegraph?
3. Who wrote the Pledge of Allegiance to the flag?
4. What is the depth of the Dead Sea?
5. What are the three largest islands in the Mediterranean Sea?
6. What is the address for the League of Women Voters?
7. How long is a day on the planet Jupiter?
8. What are the world's highest and lowest elevations?

9. What is the most popular breed of dog in the United States?

10. What is the distance of the earth to the moon?

B. Using a biographical reference, answer the following questions. List the title of the reference you used to answer the question.

1. For what two things was Philip K. Wrigley famous?

2. For what is Bruce Jenner famous? Where and when was he born?

3. What well known book did Harper Lee write? Who starred in the movie version?

4. For what newspaper does Bob Woodward write? Who was his partner for what historical event?

5. Jacques Cousteau is the co-inventor of what device?

6. List the titles of three books written by Ray Bradbury.

7. How old was Dorothy Hamill when she won her Olympic Gold Medal?

8. Where and when was Joni Mitchell born?

9. What is the name of a play written by Paul Zindel?

10. Who is Robyn Smith?

The Vertical File

Many libraries have a file cabinet in which they keep an alphabetical file of pamphlets, catalogs, handbooks, booklets, and clippings about a variety of subjects. Always check the vertical file when you are writing a report or looking for information, especially on careers.

Readers' Guide to Periodical Literature

The *Readers' Guide to Periodical Literature* is a monthly index of magazine articles listed alphabetically by subject and author. It is issued twice a month from September to June, and once a month in July and August. An entire year's issues are bound in one hardcover volume at the end of the year. There are two forms of the *Readers' Guide*. The unabridged edition indexes over 135 magazines and is found mainly in high school and public libraries. The abridged edition of the *Readers' Guide* indexes 45 magazines and is generally used in junior high school libraries.

The *Readers' Guide* is a valuable source of information. It is important to read the abbreviation guide in the preface so that you will understand how to read each entry. The example on page 195 illustrates how articles are listed.

Exercises   **Using the *Readers' Guide***

A. Write the meanings of the following abbreviations used in the *Readers' Guide*:

Lib J	m	Spr	tr	w
abr	Je	+	bibl	Ag
no	cont	bi-w	il	supp

B. Use the excerpt from the *Reader's Guide* on page 195 to answer the following questions:

1. What magazines have articles on the subject of yacht racing?

2. What issue of *Good Housekeeping* carried an article on yogurt recipes?

3. What page of *Newsweek* did the article "Young at Heart" appear on? What issue did the article appear in?

4. What do the initials YWCA stand for?

5. Who wrote an article about F. Scott Fitzgerald and Ring Lardner? In what magazine did the article appear?

6. Give the complete magazine title for the following abbreviations:

  Sat R   *Sports Illus*   *Good H*   *U.S. News*

Excerpt from the *Readers' Guide*

WYOMING
  See also
  Coal mines and mining—Wyoming
  Fishing—Wyoming   — "see also" cross reference
YWCA. See Young Women's Christian Association — "see" cross reference
YACHT hijacking. See Boat hijacking
YACHT racing
  Captain outrageous; T. Turner at the America's Cup trials.
    P. Bonventre and R. Manning. il por Newsweek 90:45-6
    Jl 11 '77
  Setting sail for the defense; America's Cup trials: with report
    by N. Williamson. C. Phinizy. il Sports Illus 46:30-5 Je
    20 '77
YARDLEY, Jonathan — author entry
  Harmony in Great Neck: the friendship of Ring Lardner and
    F. Scott Fitzgerald; excerpt from Ring: a biography of
    Ring Lardner. il pors Sat R 4:23-5+ Jl 9 '77
YEAR round schools. See School year
YELLOWSTONE National Park — subject entry
  Rocky Mountain high time of your life. V. Landi. il Outdoor
    Life 159:70-5+ My '77
YOGURT
  Making yogurt the easy way; yogurt makers and recipes. il
    Good H 185:140+ Jl '77 — name of magazine
YOGURT makers. See Kitchen utensils and appliances
YOUNG, Andrew J. 1932-
  Are Young's wings being clipped? por U.S. News 82:25 — volume number
    My 2 '77
                    about
  Andy Young and the truth. J. L. Jackson. por Newsweek
    90:9 Jl 11 '77
  Andy Young is at it again. R. Carroll and others. il por — page reference
    Newsweek 89:52 Je 6 '77
  Young at heart. J. Pringle. il por Newsweek 89:44 My 30 '77
  Young mission. N. Cousins. Sat R 4:4 Jl 9 '77 — date of magazine
YOUNG adults literature
                Bibliography
  Adult books for young adults; ed by R. Moorachian. See
    issues of School library journal
  Best books for spring 1977; ed by L. N. Gerhardt and others.
    il SLJ 23:35-7 My '77 — illustrated article
  Best books for whom; or, Where have all the grown-ups
    gone? L. L. Shapiro. Wilson Lib Bull 51:803-4+ Je '77
YOUNG adults reading
  RIF for teenagers. N. L. Marqua. SLJ 23:45 My '77

Chapter 11

Interviews and Group Discussion

Talking with people is something you all enjoy doing. You talk to your friends because you have something to tell them or because they have something to tell you. This kind of talking you call *conversation*. Conversation plays an important part in your daily social life. It helps you to know the people around you better.

Conversations can also have a more specific purpose. You may need to interview someone in order to obtain new information for a report you are writing. You and several others may need to have a group discussion to plan a project you are working on. Both interviewing and group discussion are forms of conversation with a specific purpose.

This chapter will help you improve your interviewing skills and your group discussion skills.

Part 1 Interviewing Others

The interview is a special kind of conversation in which the purpose is either to *gather information* or to *supply information*. An interview gives people the opportunity to exchange questions and answers for a specific purpose. At times when you need to gather information for a report, interviewing a knowledgeable person will be very helpful. At other times, such as when you are applying for a job, you will be the one supplying most of the information.

Although interviews are basically conversational, they are also well organized because they have a specific purpose. In order to make your interview a successful one, there are certain guidelines you should follow.

Guidelines for Conducting Interviews

1. Plan the interview carefully.

a. Choose a person who has special knowledge or interesting opinions about the subject on which you are reporting.

b. Make a definite appointment by arranging a time and date that is convenient for the person being interviewed. When you request an interview, be sure to identify yourself and explain why you want the interview.

c. Do some basic research about the subject so you can ask intelligent questions.

d. Prepare clear, specific questions in advance so that you are sure to get the information you need.

2. Make a good impression.

a. Arrive for your interview on time.

b. Introduce yourself and restate your purpose for the interview.

c. Be ready to ask your questions, one at a time. If the person being interviewed wants to just talk about the subject, you may need to save your questions until the end, unless the person has already answered them.

d. Be a good listener. Keep your attention on the speaker and what he or she is saying. The person may add some information that you hadn't thought of before.

e. At the end of the interview, be sure to thank the person.

3. Get the correct facts.

a. Take notes, especially on names and figures. Make the notes brief so that you are not writing continually while the person is talking.

b. If you want to quote the person, be sure to ask permission.

c. Go over your notes as soon as possible after the interview and write your report while the information is still fresh in your mind.

Exercises   Planning an Interview

A. List five purposes for which you might conduct interviews in connection with your classwork or extracurricular activities. Name an appropriate person to be interviewed for each purpose.

B. Choose one of the interviews you selected in the first exercise and make a list of ten questions as a guide for an interview.

Part 2   Group Discussion

Group discussion is an easy way to find an answer to a problem, to come up with a new idea, or simply to exchange information. This discussion can be either formal or informal, depending on the subject and purpose of the discussion. One of the best things about group discussion is that everyone is supposed to get a chance to talk and give his or her opinion.

There are two basic types of group discussion: **informal group discussion** and **formal group discussion.** It is important that you know which kind of discussion you are involved in because each has a specific purpose and a certain procedure to follow.

Informal Group Discussion

An informal group discussion usually takes place as soon as a problem or the need for a decision arises. Consider the following situations:

> Suppose your family has decided to go on a vacation, but you all want to go to different places?

> Suppose your intramural team has to decide on the best day and time to practice together?

> Suppose you and your friends want to go somewhere, but you just can't decide where to go?

The best solution to your problem is to have an informal discussion. Why? Because you need to exchange your ideas and talk about the pro's and con's of each idea for the purpose of arriving at a decision, solution, or plan of action that satisfies the group.

Most discussions in which you participate are informal. They usually occur spontaneously, so you don't have to prepare for them. The subjects you discuss are usually those that members of the group know something about from their common knowledge or experience. This is why informal discussions are often organized by the people themselves.

Sometimes a class or club will break into small informal groups so that everyone will have a chance to express his or her ideas in a shorter amount of time. When this method is used, you may need to select a temporary leader to help keep the discussion organized so that your purpose is accomplished.

Even though informal discussion may seem like a conversation among friends, it is more organized and has a specific purpose to accomplish.

Informal Discussion

Subjects:	General knowledge
Preparation:	Not required
Organization:	Small groups with no audience; a temporary leader may be selected.
Purpose:	To exchange ideas in order to make a group decision or plan of action.

Formal Group Discussion

A formal discussion requires more preparation and organization than an informal discussion does. Consider the following topics for discussion:

Should space exploration be continued?

Is a college education necessary to achieve success?

How stable are professional sports as a career?

How does Jack London use the theme of man vs. nature in his stories?

You probably know something about each of the preceding topics, but how much of what you know is only opinion and how much is *fact*? If you were asked to discuss one of these topics, you would first have to do some research. One of the major differences, then, between an informal discussion and a formal discussion is that a formal discussion requires *preparation.*

Logically, then, another major difference between the informal and the formal discussion is the subject to be discussed. Generally, the subject of a formal discussion is either assigned to you or is selected by your group according to the needs or interests of the audience. Since you do discuss your information in front of an audience, you can see how important it is to be prepared.

The formal discussion is highly organized. First, one person in the group is selected to be the chairperson. The chairperson states the problem or subject, keeps the discussion on the subject, makes sure that everyone has a chance to speak, and keeps the discussion moving.

Each member of the group must present his or her information. The best way to prepare your information is to use the many references that are available to you in your school library. Use Chapter 10, "Using the Library," for more specific details about references you can use.

Even though you plan the formal discussion *before* it is presented, it is important that the members of your group freely exchange ideas based on the information you have prepared. In this way, both the members of the group and the audience will learn more. That is the purpose of a formal group discussion. It is not a report but a discussion among people to inform the audience as well as each other.

Formal Discussion

Subjects:	Assigned or determined by the needs or interests of the audience.
Preparation:	Very important; researched facts are needed.
Organization:	A chairperson is selected; discussion is presented in front of an audience.
Purpose:	To exchange ideas and information in order to inform the audience.

Exercises   Informal and Formal Group Discussion

A. Look at the following list of subjects. Tell which you think should be discussed formally, and which should be discussed informally. Then explain the reasons for your decision.

Which team will win the Super Bowl or World Series?

Should schools be air-conditioned?

Should people use seat belts?

What is approximately the average time that teenagers spend watching TV per day?

What should be the theme for the spring dance?

What are some good suggestions for a new school mascot?

What are the best ways of conserving energy?

How does Edgar Allan Poe create suspense in his short stories?

B. Try the following informal discussion. First, divide the class into three groups. Now follow these directions:

You are to calculate the average height in feet and inches of the members of your group. If you don't know your exact height, you may estimate. The group must agree on the answer and submit it to the teacher.

Once you have finished your calculations and the exercise, discuss the following questions about the exercise. This will help you to understand about organizing a group.

Did anyone take over leadership?

Was he or she elected by the group?

Was a leader needed? Why or why not?

What responsibility did each member have?

Did anything slow down the group?

How could the group solve the problem faster or better next time?

Part 3 Roles of Responsibility

From your own experience in different classes and organizations, you've probably noticed that when one person talks too much, nothing ever gets accomplished. Sometimes a simple discussion turns into an argument and still nothing gets accomplished. For a group discussion to be successful, everyone in the group must accept some responsibility.

When you are a member of either an informal discussion or a formal discussion, you will find that it will be much easier to achieve the purpose of the discussion if the following five roles of responsibility are accepted by the group. Each of these roles has a specific purpose which helps to organize the discussion by making you more aware of the importance of what you say.

The Chairperson or Temporary Leader

The role of chairperson or temporary leader carries a lot of responsibility. In this position, each member of the group looks to you for guidance. You must know your subject well, be fair with all members, and see that the purpose of the discussion is accomplished. The chairperson:

1. Starts the discussion by defining the problem or by offering the first bit of information. For example:

> "The purpose of our discussion is to decide the importance of using seat belts. There are many areas to consider in this issue such as safety, insurance benefits, government standards, and the results of manufacturers' tests. Barry, will you tell us what information you have found about this issue?"

> "If we're going to discuss what gift the student council should buy the school, let's first make a list of things that are needed. I would like to suggest a new and larger trophy case."

2. Organizes the group into task forces if the subject involves a lot of material or if more than one decision is needed.

"Andrea will discuss the insurance benefits of using seat belts, Paul will tell us about government standards that are required, and David and Sharon will discuss the results of the manufacturers' testing to provide safety precautions."

"Since we have enough money to buy two gifts and since our ideas fall into two main categories, the gym and the library, let's divide into two groups to make our final decision."

3. Keeps the discussion on the subject so that time and ideas won't be wasted.

"I think we're talking too much about the performance of individual cars rather than the use of seat belts in those cars. Let's get back to the importance of using seat belts."

"Instead of complaining about what's wrong with the gym, how about some good suggestions for gifts to make it better?"

4. Makes sure that everyone has a chance to talk so that all information and ideas are exchanged.

"Andrea, I think now would be a good time for you to tell us about the insurance benefits you receive when you use seat belts."

"Ed, we haven't heard your ideas yet about what we should buy as a gift. What is your suggestion?"

The Initiator

In an active discussion, everyone should "initiate" new ideas and facts. However, some people will serve only as an initiator while others choose to also serve in another role. The initiator:

1. Offers new ideas for discussion.

"Also, I think we should consider the safety of a small child in a car seat that has a seat belt."

"My idea is that the student council should buy some typewriters for the library. Everyone could benefit from that gift."

2. Gives additional information to support someone else's idea.

"The *Newsweek* article I read agrees with your statement that it's just as important for people in the back seat to use seat belts."

"I agree with Ann. The library needs more typewriters. It seems they are always taken when my friends and I need to type a report."

The Clarifier

As the clarifier, you help other group members to support their information and to think of new ideas. The responsibility of the clarifier is to stimulate thought, help others to make their ideas and information clear, and to initiate new ideas. The clarifier:

1. Asks questions about other people's information.

"Sharon, how do we know that the test results for that particular manufacturer are true for all cars?"

"A new trophy case might be a good idea, but do you really think it's something the whole school would care about?"

2. Asks for additional information.

"Paul, do you have more current statistics to prove that the majority of people seriously hurt in car accidents were not wearing seat belts?"

"We have a lot of good ideas, but do we have to spend all of the money?"

The Summarizer

The summarizer keeps everyone in touch with what's happening during the discussion. It is important for you to listen carefully in order to keep track of the main points that have been made. It may help you to take notes during the discussion in order to keep the group informed of its progress. The summarizer:

1. States the main points that have been made so that the group is aware of its progress and what it still has to cover.

> "So far we have discussed the government regulations for seat belts and the manufacturers' testing results showing why people should use seat belts. Who has some accident statistics that will bring us closer to our goal?"

> "We know that we have enough money to buy more than one gift, and that we have several good ideas and the approximate price of each. Now we need to make a final decision about what to buy."

2. Points out areas of disagreement based on information from different sources or different group members. This helps to prevent arguments and helps the group to remember what is really important about the information.

> "Government regulations state that there should be enough seat belts in every car for the number of people it can hold. But David's research shows us that several manufacturers put only two seat belts in the back seat."

> "Joe says that a new trophy case is a good idea because the whole school is proud of its winning teams. But Ann says that the hall is always so crowded near the trophy case that most people don't ever bother to look at it."

The Evaluator

The responsibility of the evaluator is to state the conclusions of the group at the end of the discussion. This doesn't mean that the evaluator is not allowed to say anything until the end. During the discussion, the evaluator can choose another role to play so that his or her opinions can be expressed. The evaluator:

States the conclusions of the group at the end of the discussion.

"The information presented by this group shows that the government, car manufacturers, and insurance agencies are all interested in the safety that seat belts give. The information also proves that you have a better chance of not getting hurt as seriously in an accident and that your insurance is cheaper if you use seat belts. Therefore, it is important for you to use seat belts for your own safety."

"We have enough money to buy two gifts. Since most of the ideas were gifts for the gym and the library, our final decision is to buy six new gymnastic mats for the gym and two new typewriters for the library."

The more group discussion you have a chance to participate in, the easier it will be to see the importance of the five roles of responsibility. You may find that you are especially good at one role, or you may want to change roles in different discussions. The role you choose will depend on the amount of information you have, how well prepared you are, and how well you listen. The main thing to remember is that the five different roles help you to achieve the purpose of your discussion and help you to make important contributions to the group.

Exercises   Roles of Responsibility

A.   Read each of the following statements and identify which of the five roles is speaking: the chairperson or temporary leader, the initiator, the clarifier, the summarizer, or the evaluator.

1. "What we need to do is to divide into groups to get each part of this problem solved."

2. "Do you have more facts to prove that point?"

3. "Our final decision is to hold the Christmas student council dance on Friday, December 18, from 7:30 to 10:00 in the school gym."

4. "I would recommend any of Jack London's books for good reading, especially *The Call of the Wild*."

5. "So far we have three books that we all agree to recommend, but we still need two more titles."

6. "My idea for the theme of the dance is Winter Wonderland."

7. "Using only one source is not enough to prove that point. Do you have more information?"

8. "Mr. Jensen wants us to set up the schedule for the intramural team practice. We have eight different teams to consider."

B. Divide the class into groups of six to eight people each. Distribute slips of paper, each of which indicates the role the student is to play in the discussion. Make sure all roles are represented in each group. Then give each group a topic such as:

Should the school year be twelve months long?

Should schools be air-conditioned?

What are three of the most popular TV shows for kids your age?

Make a list of five books for recommended reading.

Should teenagers have to pay adult movie prices?

A time limit of approximately 20 minutes should be imposed so that a discussion of roles can follow the exercise. Try the exercise again with a new topic. This time try for a different role.

C. Plan a formal discussion with four or five other people to present to your class. Choose a topic that all of you are interested in and that can be easily researched in your school library. Elect a chairperson and decide what information about the subject each person will be responsible for. Do your research carefully and keep accurate records of all your sources. Present your discussion to the class.

Grammar and Usage

Section 1.   **The Simple Sentence**   3

Section 2.   **Using Nouns**   33

Section 3.   **Using Pronouns**   45

Section 4.   **Using Verbs**   73

Section 5.   **Using Modifiers**   109

Section 6.   **Using Prepositions and Conjunctions**   135

Section 7.   **Using Compound and Complex Sentences**   151

Section 8.   **Making Subjects and Verbs Agree**   185

Section 9.   **Using Verbals**   197

The Mechanics of Writing

Section 10.   **Capitalization**   209

Section 11.   **Punctuation**   225

Section 12.   **Spelling**   263

A detailed Table of Contents of Sections 1–12 appears in the front of this book.

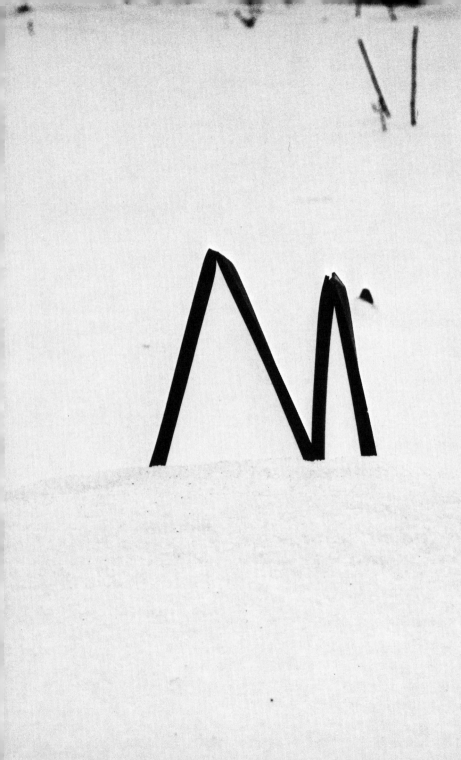

Section 1

The Simple Sentence

In conversation, you do not always have to use complete sentences. For example, you can answer a question with a word or two:

Yes. No. My sister.

You can even ask a question without using what are usually considered complete sentences:

Whose car? Which girl? What building?

In writing, you must use complete sentences to make your meaning clear, because the reader is not at hand to ask you to repeat, to explain, or to fill in words you have left out.

Sentences are clear when all the parts are properly put together. In this chapter you will study the different parts of sentences. You will also learn how to put these parts together most effectively.

Part 1   Sentences and Sentence Fragments

The surest way to get your meaning across is to use complete sentences.

A sentence is a group of words that expresses a complete thought.

By "complete thought" we mean the clear and entire expression of whatever you want to say. Which of the following groups of words expresses a complete thought?

1. Karen found
2. Found a kitten
3. Karen found a kitten.

The third group of words expresses a complete thought. It is a complete sentence.

Sentence fragments do *not* express a complete thought. They are usually the result of carelessness. The writer's thoughts come faster than he or she can write them. The writer goes on to a new sentence without finishing the sentence he or she has started. The effect is something like this:

1. Last night a funny thing   2. We were sitting around the dinner table   3. Suddenly, a loud bang

The first and third groups of words above are sentence fragments.

Other fragments are the result of incorrect punctuation. Parts of sentences are written as if they were whole sentences:

1. About 3,300 feet down   2. In one of the world's deepest mines in Idaho   3. In the warmth and dampness 4. The miners have grown a lemon tree   5. About seven feet tall   6. Under light bulbs

Which of these six groups of words are sentences and which are fragments?

You can usually understand sentence fragments if they fit in with what a speaker has already said. You often use fragments in spoken conversation. You also use them in written conversation. In other writing, however, you should avoid sentence fragments.

Exercises   Recognize sentences and fragments.

A. Number your paper 1–10. For each group of words that is a sentence, write **S.** For each sentence fragment, write **F.** In class be ready to add words to change the fragments into sentences.

1. I saw a TV show last Sunday afternoon
2. The show was about dolphins
3. Actually a kind of small whale
4. Dolphins are very intelligent
5. Playful animals
6. Under the water in the big tank
7. It is very entertaining to watch the dolphins
8. Just for fun
9. Dolphins can hear very well
10. Because dolphins breathe air

B. Follow the directions for Exercise A.

1. During the relay race
2. A very high wind and then some flashes of lightning
3. Tracy Austin is one of the best young tennis players in the United States

5

4. A report about car fumes in an underground parking lot
5. Mr. Troy, owner of Troy and Brown Sports Shop
6. Whose work on the blackboard?
7. Ella T. Grasso, the governor of Connecticut
8. Martha Jane Canary was better known as "Calamity Jane."
9. The fire engines rushed down the street
10. No one else gave a report on solar energy

Part 2   Subjects and Predicates

Every sentence has two basic parts: the subject and the predicate. The **subject** tells whom or what the sentence is about. The **predicate** tells something about the subject.

Subject (Who or what)	Predicate (What is said about the subject)
Hungry dogs	bark constantly.
A cold rain	fell all through the night.
My brother	laughed at his own mistake.

Each of these sentences expresses a complete thought. Each of them tells something (**predicate**) about a person, place, or thing (**subject**).

An easy way to understand the parts of a sentence is to think of the sentence as telling who did something, or what happened. The subject tells *who* or *what*. The predicate tells *did* or *happened*. You can divide sentences, then, in this way:

Who or What	Did or Happened
The runner	crossed the finish line.
My parents	planted a garden.
The car	skidded on the wet pavement.
The bike	needs air in its tires.

The subject of the sentence names someone or something about which a statement is to be made.

The predicate of the sentence tells what is done or what happens.

Exercises   Find the subjects and predicates.

A.   Head two columns on your paper *Subject* and *Predicate.* Write the proper words from each sentence in the columns.

Example: My sister is fixing her bicycle.

Subject	Predicate
My sister	is fixing her bicycle.

1. Gayle made limeade.
2. The Packers will play the Bears on Sunday.
3. Beth went bowling with Jenny.
4. My parents were fishing in Maine.
5. Heavy white smoke came out of the chimney.
6. Calligraphy is the art of fine handwriting.
7. I like short stories.
8. Rebecca learned to sail last summer.
9. Rugby is a very rugged sport.
10. Rugby is a British sport similar to our football.

B.   Follow the directions for Exercise A.

1. Monarch butterflies migrate every year.
2. Sugarcane is the chief product of Hawaii.
3. North Dakota produces barley, wheat, and flaxseed.
4. Kathy ate all the brownies.
5. The bike-a-thon raised money for muscular dystrophy.
6. Our homeroom will play intramural hockey tomorrow.

7. "Welcome Back, Kotter" is my favorite TV show.
8. Tim built a rock garden.
9. Photography is Elizabeth's main interest.
10. Our 4-H Club showed black angus cattle at the State Fair.

Part 3 Simple Subjects and Predicates

In every sentence there are a few words that are more important than the rest. These key words make the basic framework of the sentence. Study these examples.

Hungry **dogs**	**bark** constantly.
A cold **rain**	**fell** throughout the night.
My **brother**	**laughed** at his own mistake.

The subject of the first sentence is *Hungry dogs*. The key word in this subject is *dogs*. You can say *dogs bark constantly*. You cannot say *hungry bark constantly*.

The predicate in the first sentence is *bark constantly*. The key word is *bark*. Without this word you would not have a sentence.

The key word in the subject of a sentence is called the simple subject. It is the subject of the verb.

The key word in the predicate is called the simple predicate. The simple predicate is the **verb.** Hereafter we will use the word *verb* rather than the phrase *simple predicate*.

Finding the Verb and Its Subject

The verb and its subject are the basic framework of every sentence. All the rest of the sentence is built around them.

To find this framework, first find the verb. Then ask *who* or *what* before the verb. This will give you the subject of the verb.

Examples: My brother's cookies melt in your mouth.

Verb: melt
What melts? cookies
Simple subject: cookies

The coat in the closet belongs to me.

Verb: belongs
What belongs? coat
Simple Subject: coat

You will be able to tell a fragment from a sentence easily if you keep your eye on subjects and verbs.

A group of words without a subject makes you ask *Who did? What did? Who was? What was?* A group of words without a verb makes you ask *What about it? What happened?*

Fragment: Ran down the street (Who ran down the street?)
Fragment: A cold rain (What about it? What happened?)

Looking at the Sentence as a Whole

The **complete subject** is the simple subject with any words that modify or describe it.

Example: Hungry dogs bark constantly.

Hungry dogs is the complete subject. What is the simple subject?

The **complete predicate** is the verb with any words that modify or complete its meaning. What is the complete predicate in the sentence above?

Diagrams of Subjects and Predicates

1.

Subject	Predicate
Hungry dogs	**bark constantly.**

2.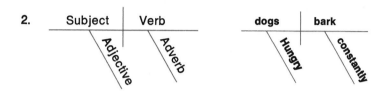

You will remember that adverbs may modify adjectives or other adverbs. Here is how they appear in a diagram.

3.

Exercises Find the verb and its subject.

A. Head two columns *Verb* and *Simple Subject.* Number your paper 1–10. For each sentence, write the verb and its simple subject.

1. A crate of oranges arrived from Florida.
2. The new IBM computer printed our class schedules.
3. A tiny, gray kitten perched itself on our windowsill.
4. The bike in the garage has a flat tire.

5. The jubilant, cheering crowd rose to its feet to greet the team.

6. The tall, wiry center sank the winning basket.

7. The locker next to the library belongs to Miki and me.

8. My sister Laura won an award at the art fair.

9. The woman in the pinstriped suit is my math teacher.

10. The aluminum cans in those plastic bags go to the recycling center.

B. Follow the directions for Exercise A.

1. The chestnut-brown thoroughbred trotted victoriously around the track.

2. An abandoned nest in the old oak tree became home for three little sparrows.

3. The corridor outside the cafeteria leads to the music room.

4. A shaggy white puppy wandered aimlessly into the gym.

5. The new booklet on bicycle rules explains the need for safety in cycling.

6. A tiny, tiger-striped kitten chased playfully after the huge ball of yarn.

7. The sound-slide show on energy conservation explained the importance of natural resources.

8. The friendly driver assisted the passenger off of the bus.

9. A continuous, heavy snow delighted the skiers.

10. The drought reduced the falls to a trickle.

Part 4   The Parts of a Verb

A verb may consist of one word or of several words. It may be made up of a **main verb** and **helping verbs.** In naming the verb of any sentence, be sure to name all the words that it is made of.

Helping Verbs	+	Main Verb	=	Verb
might have		gone		might have gone
will		see		will see
are		driving		are driving
could		go		could go

Sometimes the parts of a verb are separated from each other by words that are not part of the verb. In each of the following sentences, the verb is printed in red. The words in between are not part of the verb.

I **have** never **been** to Disney World.
We **did** not **see** the accident.
The bus **has** often **been** late.

Some verbs are joined with other words to make contractions. In naming verbs that appear in contractions, name only the verb. The word *not* is an adverb. It is never part of a verb.

Contraction	Verb
hasn't (*has not*)	*has*
weren't (*were not*)	*were*
I've (*I have*)	*have*
we'd (*we had* or *would*)	*had* or *would*

Exercises   Find the verb.

A. Number your paper 1–10. List the verbs in the following sentences.

1. We have not gone to the lake once this summer.
2. This report has not been completed.
3. The buses often do arrive late.
4. I have never been to Martha's Vineyard in Massachusetts.
5. Cheryl did not see *Rocky* or *Star Wars*.
6. The 747 will arrive at midnight.
7. The hockey team is practicing on the ice until 6 P.M.

8. Our class is going on a field trip next week.

9. The package may have been delivered to the wrong house.

10. I am going to a ski lodge next weekend.

B. Follow the directions for Exercise A.

1. We aren't giving our panel discussion today.

2. I don't really like Barry Manilow or Linda Ronstadt.

3. The ambulance was cautiously approaching every intersection.

4. Jim and I will finish this job later.

5. It hasn't rained for a month.

6. Our play rehearsal wasn't very successful.

7. Raul was carefully walking around the fountain.

8. We haven't planted a flower garden this year.

9. My sister and I made a rock garden, however.

10. The counselors had quickly collected the test booklets.

Part 5   Subjects in Unusual Positions

Sentences Beginning with *There*

Many sentences begin with the word *there*. Sometimes *there* is used as an adverb modifying the verb to tell *where* something is or happens.

> There stood the boy. (The boy stood *there*.)
> There is our bus. (Our bus is *there*.)

In other sentences, *there* is only an introductory word to help get the sentence started.

> There is no candy in the machine. (No candy is in the machine.)
> There are some mistakes here. (Some mistakes are here.)

In diagraming sentences that begin with *there*, it is necessary to decide whether *there* is used as an adverb or whether it is simply an introductory word. When *there* modifies the verb, it is placed on a slant line below the verb. When *there* is an introductory word, it is placed on a straight line above the sentence line.

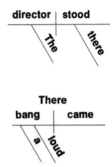

In most sentences beginning with *there*, the subject comes after the verb. To find the subject, first find the verb. Then ask *who* or *what*.

Exercises   Find the verb and its subject.

A. Write down the simple subject and the verb in each sentence. Tell whether *there* is used as an adverb or as an introductory word.

1. There he goes.
2. There stood the trophy.
3. There they are.
4. There will be basketball practice tomorrow.
5. There go the runners.
6. There I sat.
7. There I waited in line for over an hour.
8. There will be a picnic tomorrow.
9. There was a sudden pause.
10. There will be pony races.

B. Follow the directions for Exercise A.

1. There goes the runner.
2. There is cheesecake for dessert.
3. There will be no school on Monday.
4. There is the lock for your bicycle.
5. There are plenty of napkins.
6. There might be a thunderstorm later tonight.
7. There is a swimming meet on Friday.
8. There came a chilly wind.
9. There will be an assembly at noon.
10. There are several students in line.

Other Sentences with Unusual Word Order

The usual order of words in a sentence is *subject–verb.* In many sentences, however, the subject comes after the verb or between parts of the verb. You have seen one example of this arrangement in sentences beginning with *there.* Here are some others.

1. Sentences beginning with *here*

Here is your hat. (Your hat is here.)
Here are the keys. (The keys are here.)

Unlike *there,* the word *here* is always an adverb telling *where* about the verb.

2. Questions

Are you leaving? (You are leaving?)
Has the mail come? (The mail has come?)

3. Sentences beginning with phrases or adverbs

Onto the field dashed the team. (The team dashed onto the field.)
Finally came the signal. (The signal finally came.)

To find the subject in a sentence with unusual word order, first find the verb. Then ask *who* or *what*.

Example: Here comes the parade.

Verb: comes
Who or *what comes?* the parade
Subject: parade

To diagram sentences with unusual word order, find the verb and its subject. Place them in their proper positions. Then place the modifiers where they belong.

Imperative Sentences

In imperative sentences, which state commands or requests, the subject is usually not given. Since commands and requests are always given to the person spoken to, the subject is *you*. Since the *you* is not given, we say that it is *understood*.

(*You*) Bring me the newspaper.   (*You*) Wipe your feet.

In the diagram of an imperative sentence, the subject is written in parentheses.

(You)	Have	patience

Exercises   **Find the verb and its subject.**

A. Label two columns *Subject* and *Verb*. Number your paper 1–10 and write down the subject and verb for each sentence.

1. Hang on!
2. Are there two minutes left?
3. Did you read the article about mopeds?
4. Economy is one advantage of the moped.

5. Down the slopes raced the skiers.
6. Down came the rain.
7. Is our team in the play-offs?
8. There comes the bus.
9. On the porch hung several plants.
10. Have you seen that movie?

B. Follow the directions for Exercise A.

1. Are these books due today?
2. Out came the sun.
3. Here are the T-shirts for the Pep Club.
4. Have you heard the new Fleetwood Mac album?
5. All along the shoreline swimmers basked in the sun.
6. After the storm a beautiful rainbow appeared.
7. Over the phone came the reply.
8. Don't just stand there.
9. Here comes the mail.
10. Do you like frozen yogurt?

Part 6 Objects of Verbs

Some verbs complete the meaning of a sentence without the help of other words. The action that they describe is complete.

> The boys *came*.
> We *are going*.

Some verbs, however, do not express a complete meaning by themselves. They need other words to complete the meaning of a sentence.

> Sue hit _____. (Hit what? Sue hit the *ball*.)
> Jane raised _____. (Raised what? Jane raised the *window*.)

Direct Objects

The word that receives the action of a verb is called the **direct object** of the verb. In the sentences above, *ball* receives the action of *hit*. *Window* receives the action of *raised*.

Sometimes the direct object tells the *result* of an action.

> We dug a *hole*.
> Edison invented electric *lights*.

To find the direct object, first find the verb. Then ask *whom* or *what* after it.

> Carlos saw the President.   Anne painted a picture.
> *Verb:* saw   *Verb:* painted
> *Saw whom?* President   *Painted what?* picture
> *Direct Object:* President   *Direct Object:* picture

A verb that has a direct object is called a **transitive verb.** A verb that does not have an object is called an **intransitive verb.** A verb may be intransitive in one sentence and transitive in another.

> **Intransitive:** We were watching.
> **Transitive:** We were watching the race.

Direct Object or Adverb?

Many verbs used without objects are followed by adverbs that tell *how, where, when,* or *how much.* These words are adverbs that go with or modify the verb. Do not confuse them with direct objects. The direct object tells *what* or *whom.*

To decide whether a word is a direct object or a modifier of the verb, decide first what it tells about the verb. If it tells *how, where, when* or *how much,* it is an adverb. If it tells *what* or *whom,* it is a direct object.

> Don worked *quickly.* (Quickly is an adverb telling *how.*)
> Sue worked the *problem.* (*Problem* is a direct object.)

Number your paper 1–10. Decide what the italicized word is in each sentence. Write *Adverb* or *Direct Object* beside each number.

1. Several guests left *early*.
2. Someone left a red *sweater*.
3. The band plays *often*.
4. The band plays *well*.
5. The band plays good *music*.
6. I liked that delicious *pie*.
7. Please return *soon*.
8. Please return my *camera*.
9. Michele tried *again*.
10. Mark tried the *door* again.

Indirect Objects

Some words tell *to whom* or *for whom* something is done. Other words tell *to what* or *for what* something is done. These words are called the **indirect objects** of the verb.

> We gave **Mary** some *money*. (Gave *to* Mary)
> Anne knitted **Kim** a *sweater*. (Knitted *for* Kim)
> We gave the **boat** a *coat* of paint. (Gave *to* the boat)

In the sentences above, the words in red type are the indirect objects. The words in italics are the direct objects.

The words *to* and *for* are never used with the indirect object. The words *to* and *for* are prepositions. Any noun or pronoun following *to* or *for* is its object.

> They baked *me* a cake. (*Me* is indirect object of *baked.*)
> They baked a cake for *me*. (*Me* is object of the preposition *for.*)

In a diagram, the direct object is placed on the main line

after the verb. Notice that the line between verb and object does not go below the main line.

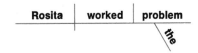

The indirect object is placed below the main line.

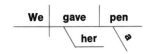

Exercises   Find the sentence parts.

A.   Number your paper 1–10. Label three columns *Verb, Indirect Object,* and *Direct Object.* For each sentence below in which they appear, write down those three parts. After each verb write *Transitive* or *Intransitive.*

Example: Todd drew us a very rough map.

Verb	Indirect Object	Direct Object
drew (transitive)	us	map

1. I brought Cindy her scarf.
2. We gave our dog a good bath.
3. Maria made us a Mexican dinner.
4. Paul gave the beans a stir.
5. I hooked Mom a rug for her birthday.
6. The principal gave the co-captains the trophy.
7. Will you bring me some ice?
8. The sun sparkled on the waves.

9. Brenda must have hoed the garden.
10. Pat got a digital watch for Christmas.

B. Follow the directions for Exercise A.

1. Our class cleaned the courtyard.
2. Jill loaned me her thesaurus.
3. Steve gave Paula the tickets.
4. Judy was whistling an old Beatles song.
5. Uncle Don gave the cactus to me.
6. Did you buy me some more film?
7. Liz shouted down the stairs.
8. Did you adjust the thermostat?
9. Please get me some stamps.
10. We fixed the antenna for my CB.

C. Look at the verbs in the following sentences. If the verb has no object, write a sentence with the same verb and an object. If the verb already has an object, write a sentence with the same verb but no object.

Example: An old highway looped around the mining town.

Verb: *looped* (no object)
Bob looped the rope twice.

1. Dad had already packed.
2. We reached the airport about 2 o'clock.
3. I ran a mile without stopping.
4. The plane climbed another 2000 feet.
5. Elizabeth painted the garage door.
6. The driver delivered the package to the hospital.
7. Our group had already finished.
8. Long waves rolled up the beach.
9. Did you finish your collage?
10. Juan designed the cover for the yearbook.

Part 7   Predicate Words and Linking Verbs

Some verbs do not expess action. They tell of a state of being. These verbs link the subject of a sentence with a word or group of words in the predicate. Because they link the subject with some other word or words, they are often called **linking verbs.**

> He *is* a doctor.
> They *are* good swimmers.

The most common linking verb is the verb *to be*. This verb can have many forms. Study these forms of *to be* to make sure you recognize them:

be	been	is	was
being	am	are	were

The verbs *be, being,* and *been* can also be used with helping verbs. Here are some examples:

might be	is being	have been
could be	are being	might have been
will be	was being	would have been

The words linked to the subject by a linking verb like *be* are called **predicate words.** There are **predicate nouns, predicate pronouns,** and **predicate adjectives.**

> *Renée* is a *swimmer*. (Predicate noun)
>
> *This* is *she*. (Predicate pronoun)
>
> *Bill* was *happy*. (Predicate adjective)

Notice how the subjects and the predicate words in the above sentences are linked by *is* or *was*.

Here are some other common linking verbs:

seem   feel   become   look
appear   taste   grow   sound

Like *be*, these verbs can have various forms (*seems, appears, felt*), or they can be used with helping verbs (*will appear, could feel, might have become*).

The *music* sounded *beautiful*. (Predicate adjective)

The *plants* grew *taller*. (Predicate adjective)

I have become an *expert*. (Predicate noun)

In diagrams, the predicate words appear on the main line with subjects and verbs. Note that the line between the verb and the predicate word slants back toward the subject.

| Whales | are \ mammals | (Predicate noun) |

| It | was \ she | (Predicate pronoun) |

| Ted | looked \ tired | (Predicate adjective) |

Exercises Find predicate words and linking verbs.

A. As your teacher directs, point out the subject, linking verb, and predicate word in each sentence.

1. Snakes are reptiles.
2. The singing sounded good.
3. This is he.
4. The flowers looked wilted.
5. Has Kathy been sick?

6. The driver was angry.
7. The house seemed empty.
8. Karen felt lonesome.
9. Was it she?
10. Sue became chairperson.

B. Make four columns on your paper. Number 1–12 down the columns. Head the columns *Subject, Verb, Direct Object,* and *Predicate Word.* Find these parts in the sentences below and place them in the right columns.

1. Our new puppy has behaved badly.
2. We left him in his pen today.
3. We left him some water.
4. He looked miserable.
5. On returning we were angry.
6. The puppy had spilled the water.
7. He had escaped from the pen.
8. He had chewed the sofa pillow.
9. Feathers covered the floor.
10. The puppy looked very happy.
11. He had taught us a lesson.
12. We will never leave him inside again.

Part 8   Compound Sentence Parts

The word *compound* means "having two or more parts."
Every part of the sentence we have studied in this chapter can be compound—subjects, verbs, direct objects, indirect objects, and predicate words.
If the compound form has only two parts, there is usually a conjunction (*and, or, but*) between them. If there are three or more parts, the conjunction usually comes between the last two.

Compound Subjects

The *dog* and the *cat* are good friends.
Soap, butter, and *potatoes* spilled from the bag.

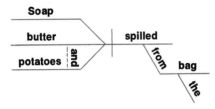

Compound Verbs

The skier *swerved, dodged,* and *careened* down the icy slope.
Dr. Rosen *called* and *asked* for you.

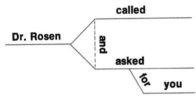

Compound Objects of Verbs

We saw the *President* and his *family.* (Direct objects)
The boss showed *Nancy* and *me* the shop. (Indirect objects)

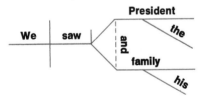

Compound Predicate Words

The backpackers were *tired and hungry.* (Predicate adjectives)
The winners were *Rebecca* and *Sherry.* (Predicate nouns)

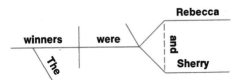

Exercises Find the compound sentence parts.

A. As your teacher directs, show the compound parts in the following sentences. Tell whether they are compound subjects, verbs, objects, or predicate words.

1. The water was cool and refreshing.
2. Last weekend we skated and skied.
3. The engine hesitated and then purred.
4. Tara and Charlene painted the scenery.
5. Jeff and I washed and waxed the car.
6. We brought Fritos and popcorn to the picnic.
7. Did you give Cindy the posters and the flyers?
8. Marla and Robin made hanging planters in shop class.
9. We suspended the balloons and the prizes from the ceiling.
10. The gymnasts showed discipline and control.

B. In each of the following sentences, make the part noted in parentheses compound.

Example: We unpacked the crates. (*direct object*)
We unpacked the crates and the cartons.

1. Jon carried the groceries into the house. (*direct object*)
2. The pizza was spicy! (*predicate word*)
3. Did you remember the Kleenex? (*direct object*)
4. There are pickles over here. (*subject*)
5. The hypnotist's performance was fascinating. (*predicate word*)
6. Mrs. Lopez gave Janelle a bracelet. (*direct object*)
7. Next came the President's car. (*subject*)
8. Linda fixed the handlebars. (*direct object*)
9. Mr. and Mrs. Karnatz gave Meredith a job at the store. (*indirect object*)
10. There are ten divers competing. (*subject*)

Additional Exercises

The Simple Sentence

A. Recognize sentences and sentence fragments.

Number your paper 1–10. For each group of words that is a sentence, write **S.** For each sentence fragment, write **F.** In class be ready to add words to change the fragments into sentences.

1. Because of the driving snow
2. A special track was designed and built for the skateboard races
3. A big wave broke over the side of the boat
4. Thousands of people along the parade route
5. Bill's new yellow car out in the driveway
6. A heavy gray sky over the lake
7. The coach explained the basic rules
8. A cheer from the grandstand
9. A helicopter over the traffic jam
10. Brownies and Dutch chocolate ice cream for dessert

B. Find complete subjects and complete predicates.

Number your paper 1–10. Make two columns *Complete Subject* and *Complete Predicate.* Write the proper words in each column.

1. Rick caught the ball easily.
2. The atomic submarine surfaced before dawn.
3. A red-tailed hawk circled the field.
4. My uncle uses mulch on his tomato plants.

5. A new apartment building was constructed near the shopping center.

6. Our janitor was cleaning the basement.

7. They unloaded the elephants in the pouring rain.

8. My sister and I went canoeing on Sunday.

9. The tall brunette in the front row spiked the ball over the net.

10. You could hear the crickets outside the cabin.

C. Find the verb and its simple subject.

Number your paper 1–10. Write the simple subject and the verb in each sentence. Tell whether *there* is used as an adverb or as an introductory word.

1. There is the library.
2. There will be band practice in the morning.
3. There is an MGB parked in the driveway.
4. There wasn't a cloud in the sky.
5. There was no play rehearsal today.
6. There was no more room in the stadium.
7. There will be a dance next Friday.
8. There sat the box by the bus stop.
9. There were only two commercials during the show.
10. There will be a slight delay before take-off.

D. Find the verb and its subject in unusual kinds of sentences.

Number your paper 1–10. Make two columns *Subject* and *Verb*. Write down the subject and verb for each sentence.

1. Through the back door Jim and his dog scampered.
2. Over the hill the motorcyclists raced.
3. Did the rocket misfire?

4. Find the villain.
5. Here is the newspaper.
6. Out swarmed the bees.
7. Here are the results of the test.
8. Onto the field the marching band paraded.
9. Fire this ceramic vase in the kiln.
10. Did you read the editorial in the newspaper?

E. Recognize direct objects and adverbs.

Number your paper 1–10. Decide what the italicized word is in each sentence. Write *Adverb* or *Direct Object* beside each number.

1. The telephone rang *loudly*.
2. The lightning flashed *overhead*.
3. Pelé scored the winning *goal*.
4. The crowd cheered *wildly*.
5. Paula lost her *wallet*.
6. The laundromat charges 35 *cents*.
7. My horse won *again*.
8. The newscaster smothered a *yawn*.
9. Mrs. Brock checked the *meter*.
10. Steve rose *quickly* from his chair.

F. Find the sentence parts.

Number your paper 1–10. Make three columns *Verb, Indirect Object,* and *Direct Object.* For each sentence below in which they appear, write down those three parts. After each verb write *Transitive* or *Intransitive.*

1. Two tugboats were pulling the barge through the canal.
2. The crowd gave the coach a big hand.
3. That cub scooped a fish out of the water.
4. Something is making a noise on the top shelf.

5. Write us a letter.
6. Sonia made Dad a lamp in shop class.
7. Mary threw the dog the Frisbee.
8. The center knocked the puck into the net.
9. I brought Chris her assignments from school.
10. I developed the film in the photo lab.

G. Find predicate words, linking verbs, and objects.

Number your paper 1–10. Make four columns *Subject, Verb, Direct Object,* and *Predicate Word.* Fill in the parts that you find for each sentence. You will find either a direct object or a predicate word in each sentence.

1. Nine men moved the piano.
2. The sky to the west looks strange.
3. The muffins in the oven smell delicious.
4. My mother canned peaches all morning.
5. The gulls on the beach faced the wind.
6. We picked apples from the orchard trees.
7. Their fishing boat weathered the storm.
8. From the airplane the toll road appeared empty.
9. The center snapped the ball to the quarterback.
10. The boughs on the mantel look lopsided.

H. Finding the compound parts in a sentence.

As your teacher directs, show the compound parts in the following sentences. Tell whether they are compound subjects, verbs, objects, or predicate words.

1. Your backstroke is better and stronger.
2. Three monkeys and their trainers were juggling oranges.
3. Emily and Ken can walk on stilts.
4. The photography club furnished the doughnuts and cider.

5. A marathon runner must be well prepared and determined.

6. A landslide uprooted those trees and rocks.

7. The roadrunner looked fierce and determined.

8. The December wind was cold and biting.

9. The Ford Fiesta and the Chevy Chevette are American economy cars.

10. Laplanders and Finns traditionally hunt reindeer.

Section 2

Using Nouns

Geologists, seeking oil or uranium, study samples of rock or soil. They can recognize different kinds of rock or soil at once, because most rocks and soils have been carefully analyzed and put into different classes.

Scholars have analyzed and classified the various elements of language. They have found that all the words used in sentences fall into certain groups or classes.

People can use words without knowing very much about these groups or classes. Skillful writers and speakers, however, have a good understanding of the groups or classes into which words fall.

In this section you will study in detail one very important group of words: nouns.

Part 1 What Are Nouns?

One important use of language is to name the people, places, and things around us. Words used to name are called **nouns.**

A noun is a word used to name a person, place, or thing.

The classes into which words are grouped are called **parts of speech.** Nouns are one of the most important parts of speech.

Nouns name all sorts of things. They name things you can see, such as horses, boats, and footballs. They name things you cannot see, such as feelings, beliefs, and ideas.

Persons	Places	Things
doctor	Spain	book
Kimberly	home	building
Michelle	Chicago	loyalty

Exercise   Find the nouns.

Make three columns on a sheet of paper. Use these headings: (1) *Names of Persons,* (2) *Names of Places,* (3) *Names of Things.* Under the proper heading, list each noun in the following paragraph:

> An unusually strong earthquake occurred in China in 1976. Tremors from the quake were felt hundreds of miles away. In the severely damaged city of Tientsin, thousands of Chinese evacuated collapsing buildings. The industrial city of Tangshan was devastated, and its nearby mines were also damaged. An estimated 655,000 people lost their lives.

Proper Nouns and Common Nouns

Look at the drawings of dogs. How do the nouns differ from each other? How does *dog* differ from *Lucky?*

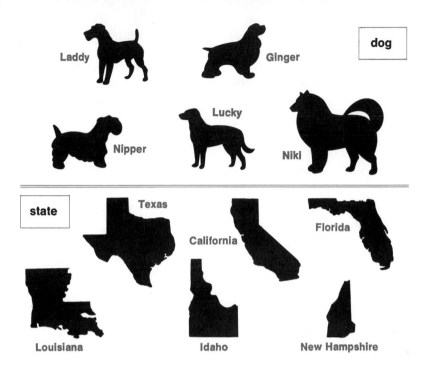

There are two kinds of nouns. A **common noun** is a name common to a whole group of things. *Dog* is a common noun. But the names *Laddy*, *Nipper*, and *Ginger* are names of individual dogs. They are **proper nouns.**

1. A common noun is the name of a whole group of persons, places, or things. Is is a name that is common to the whole group.

2. A proper noun is the name of a particular person, place, or thing.

Look at the drawings of states. Which nouns are proper nouns? Why do you think so? Are there any common nouns in the picture?

Look at the drawings again. Read the nouns that are capitalized. Notice that the common nouns *dog* and *state* are not capitalized. Remember this rule:

A proper noun always begins with a capital letter.

A. Make two columns on your paper. Head one column *Common Nouns* and the other *Proper Nouns*. Decide whether the nouns below are common or proper. Place each in the right column. Capitalize the proper nouns.

1. salt lake city, las vegas, town, atlanta, city

2. dancer, maria tallchief, martha graham, opera, beverly sills

3. pamphlet, reader's digest, magazine, sports illustrated, seventeen

4. montana, kansas, state, indiana, region

5. crater lake, lagoon, gulf of mexico, white's pond, lake champlain

6. continent, africa, europe, peninsula, korea, italy

7. track meet, XXI olympic games, cincinnati reds, hockey, world series

8. mountain, andes, old smoky, mount popocatepetl, hills

9. artist, georgia o'keeffe, sculptor, alexander calder, louise nevelson

10. monument, mount rushmore, statue of liberty, building, empire state building

B. Write five sentences of your own, using at least one proper noun in each sentence.

Part 2 Forming the Singular and Plural of Nouns

The noun *shoe* is singular. It stands for only one shoe. The noun *shoes* is plural. It stands for more than one shoe.

When a noun stands for one person, place, or thing, it is **singular.** When it stands for more than one person, place, or thing, it is **plural.**

Forming Plurals

The first two rules below cover most English nouns. The other five rules deal with words that you use frequently.

1. To most singular nouns, add *s* to form the plural:

ropes   boots   books   desks

2. When the singular form ends in *s, sh, ch, x,* or *z,* add es:

glasses   bushes   coaches   boxes   buzzes

3. When a singular noun ends in *o,* add *s* to make it plural:

rodeos   photos   solos
studios   Eskimos   pianos

For a few words ending in o, preceded by a consonant, add *es:*

potatoes   cargoes   tomatoes
heroes   echoes

4. When the singular noun ends in *y* with a consonant before it, change the *y* to *i* and add es*:*

city—cities   lady—ladies   country—countries

If the *y* is preceded by a vowel (*a, e, i, o, u*), do not change the *y* to *i*. Simply add *s:*

toy—toys   play—plays   day—days

5. Some nouns ending in *f* simply add *s:*

beliefs   chiefs   dwarfs   handkerchiefs

Many words ending in *f* or *fe* change the *f* to *v* and add *es* or *s*. Since there is no rule to follow, these words have to be memorized. Here are some examples of such words:

thief—thieves   leaf—leaves   life—lives
shelf—shelves   half—halves   calf—calves
loaf—loaves   wife—wives   knife—knives

6. Some nouns have the same form for both the singular and plural. Memorize these:

deer   salmon   trout   sheep   moose
tuna   cod   pike   bass   elk

7. Some nouns form their plurals in special ways:

child—children   goose—geese   man—men
mouse—mice   ox—oxen   woman—women

Here is a dictionary entry for the word *knife*. Notice that the entry shows the plural, *knives*. Most dictionaries show the plurals of nouns if the plurals are formed in an irregular way.

---

plural
knife (nif) **n.,** *pl.* **knives** [OE. *cnif*: for IE. base see KNEAD] **1.** a cutting or stabbing instrument with a sharp blade, single-edged or double-edged, set in a handle **2.** a cutting blade, as in a machine —**vt. knifed, knif'ing 1.** to cut or stab with a knife ☆**2.** [Colloq.] to use underhanded methods in order to hurt, defeat, or betray — ☆**vi.** to pass into or through something quickly, like a sharp knife— ☆**under the knife** [Colloq.] undergoing surgery —**knife' like' adj.**

When you are in doubt about plurals, consult a dictionary!

Exercises **Form the plurals of nouns.**

A. Write the plural of each of these nouns. Then use your dictionary to see if you are right.

1. church	6. dish	11. company	16. baby
2. brush	7. elk	12. watch	17. city
3. elf	8. sheep	13. bookshelf	18. mouse
4. wish	9. fox	14. chimney	19. witch
5. potato	10. tooth	15. lady	20. radio

B. All but one of the following sentences have at least one error in plurals. Write the sentences correctly.

1. We placed all of the dishs on the benchs in the hallway.
2. Several different companys make CB radioes.
3. The thieves took several loaves of bread.
4. The babys were getting new tooths.
5. Several companys sell frozen mashed potatos.
6. First, cut the loafs in halves.
7. The deers were eating the green shoots on the bushs.
8. Use these brushs to stain the bookshelfs.
9. The larger boxes had scratchs on them.
10. My blue jeans are covered with patchs.

Part 3 Forming the Possessive of Nouns

Most living persons own or possess something. We say:

Carol's coat   the doctor's bag   a lawyer's case

To show that something belongs to or is a part of a person, we use the same form:

Jill's face   Ann's tooth   Bill's worries

We usually speak of ownership, belonging, or possession for people and animals. Occasionally, however, things are also used in the possessive. We speak of a *city's problems, the day's end,* or *a stone's throw.*

Forming Possessives

There are two rules for making the possessive of nouns:

1. If the noun is singular, add an apostrophe and *s:*

Bess's slicker   Mother's briefcase   Charles's bike

2. If the noun is plural and ends in *s*, add just the apostrophe:

the Hoffmans' car   students' projects   babies' toys

If the noun is plural but does not end in *s*, add both the apostrophe and *s*.

children's books   men's sweaters   women's jewelry

Exercises   Form the possessive of nouns.

A.   Write the possessive form of these nouns:

1. bee	6. princess	11. Thomas	16. winner
2. Mary	7. mouse	12. Les	17. Tracy
3. carpenter	8. Andrea	13. mirror	18. singer
4. child	9. watchman	14. conductor	19. lake
5. Marsha	10. waitress	15. Tricia	20. Vince

B.   Write the possessive form of these nouns:

1. watchmen	6. birds	11. countries	16. stereos
2. teachers	7. sheep	12. dogs	17. foxes
3. women	8. schools	13. socks	18. ducks
4. children	9. boys	14. churches	19. engineers
5. people	10. ladies	15. dresses	20. statues

C. Write the possessive form for each italicized word:

1. Our *class* assignment sheets were sitting on the *teacher* desk.
2. The Student *Council* decision to have a walk-a-thon was supported by the *teachers* committee and the *principal* office.
3. Mrs. *Thomas* car was parked in the driveway.
4. My *brother* short story won first prize in the Young Writers Contest.
5. *Maurita* and *Amy* paintings were on display in the art room.
6. The *farmer* newly planted field was washed out by the heavy rain.
7. The *painter* ladders were on our front porch.
8. *Jonathan* bicycle needs new brakes.
9. Our *neighbor* treehouse is one of the best I've ever seen.
10. *Janine* time broke the school record for the 100-yard dash.

Additional Exercises

Using Nouns

A. Find the common and proper nouns.

Make two columns *Common Nouns* and *Proper Nouns.* Decide whether the following nouns are common or proper. Place each in the right column. Capitalize the proper nouns.

1. sun valley, ravine, grand canyon, death valley, pike's peak
2. golden gate bridge, overpass, st. louis arch, brooklyn bridge
3. executive, doctor, president carter, judge, cardinal bonzano
4. musician, barry manilow, judy collins, guitar, andrés segovia
5. stream, des plaines river, niagara falls, rapids, colorado river
6. intersection, holland tunnel, haggar's corners, highway
7. nation, france, country, united states, scotland, india
8. queen, princess grace, prince shah pahlavi of iran, queen elizabeth
9. forest, yellowstone national park, westbrook park, lincoln park
10. language, swahili, finnish, travel, spanish, greek

B. Form the plurals of nouns.

Write the plural of each of these nouns.

1. tomato	3. auto	5. ditch	7. shelf
2. donkey	4. track	6. wolf	8. party

9. peach	12. studio	15. play	18. switch
10. foot	13. scratch	16. toy	19. leaf
11. auto	14. cry	17. perch	20. deer

C. Form the possessive of nouns.

Write the possessive form in the singular or plural as indicated.

1. the horse (plural) mouths
2. Lisa (singular) equipment
3. the child (plural) beds
4. the cat (plural) paws
5. a doctor (singular) appointment
6. the bird (plural) beaks
7. one weatherman (singular) forecast
8. the water (singular) edge
9. Ms. Marsh (singular) business
10. the caddy (plural) hours
11. the gull (plural) cries
12. America (singular) resources
13. the bungalow (singular) owners
14. a bride (singular) bouquet
15. some duck (plural) backs
16. Sara (singular) singing
17. the President (singular) power
18. the moose (plural) antlers
19. the ship (singular) captain
20. Max (singular) shoes

Section 3

Using Pronouns

Our speech and writing would be very awkward if we had only nouns to refer to persons, places, or things. We would have to talk like this:

> Beth found Beth's book in Beth's locker.
> Beth took Beth's book back to the library.

Fortunately, we have words that can be used in place of

nouns. These are called **pronouns.** With pronouns we can talk like this:

> Beth found *her* book in *her* locker. *She* took *it* back to the library.

The words *her* and *she* are pronouns that stand for the noun *Beth* and are used in place of it. The word *it* is a pronoun that stands for the word *book* and is used in its place.

Part 1   Personal Pronouns

Personal pronouns are used to take the place of nouns that name persons.

Personal pronouns refer to persons in three ways:

1. When the pronoun refers to the person speaking, it is in the **first person:** *I, me, we,* and *us,* for example.

2. When the pronoun refers to the person spoken to, it is in the **second person:** *you, your, yours.*

3. When the pronoun refers to some other person or thing that is being spoken of, it is in the **third person:** *he, his, him, she, her, it, they, their, them,* for example.

> Examples: The letter was addressed to *me.* (*Speaker—first person*)
> The phone call is for *you.* (*Person spoken to— second person*)
> The boys are looking for *him.* (*Person spoken of—third person*)

The word *it* is also called a personal pronoun, even though it is never used in place of a person's name.

Pronouns in the third person that refer to male persons are said to be in the **masculine gender.** Pronouns that refer to female persons are said to be in the **feminine gender.** Pronouns that refer to things are said to be in the **neuter gender.**

Examples: Bob bought *his* ticket yesterday. (*His* is masculine in gender.)

Marie says that book is *hers*. (*Hers* is feminine in gender.)

Jill reached for the paddle, but *it* floated out of reach. (*It* is neuter in gender.)

Animals are often referred to by *it* or *its*. They may also be referred to by *he, his, she, her*, or *hers*.

Exercises   **Find the pronouns.**

A.   Number your paper 1–10. Write the pronouns you find in the following sentences. After each pronoun, write the noun or nouns it stands for (except for first-person pronouns).

1. Sue left her math book in her locker.

2. Snow was all over the ball park this morning, but it melted.

3. John and Ginny visited their cousins in Texas.

4. Ken came by and picked up his soccer ball before supper.

5. The store owners said that they would sponsor our hockey team.

6. The Sierra Nevadas are mountains in California. They include Mount Whitney.

7. Dorinda lost her gloves.

8. The cat cared for its new baby kittens.

9. Linda and her best friend are going to New York, and they will compete in a speech contest there.

10. Jay opened the envelope, but he found nothing in it.

B. Follow the directions for Exercise A.

1. Jeff, would you like to play tennis with Carol and Sue?

2. A seismograph records earthquakes. It indicates their intensity.

3. Last summer, the neighbors painted their house, and Dad built a patio.

4. Joel and Jim Hertz raised tomatoes. They sold them to the neighbors and made money.

5. The Owens parked their cars in the driveway while the workers repaired their garage roof.

6. Mom and Dad have their tickets for the school concert tonight.

7. Mary, have you found your umbrella?

8. Bill looked for his books but couldn't find them.

9. The sun had sun dogs, a circle of bright rainbow spots, around it. They were formed from ice particles.

10. Did Pam and Mary find the packages they had wrapped?

Part 2 Compound Personal Pronouns

A **compound personal pronoun** is formed by adding *-self* or *-selves* to certain personal pronouns:

First person:	myself	ourselves
Second Person:	yourself	yourselves
Third Person:	himself herself } itself	themselves

Exercises   Use compound personal pronouns.

A. Number your paper 1–10. Beside each number write the correct compound personal pronoun for each of the following sentences. After it, write the noun or pronoun to which it refers.

> Example: He made (pronoun) a T-shirt in sewing class.
>   himself, he

1. Cut (pronoun) a bigger piece of pie.
2. We made the loom (pronoun).
3. Bret let (pronoun) down by the rope.
4. The fans shouted (pronoun) hoarse.
5. The cat tried to clean (pronoun) off after wandering through the shrubs.
6. I will finish washing the car by (pronoun).
7. Mrs. Adel suggested we do the painting (pronoun).
8. Nancy, Carrie, and Sue made the movie (pronoun).
9. We don't weigh (pronoun) very often.
10. I built and stained these bookcases by (pronoun).

B. Follow the directions for Exercise A.

1. The door just locked (pronoun).
2. Diane must not have counted (pronoun) when she took the lunch count.
3. Jamie, don't rush (pronoun).
4. We always can the peaches (pronoun).
5. Will you two be able to finish the job (pronoun)?
6. Bridget organized the presentation by (pronoun).
7. Read the article (pronoun); I think you'll both find it intriguing.
8. We just bought (pronoun) a pumpkin.
9. The store more than pays for (pronoun).
10. He wasn't sure of (pronoun) on a high ladder.

Part 3 Indefinite Pronouns

Pronouns like *anyone* and *nobody* do not refer to any definite person or thing. They are called **indefinite pronouns.**

Most indefinite pronouns are singular in number. They refer to only one person or thing. Here they are:

another	each	everything	one
anybody	either	neither	somebody
anyone	everybody	nobody	someone
anything	everyone	no one	

Examples: Everyone has *his* invitation.
(*Not:* Everyone has *their* invitation.)

Everyone has *his or her* invitation.
(When the indefinite pronoun refers to both males and females, *his or her* is acceptable.)

A few indefinite pronouns are plural. They refer to more than one person or thing:

both   many   few   several

The pronouns *all, some,* and *none* may be singular or plural, depending upon their meaning in the sentence.

Examples: All the pie *is* gone.
All of the members *are* here.

Some of the milk *is* sour.
Some of the apples *are* ripe.

None of the time *was* wasted.
None of the flowers *were* left.

Exercises **Find the indefinite pronouns.**

A. Number your paper 1–10. For each sentence write down the indefinite pronoun or pronouns.

1. Is anything the matter?
2. Both of the games were postponed because of rain.
3. All of the photographs for the yearbook were too dark.
4. Somebody has left his or her jacket on the bus.
5. Either of the counselors will help you with your schedule.
6. In the spring, almost everyone rides his or her bike to school.
7. During the noon hour, anyone can go home to eat lunch.
8. All of the eighth-grade students went to the high school for orientation.
9. Each of the students filled out his or her registration cards.
10. Everyone was taking the high school placement test on Saturday.

B. Number your paper 1–10. For each sentence write down the indefinite pronoun and pick the verb in the parentheses that agrees with it.

1. Neither of the keys (fits, fit) the lock.
2. Just a few of my relatives (is, are) coming.
3. Some of the band members (is, are) competing in the music contest.
4. Each of the countries (send, sends) two representatives.
5. Neither of the encyclopedias (explain, explains) the subject very well.
6. All of the runners (was, were) lined up for the race.
7. All of the bookcases (have, has) assembling instructions.
8. Several of those days last week (was, were) scorchers.
9. Neither of my shoes (is, are) wet.
10. Both of my brothers (works, work) at the ice cream parlor.

Part 4   Demonstrative Pronouns

The pronouns *this, that, these,* and *those* are used to point out which persons or things are referred to. They are called **demonstrative pronouns.**

This and *these* point to persons or things that are near. *That* and *those* point to persons or things farther away.

> **This** is the right road.   **These** belong to Jim.
> **That** is my camera.   **Those** are my boots.

Exercise   Use demonstrative pronouns.

Number your paper 1–10. Write the correct demonstrative pronoun for the blank space in each sentence.

1. _____ are my boots over there.
2. _____ was Kate on the telephone.
3. _____ were the books I was telling you about.
4. _____ is the metric table we have to learn.
5. _____ are the tools you wanted to borrow.
6. _____ was my brother who read the announcements.
7. _____ are the chapters I read last night.
8. _____ are probably better than those.
9. _____ is my bike parked over there.
10. _____ was Ryan in the doorway.

Part 5   Interrogative Pronouns

The pronouns *who, whose, whom, which,* and *what* are used to ask questions.

Examples: *Who* rang the bell?   *Which* is your paper?
  Whose are those shoes?   *What* did you say?
  Whom do you mean?

Exercise **Find and use different kinds of pronouns.**

Number your paper 1–10. Write all the pronouns in these sentences. After each pronoun, write *Indefinite, Demonstrative,* or *Interrogative* to show what kind it is.

> Example: Are these for everybody?
>
> *These*—demonstrative pronoun
>
> *Everybody*—indefinite pronoun

1. Those are the best skates to buy.
2. Which of the new TV shows do you enjoy?
3. This is Jay's cassette player.
4. No one knew the answer to either of the questions.
5. What is everybody waiting for?
6. Which is the one Ann chose?
7. Nobody can solve the problems.
8. To whom do you wish to speak?
9. Which of the shelves do you want painted?
10. These are the ones to be painted.

Part 6 The Cases of Pronouns

The **case** of a word is a special form of the word used to show whether the word is a subject, object, possessive, and so on.

In English, the only kinds of words that have case forms are nouns and personal pronouns. English nouns have just one special case form, the possessive (the **possessive case**). You have already studied the possessive form of nouns.

You will now study the possessive forms of pronouns. You will also study the other special forms that English personal pronouns have.

English personal pronouns have three special forms (three cases). Like nouns, they have a possessive case. In addition, they have two other cases: the **nominative case** and the **objective case.**

The Nominative Case of Pronouns

Personal pronouns are used in the nominative case (1) when they are subjects and (2) when they follow linking verbs. Here are the nominative case forms of each of the personal pronouns:

I	we
you	you
he, she, it	they

Examples: Personal pronoun used *as subject*
$$\begin{cases} \textit{I} \text{ agree with you.} \\ \textit{She} \text{ is not going.} \\ \textit{We} \text{ understand.} \end{cases}$$

Personal pronoun used *after linking verb*
$$\begin{cases} \text{This is } \textit{he.} \\ \text{It was } \textit{I.} \\ \text{It is } \textit{they.} \end{cases}$$

The Objective Case of Pronouns

Personal pronouns are used in the objective case (1) when they are direct or indirect objects of verbs and (2) when they are objects of prepositions. Here are the objective case forms of the personal pronouns:

me	us
you	you
him, her, it	them

Examples: Direct Object
$$\begin{cases} \text{The dog bit } \textit{him.} \\ \text{Jack helped } \textit{them} \text{ with the work.} \end{cases}$$

Indirect Object   I gave *her* a gift.

$$\text{Object of Preposition} \begin{cases} \text{The candy is for } me. \\ \text{Write a letter to } them. \\ \text{The money came from } her. \end{cases}$$

The Possessive Case of Pronouns

Personal pronouns are used in the possessive case to show ownership or possession. Personal pronouns in the possessive case consist of two groups: (1) Pronouns used, like adjectives, to modify nouns; (2) Pronouns used, like nouns, as subjects of verbs, as predicate words, or as objects of verbs or prepositions.

Here are the possessive case forms of the personal pronouns when they modify nouns:

my	our
your	your
his, her, its	their

Examples: *my* sister   *our* car
           his book   *its* wheels
           her mother   *their* money

Here are the possessive case forms of the personal pronouns when they are used as subjects of verbs, as predicate words, or as objects of verbs or prepositions:

mine	ours
yours	yours
his, hers, its	theirs

Examples: This book is *mine*. (predicate word)
           Yours is on the desk. (subject of verb)
           I don't see *hers*. (object of verb)
           Look at the pictures in *ours*. (object of preposition)

A.   Choose the right pronoun from the parentheses. Be ready to explain how it is used in the sentence.

1. Does this copy belong to (he, him)?
2. That was (her, she).
3. Mrs. Walsh gave the job to (I, me).
4. Donna and I helped (they, them) with the yard work.
5. Hasn't anybody seen (he, him)?
6. It was (her, she) who answered the call.
7. Was it (they, them) who called?
8. Is there anything of (your, yours) to go home?
9. This is (he, him).
10. Will you give these books to (she, her)?

B.   Choose the right pronoun from the parentheses. Be ready to explain how it is used in the sentence.

1. The principal wanted to talk to Kelly and (I, me).
2. Could it have been (they, them)?
3. I have both of (theirs, their).
4. That looks more like (me, I).
5. Mother asked (me, I) for the key.
6. The award was given to (she, her) for outstanding achievement.
7. Each of (us, we) had a look at it.
8. I'm sure it was (he, him) on the telephone.
9. The test results were given by (they, them) at a special meeting.
10. (Me, I) am going to the museum.

C.   The personal pronouns in the following sentences are in italics. Write each one. After it, write *Nominative* or *Objective*.

1. The puck just missed *him*.

2. Ms. Anderson gave *us* several problems for homework.
3. *I* gave *you* the schedule.
4. *They* were taking *her* to dinner.
5. *He* gave the gifts to *them*.
6. *We* have been waiting for *him*.
7. The manager sold *us* the T-shirts at a discount.
8. Carl couldn't hear *me*.
9. Did Aunt Ellen get a good picture of *us*?
10. The third one in the front row is *she*.

Part 7 Pronouns in Compound Sentence Parts

You seldom make mistakes when you use one personal pronoun by itself. You would never say "Give *I* the pencil."

Trouble arises when two pronouns or a pronoun and a noun are used together in compound sentence parts. Would you say "Brian and me built a radio" or "Brian and I built a radio"?

Have you heard people say "between you and I"? Does this sound right? Should it be "between you and me"? How can you tell? Let's look at some sentences with pronouns correctly used in compound parts.

> **Compound Subject:** *Terry and she* went to the rink.
> **Compound Direct Object:** We visited the *Browns and them*.
> **Compound Indirect Object:** Mrs. Hill gave *Sue and me* a job.
> **Compound Object of Preposition:** The package was for *Jack and me*.

Now read the sentences above a second time. This time drop out the noun in each compound part. For example, read "*She* went to the rink." Each sentence will sound right and sensible to you.

Whenever you are in doubt about which form of the pronoun to use in a compound sentence part, drop out the noun. Read the sentence with just the pronoun, and you will usually choose the right one.

If there are two pronouns in the compound part, read the sentence for each pronoun separately.

> Mrs. Huber will call for you and (she? her?).
> Mrs. Huber will call for you.
> Mrs. Huber will call for *her*.

Caution: After forms of *be*, use only *I*, *we*, *he*, *she*, or *they* as predicate pronouns.

Exercises Choose the right pronoun in compound sentence parts.

A. Choose the right pronoun from the parentheses in each sentence.

1. Dawn and (her, she) will bring the peanuts.
2. Can you give Sandy and (we, us) a ride?
3. Gayle and (her, she) are trying out for cheerleading.
4. The doorman gave Al and (I, me) a pass.
5. There is no difference in weight between (him and me) (he and I).
6. Wait for Lori and (I, me) after school.
7. Jeff lives between (they and I) (them and me).
8. (Her, She) and I are the newspaper editors.
9. The ushers were Marla and (her, she).
10. Just between you and (me, I), that speaker wasn't very good.

B. All but one of the following sentences contain a pronoun error. Write the sentences, correcting the errors.

1. My parents and me are going to the ice show tonight.

2. Larry and them have gone to Detroit.

3. The telephone must be for either you or she.

4. Everyone had enough except Janet and she.

5. The packages were divided evenly between Tanya and I.

6. Judy and her just went out the back door.

7. Mrs. McGowan made Meg and I a sandwich.

8. The gas station attendant gave Mary Beth and I directions.

9. Peggy and Linda sat next to Lauri and I at the concert.

10. The helicopter kept circling around Pam and me.

Part 8   *Who* and *Whom*

The words *who, whose,* and *whom* are used to ask questions. When used in this way, they are called **interrogative pronouns.**

> *Who* told you that story? (*Who* is subject of *told.*)
> *Whose* is the yellow sweater? (*Whose* is subject of *is.*)
> *Whom* did you meet? (*Whom* is object of *did meet.*)
> To *whom* did you go? (*Whom* is object of preposition *to.*)

Who is the nominative form. It is used as the subject of a verb.

Whom is the objective form. It is used as the direct object of a verb or as the object of a preposition.

Whose is the possessive form. Like other possessives, it can be used with a noun to modify the noun: *Whose bike* is missing? When it is used without a noun, it may be the subject or object of a verb.

> *Whose* house is that? (*Whose* modifies *house.*)
> *Whose* were you using? (*Whose* is object of *were using.*)
> *Whose* are those boots? (*Whose* is subject of *are.*)

Exercises **Choose the right interrogative pronoun.**

A. Choose the right interrogative pronoun from the two given in parentheses.

1. (Who, Whose) move is it?
2. (Whose, Who) are these binoculars?
3. (Who, Whom) are these people?
4. (Whom, Who) were you thinking of?
5. (Whom, Who) do these Adidas belong to?
6. (Who, Whom) swam ten lengths?
7. (Whom, Whose) speech did you like the best?
8. (Whose, Whom) is this?
9. (Whom, Whose) country has that flag?
10. For (who, whom) does the bell toll?

B. Choose the right interrogative pronoun from the two given in parentheses.

1. To (whom, who) did you give the library books?
2. (Who, Whom) is this letter from?
3. (Whom, Who) painted this picture?
4. (Who, Whom) do you know in Alaska?
5. (Who, Whom) is Randy talking to?
6. (Whose, Who) are these initials?
7. To (who, whom) should I give these letters?
8. For (who, whom) shall I ask?
9. (Whom, Who) did you ask for?
10. (Who, Whom) will get the MVP award in hockey?

Part 9 Possessive Pronouns and Contractions

Some contractions are formed by joining a pronoun and a verb, and omitting one or more letters. The apostrophe is used to show where letters are left out.

> it + is = it's   they + are = they're
> you + are = you're   who + is = who's

The possessive forms of the pronouns *its, your, their,* and *whose* sound the same as these contractions: *it's, you're, they're,* and *who's.* Because they sound alike, the contractions and possessives are sometimes confused.

> **Wrong:** The groundhog saw it's shadow.
> **Right:** The groundhog saw its shadow.
>
> **Right:** You're (You are) late for your appointment.
> **Right:** They're (They are) planning to show their slides.
> **Right:** Who's (who is) the boy whose coat you are wearing?

There are two simple rules to follow to make sure that you use possessive pronouns and contractions correctly.

1. When you use one of these words that sound alike, ask yourself whether it stands for one word or two. If it stands for two words, it is a contraction and needs an apostrophe.

2. Never use an apostrophe in a possessive pronoun.

Exercises   Possessive pronouns and contractions.

A. Choose the right word from the two in parentheses.

1. The amusement park gave free passes to (it's, its) first 500 entrants.

2. (Whose, Who's) bike is chained to the tree?

3. (You're, Your) idea might work.

4. Are you sure that (they're, their) coming?

5. (Whose, Who's) going to the Ridgetown Fair?

6. (They're, Their) glad (its, it's) Friday.

7. (Whose, Who's) going to mow the lawn?

8. (Their, They're) going to pick up (their, they're) uniforms at noon.

9. Have you made up (you're, your) mind?

10. (Who's, Whose) got a dime that I can borrow?

B. Write the words each contraction below stands for.

1. It's twenty miles from this town to Omaha.

2. Who's next?

3. We've walked the whole way.

4. Who'd have thought it would snow in April?

5. They've come to repair the water main.

6. Who's been in my locker?

7. You've got a good sense of humor.

8. It's your turn now.

9. The book is called *Who's Who*.

10. When's the pizza being delivered?

Part 10   Special Pronoun Problems

Compound Personal Pronouns

The compound personal pronouns (*myself, yourself,* etc.) must not be used in place of personal pronouns. They are used *in addition* to personal pronouns. It is a good rule to use a compound personal pronoun only when the word it refers to has been used in the same sentence.

> I saw the weather balloon *myself*. (*Myself* refers to *I*.)
> You can judge for *yourself*. (*Yourself* refers to *you*.)
> She *herself* knows what should be done. (*Herself* refers to *she*.)

We Boys—Us Boys; We Girls—Us Girls

When you use phrases like *we girls* and *us boys*, you must be sure that you are using the right case of the pronoun. You can tell which pronoun to use by dropping the noun and saying the sentence without it.

> **Problem:** (We, Us) girls will be at Jan's house.
> **Correct:** We will be at Jan's house.
> **Correct:** We girls will be at Jan's house.
>
> **Problem:** Will you call for (us, we) boys?
> **Correct:** Will you call for us?
> **Correct:** Will you call for us boys?

Them and *Those*

The word *them* is always a pronoun. It is always used as an object of a verb or preposition.

Those is sometimes a pronoun and sometimes an adjective. If a noun appears right after it, *those* is probably an adjective. Used without a noun, it is a pronoun.

> We found *them* here. (Object of verb)
> We have heard from *them*. (Object of preposition *from*)
> We like *those* best. (Object of verb)
> *Those* birds are cardinals. (Adjective modifying *birds*)
> We will order *those* cakes. (Adjective modifying *cakes*)

Exercises **Use the right form.**

A. Fill in the blank with the correct compound personal pronoun.

1. I finished building the end table _____.

2. You can both see for _____ that the experiment worked.

3. We went to the movies by _____.

4. If you jog, you compete only with _____.

5. Janelle planted the flower bed by _____.

6. They can read for _____ that the track meet was cancelled.

7. I went by _____ to the art exhibit.

8. We treated _____ to hot fudge sundaes.

9. Will you take the Amtrak to St. Louis by _____?

10. David directed the play _____.

B. Choose the correct word from the two words given in parentheses.

1. Do you want to go to the beach with Diana and (me, myself)?

2. (We, Us) Scouts would like to sponsor a canoe trip.

3. (Them, Those) portraits look very old.

4. (We, Us) players are going to the Knicks-Bulls basketball game.

5. Will you call for (we, us) boys on the way to the stadium?

6. Who piled all (them, those) boards up?

7. Would you like to sit with (us, we) girls at the play?

8. Most of (us, we) boys will help paint the bleachers.

9. You won't need all of (them, those) pencils.

10. (We, Us) students held a pep rally yesterday.

Part 11 Pronouns and Antecedents

A personal pronoun, you remember, is used in place of a noun. This noun is the word to which it refers. The noun usually comes first, either in the same sentence or in the preceding sentence. The noun for which a pronoun stands is called its **antecedent.**

> We waited for Kay. *She* was making a phone call.
> (*She* stands for *Kay. Kay* is the antecedent.)
> The men had taken off *their* coats.
> (*Their* stands for *men. Men* is the antecedent.)

Pronouns themselves may be the antecedents of other pronouns:

> Does everyone have *his* books?
> (*Everyone* is the antecedent of *his.*)
> Do you have *your* music lesson today?
> (*You* is the antecedent of *your.*)

A pronoun must agree with its antecedent in number.

Here the word *agree* means that the pronoun must be the *same in number* as its antecedent. The word *number* here means *singular* or *plural.* The pronoun must be singular if the word it stands for is singular. It must be plural if the word it stands for is plural.

> The runners took *their* places.
> (*Runners* is plural; *their* is plural.)
> The scientist told of *his* early experiences.
> (*Scientist* is singular; *his* is singular.)
> Everybody brought *his* own records.
> (*Everybody* is singular; *his* is singular.)
> One of the girls left *her* project in the shop.
> (*One* is singular; *her* is singular.)

Exercises Pronouns and antecedents.

A. The personal pronouns in these sentences are italicized. Find the antecedent of each pronoun. Write it.

1. One of the boys had a cast on *his* arm.
2. You usually bring *your* own towel to the pool.
3. The box isn't pretty, but the paper around *it* is.
4. Everyone in the audience had tears in *his* eyes.
5. Both of the owls had *their* eyes half shut.
6. Everyone thinks *you* can do it, Sarah.
7. One of the glasses had a crack in *it*.
8. Brenda bought *her* own materials.
9. The members of the cast took *their* places.
10. One of the storm shelters had *its* entrance boarded up.

B. Choose the right pronoun from the parentheses.

1. Has everyone taken (his, their) turn?
2. If anyone wants to go, tell (him, them) to see Paul.
3. Few were able to finish (his, their) work.
4. Most of the cans had lost (its, their) labels.
5. Somebody has left (his, their) wallet on my desk.
6. Everyone had an opportunity to state (their, his) opinion.
7. None of the bottles had (its, their) label removed.
8. Nobody expected to hear (his, their) own name over the loudspeaker.
9. None of the actors could remember (his, their) lines at the first rehearsal.
10. Each of the students explained (his, their) collage to the class.

Additional Exercises

Using Pronouns

A. Find the pronouns.

Number your paper 1–10. Write the pronouns you find in each of the following sentences. After each pronoun, write the noun or nouns it stands for.

1. Mike said he would set the dinner table.
2. There's no stamp on the envelope. It must have come off.
3. One rancher drove his jeep ten miles out on the range.
4. There's the box. Its lid has a picture of a cornfield.
5. Brad and Joe said Scott could use their tent.
6. Claire and Joy put the camping equipment in their car.
7. Mr. Hernandez attached his trailer to the back of his van.
8. Two archaeologists told how they had discovered the ruins.
9. Sue and Wendy missed the bus, and then they got caught in the rain.
10. There's the tree where Megan snagged her kite.

B. Use compound personal pronouns.

Number your paper 1–10. Beside each number write a correct compound personal pronoun for each of the following sentences. After it, write the noun or pronoun to which it refers.

1. The boys decorated the gym by (pronoun).
2. Julie cleaned the fish (pronoun).
3. I moved the plants (pronoun) so that they wouldn't get damaged.

4. Please help (pronoun) to more dessert.
5. The drum majorette usually led the parade (pronoun).
6. Rob made the fudge all by (pronoun).
7. Why doesn't Janet try out for the team (pronoun)?
8. We watched (pronoun) on the TV screen.
9. Ken, Rachel, and Jill painted the scenery (pronoun).
10. A lion cub sunned (pronoun) on a rock.

C. Find the indefinite pronouns.

Number your paper 1–10. For each sentence write down the indefinite pronoun and pick the verb in parentheses that agrees with it.

1. Some of the tarts (taste, tastes) like strawberry.
2. Several of the foreign exchange students (come, comes) from South America.
3. Everything in the boxes (is, are) wet.
4. None of those stars to the west (set, sets) before 10 P.M.
5. Each of the divers (perform, performs) twice.
6. One of those tires (has, have) a slow leak.
7. Somebody in the prop room always (forget, forgets) the king's cushion.
8. (Are, Is) anybody coming?
9. No one in the caves (wander, wanders) away from the guide.
10. Both of us (know, knows) the way around the swamp.

D. Find different kinds of pronouns.

Number your paper 1–10. Write all the pronouns in these sentences. After each pronoun, write *Indefinite*, *Demonstrative*, or *Interrogative* to show what kind it is.

1. How did Kirk get these out of the water?
2. No one admitted leaving the phone off the hook.

3. Several of the girls carried this from the station.
4. Why would anyone bring these to a picnic?
5. Everybody heckled the pitcher.
6. Who let the cat out of the bag?
7. Nobody knew the right answer.
8. Pete is buying these as a present.
9. What's that by the rock pile?
10. Both of the teams had practiced vigorously.

E. Choose the right pronoun.

Choose the right pronoun from the parentheses. Be ready to explain how it is used in the sentence.

1. Was it (he, him) who won the trophy?
2. It was (she, her) who painted that picture.
3. The workers demanded (their, theirs) pay immediately.
4. (We, Us) organized the pep assembly.
5. Strong winds blew the shack over on (it, its) side.
6. We thought it was (he, him) who made the announcements.
7. The manager gave Ann and (me, I) tickets to the movie.
8. Caryl and (me, I) are going to the shopping mall.
9. Jack wanted you to bring (your, yours) along.
10. Please give these music books to Darla and (she, her).

F. Use the right pronoun in compound sentence parts.

Choose the right pronoun from the parentheses.

1. (He, Him) and Sally set up the ping pong table.
2. Did you meet John and (they, them) at the exhibit?
3. A waiter showed Mrs. Ryan and (she, her) to a table.
4. (She, Her) and (me, I) were digging for clams.
5. They gave Ted and (we, us) just ten minutes to get ready.

6. My father packed Ken and (me, I) a lunch.

7. Barb waited fifteen minutes for Mr. Kopp and (they, them).

8. Bob and (us, we) had to mow and rake the lawn.

9. The setter came to Greg and (he, him) right away.

10. The lifeguard warned Patty and (we, us) about the undercurrent.

G. Choose the right interrogative pronoun.

Choose the right interrogative pronoun from the two given in parentheses.

1. (Whom, Who) came in second?

2. (Who, Whose) was the best answer?

3. (Who, Whom) left her sunglasses on the counter?

4. To (whom, who) are you giving the macramé hanger?

5. (Who, Whom) did Scott give the folder to?

6. (Whom, Who) knows how to get to the airport?

7. (Whose, Whom) phone number is that?

8. (Who, Whom) did the coach choose for the starting line-up?

9. (Whom, Who) let the cats out of the house?

10. (Whose, Whom) are these cookies for?

H. Possessive pronouns and contractions.

Choose the right word from the two in parentheses.

1. (It's, Its) too early.

2. The panther boxed (its, it's) cub's ears.

3. (Who's, Whose) team do we play next week?

4. (Your, You're) appointment with the orthodontist is tomorrow.

5. Christie and Tom said (they're, their) report was on bicycle safety.

6. (Whose, Who's) got the relish?

7. (It's, Its) Monday and it's (you're, your) turn to cook.

8. (Their, They're) ready for take-off.

9. (It's, Its) (your, your're) turn.

10. (They're, Their) always late starting the meeting.

I. Use the right form with special pronoun problems.

Choose the correct word from the two in parentheses.

1. The coach handed the trophy to (me, myself).

2. (Them, Those) are too big.

3. The principal presented (we, us) students with diplomas.

4. Please put (them, those) boxes in the trash can.

5. (Us, We) girls got special recognition for our efforts.

6. (Them, Those) posters are to be hung in the cafeteria.

7. (Them, Those) shops on Central Street are open until 9 P.M.

8. Would you like to go to the show with (us, we) girls?

J. Pronouns and antecedents.

The personal pronouns in these sentences are italicized. Write the antecedent of each pronoun.

1. The paramedics entered the fiery building carrying all of *their* equipment.

2. Chris's coat had a tear in *it*.

3. Phil fixed *his* back tire.

4. Vicki's yard has a fence all around *it*.

5. Mrs. Kohl was knitting a sweater for *her* granddaughter.

6. Bring *your* gym clothes for the intramural game tomorrow.

7. Curt looked at *his* dog dish and walked away from it.

8. Lara and Pete told *their* parents about the band concert.

9. Susie brought *her* tape recorder.

10. The swallows always make *their* nests in the barn.

Section 4

Using Verbs

Of all the parts of speech, the verb is the most important. It is the moving power, the motor, of a sentence.

Verbs are important because you need them for sentence building. They are important, too, because they help you more than any other part of speech to say exactly what you mean. See the variety of ways in which *go* can be used:

I go.	I went.
I am going.	I have gone.
I am going to go.	I had gone.
She goes.	She should have gone.

In Section 1 you studied some of the forms and uses of verbs. In this chapter you will study verbs in greater detail.

Part 1 What Verbs Are

A verb is a word that tells of an action or state of being.

Action Verbs

Some verbs tell of an action:

> Mom *started* the car.   The rain *drenched* us.

Sometimes the action is one you cannot see:

> Carlos *needed* help.   Kate *had* a good idea.

Whether you can see the action or not, an action verb tells that something is happening, has happened, or will happen.

Linking Verbs

A few verbs do not tell of an action. They merely tell that something is. They express a state of being:

> The clock *is* slow.   The sky *looks* gloomy.
> The house *seems* empty.   The gloves *feel* soft.

These verbs are called **linking verbs** because they connect the subject with some other word or words in the sentence.

Here are the most common linking verbs:

be (am, are, is, was,	look	smell
were, been, being)	appear	taste
become	feel	grow
seem	sound	

Many linking verbs can also be used as action verbs.

Linking Verb	Action Verb
The melon *looked* ripe.	Ann *looked* at the melon.

The melon *feels* ripe.   Ann *felt* the melon.
The night *grew* cold.   Tom *grows* tomatoes.

Exercises   Find the verbs.

A. Find the verb in each sentence. Write it. After the verb write *Action* or *Linking* to show what kind it is.

1. That Dutch apple pie smells delicious.
2. These candy sticks taste sour.
3. The florist appeared at the door with flowers for my sister.
4. Sherry looked in the attic.
5. Many visitors waited in line for tickets.
6. The horses raced toward the finish line.
7. Those bananas look overripe.
8. The sun broke through the smog at noon.
9. The sky looks ominous.
10. The record sounds scratchy.

B. Follow the directions for Exercise A.

1. The air smells clean and fresh after that storm.
2. The first wrestler pinned his opponent in ten seconds.
3. A beautiful rainbow appeared across the meadow.
4. Chicago and Boston are my two favorite rock groups.
5. I finished my social studies assignment in class.
6. After dinner, Erica and I cycled to the park.
7. The yearbook staff sold hot dogs and Cokes at the football games.
8. The speaker for the assembly sounds interesting.
9. The weekend at Six Flags over Mid-America was adventurous.
10. Mrs. Bauer grows cantaloupe and watermelon in her garden.

Part 2 Helping Verbs and Main Verbs

You will also remember that a great many verbs consist of more than one word. Verbs can be made up of a **main verb** and one or more **helping verbs.**

Verb	Helping Verbs	Main Verb
had gone	had	gone
was seen	was	seen
can go	can	go
might have gone	might have	gone
must have been caught	must have been	caught

There are three verbs that can be used either as main verbs or as helping verbs. Here are their forms:

do	has	is	was	be
does	have	am	were	been
did	had	are		

	Used as Main Verb	Used as Helping Verb
Examples:	Can you *do* this job?	I *do know* your sister.
	Who *has* my key?	Sue *has gone* home.
	Where *were* you?	The boys *were working*.

Here is a list of words frequently used as helping verbs.

can	shall	will	may	must
could	should	would	might	

Sometimes parts of a verb are separated from each other by words that are not part of the verb.

I *did* not *ask* the right question.
Mac *was* certainly *trying* hard.

Exercises   Find the Verbs.

A.   Find the parts of the verb in each sentence. Put them in two columns labeled *Helping Verb* and *Main Verb*.

Example: They will deliver the packages tomorrow.

Helping Verb	Main Verb
will	deliver

1. We are going to the circus tomorrow.
2. We have completed our study of the U. S. Constitution.
3. Everyone has gone home.
4. Can Manny and Liz go to the baseball game with us?
5. It must have snowed all night.
6. After the concert, we are going to the pizzeria.
7. I was writing my composition during study hall.
8. My sister is running in the marathon race.
9. Colleen and I have skated at the new roller rink.
10. The hot air balloons had landed in the stadium.

B.   Follow the directions for Exercise A.

1. Mopeds have been designed for economical transportation.
2. A moped can go up to 30 miles per hour.
3. It is considered a motorized bicycle.
4. No licenses are required for moped drivers in many states.
5. Consumers are concerned about the price of fuel.
6. Energy conservation has become everyone's responsibility.
7. Car pools and public transportation can help our energy resources.
8. Each of us must make individual efforts to save energy.
9. Solar energy can help us in the years ahead.
10. Some day we will probably heat our homes, schools, and offices with solar energy.

Part 3 Progressive Forms

Sometimes we tell the time of an action like this:

I *am* talking. (instead of I *talk*)
I *was* talking. (instead of I *talked*)

We use a form of the verb *be* with the form of the main verb that ends in *-ing*. We call these the **progressive forms** of the verb. Here are the **progressive forms** of *talk* that are used with *I*:

I am talking.	I have been talking.
I was talking.	I had been talking.
I shall (will) be talking.	I shall (will) have been talking.

Exercises Progressive forms.

A. Number your paper 1–10. Write down the verb in each sentence.

1. The Allens are raising dalmatians.
2. I will be going to Florida in April.
3. Julia was talking to Ms. O'Shea about the Science Fair.
4. I will be running for vice-president of the French Club.
5. We will be keeping in touch.
6. I was watching the Movie of the Week last night.
7. Bill, Tom, and Maria have been managing the pool.
8. We will be playing more soccer next year.
9. I was listening to the radio.
10. Raul and Marlene will be working at Indian Lake next July and August.

B. Copy these sentences, changing each verb to its progressive form.

1. This machine filters our drinking water.

2. From now on, the sun will set later and later.
3. The dishwater, as usual, had gotten cold.
4. Kurt practiced his diving.
5. Peggy has collected information on Japan.
6. I talked to my counselor about next year's class schedule.
7. We telephoned my sister at college.
8. Ray talked to Mrs. Pampel about his assignments.
9. The audience laughed at the entertainer.
10. We waited for the bus.

Part 4   The Tenses of Verbs

Verbs are time-telling words. They not only tell of an action or a state of being. They also tell *when* the action takes place. They tell whether the action or state of being is past, present, or future.

Verbs tell time in two ways:

1. By changing their spelling:

    walk—walked   sleep—slept

2. By using helping verbs:

    will creep   has crept   had crept

Verbs express six different times. Each verb has a form to express each of these six different times. The forms of a verb used to indicate time are called the **tenses** of a verb.

The Simple Tenses

The **present tense** of the verb is the same as the name of the verb:

    run   go   walk

The **past tense** of regular verbs is formed by adding *-d* or *-ed* to the present tense:

> walked   placed

The past tense of irregular verbs is usually shown by a change of spelling:

> shine—shone   swing—swung

The **future tense** is formed by using *shall* or *will* with the present tense:

> shall go   will run

The three tenses described above are called the **simple tenses.** They describe:

1. What is happening now: *present tense*
2. What happened before: *past tense*
3. What will happen later: *future tense*

The Perfect Tenses

Sometimes we have to speak of two different times, one earlier than the other. To make these times clear, we can use the **perfect tenses.** The perfect tenses are formed by using *has, have,* or *had* with the past participle.

The perfect tenses are formed as follows:

> **Present Perfect:** has run, have run
> **Past Perfect:** had run
> **Future Perfect:** will have run, shall have run

Exercises   Recognize verb tenses.

A. Find each verb in the following sentences. Tell the tense of each.

1. What have you done with the scissors?
2. We have always enjoyed these travelogs.
3. My brother and I walk to school.

4. Will you come to the party tonight?
5. Have you ever gone to a volleyball game?
6. The new ice cream parlor will open in June.
7. My parents and I have traveled to Mexico.
8. We will have eaten the cake by tomorrow.
9. When will the fair open?
10. Lynn hasn't seen the ice show.

B. Write a sentence for each of the verbs below. Use the verb in the tense indicated.

1. fill (past tense)
2. drop (past perfect tense)
3. stay (future tense)
4. glisten (past tense)
5. close (future perfect tense)
6. splash (present tense)
7. flash (present progressive tense)
8. cause (present tense)
9. attach (past perfect tense)
10. touch (future tense)

Part 5 The Principal Parts of Verbs

Every verb has certain forms on which nearly all other forms of the verb are based. These essential forms of a verb are called the **principal parts** of the verb.

The principal parts of a verb are the **present tense,** the **past tense,** and the **past participle.**

Present	Past	Past Participle
talk	talked	talked
knit	knitted	knitted
add	added	added
divide	divided	divided

The present tense and the past tense are **simple tenses** of the verb. The past participle is used for all **perfect tenses** of the verb.

As you can see, the past and the past participle forms of *talk, knit, add*, and *divide* are the same. These are **regular verbs.** In all regular verbs the past and past participle are formed by adding -*d* (*divided*) or -*ed* (*talked*) to the present form.

Many regular verbs change their spelling when -*d* or -*ed* is added to them. These changes are made in accord with regular spelling rules.

knit + ed = knitted	hurry + ed = hurried
fit + ed = fitted	try + ed = tried
pat + ed = patted	pity + ed = pitied

Some verbs change their spelling this way:

say + d = said   pay + d = paid   lay + d = laid

Exercise   Principal parts of verbs.

The verbs below are regular verbs. Make three columns on your paper. Head them *Present, Past, and Past Participle.* Place the principal parts of the verbs in the right columns.

1. worry	6. help	11. rob	16. try
2. sob	7. pass	12. like	17. flip
3. pay	8. end	13. rap	18. push
4. carry	9. slip	14. hurry	19. vary
5. grab	10. use	15. rub	20. sew

Part 6 Irregular Verbs

There are hundreds of verbs in our language that follow the regular pattern of adding -*d* or -*ed* to the present to form the past and past participle.

Those verbs that do not follow this pattern are called **irregular verbs.** There are only about sixty irregular verbs that are frequently used. Many of these have only one change. They present few problems.

buy	bought	bought
make	made	made
feel	felt	felt

A few irregular verbs do not change at all from one principal part to another. They offer no problems in usage.

hit   let   set   shut

Most verb problems come from the irregular verbs that have three different forms:

throw	threw	thrown
ring	rang	rung

If you are not sure about a verb form, look it up in a dictionary. If the verb is regular, only one form will usually be listed.

If the verb is irregular, the dictionary will give the irregular forms. It will give two forms if the past and past participle are the same: *say, said.* It will give all three principal parts if they are all different: *sing, sang, sung.*

Dictionary Entry for Begin

present
|

be·gin (bi gin′), **v.** to start being, doing, acting, etc.; get under way
[Work *begins* at 8:00 A.M. His cold *began* with a sore throat.]
—**be·gan′,** *p.l.;* **be·gun′,** *p.p.*
| |_____ past participle
|
past

The Most Common Irregular Verbs

Present	Past	Past Participle	Present	Past	Past Participle
begin	began	begun	lay	laid	laid
break	broke	broken	lie	lay	lain
bring	brought	brought	ride	rode	ridden
choose	chose	chosen	ring	rang	rung
come	came	come	rise	rose	risen
do	did	done	run	ran	run
drink	drank	drunk	see	saw	seen
eat	ate	eaten	sing	sang	sung
fall	fell	fallen	speak	spoke	spoken
freeze	froze	frozen	steal	stole	stolen
give	gave	given	swim	swam	swum
go	went	gone	take	took	taken
grow	grew	grown	throw	threw	thrown
know	knew	known	write	wrote	written

There are two general rules for using irregular verbs:

1. With the past participle, use a helping verb such as *has,* *have,* or *had.*

> have ridden   has swum
> has broken   had thrown

2. With the past tense, use no helping verb.

> The show *began* early.
> The books *lay* on the table.

Practice Pages on Irregular Verbs

Irregular verbs can cause problems in writing as well as in speaking. Pages 87–99, with red borders, provide practice in the correct use of irregular verbs.

How well do you use these verbs? The following exercise will tell you.

If the exercise shows that you need more practice with certain verbs, your teacher may ask you to turn to those verbs on the following pages. For each verb there are many sentences that will help you to "say it right," "hear it right," and "write it right."

Exercise **Using Irregular Verbs.**

Number your paper 1–30. For each sentence, write the correct word from the two given in parentheses.

1. The party (began, begun) about seven o'clock.
2. The gate had been (broke, broken) long ago.
3. Who (bring, brought) these posters to class?
4. Has everyone (chosen, chose) a topic for his or her report?
5. Jack (came, come) home after the debate.
6. Rob has never (did, done) such a good job.
7. At camp, we (drunk, drank) a quart of milk every day.
8. Someone had (ate, eaten) all the brownies.
9. The temperature had (fell, fallen) very quickly.
10. Have you ever eaten (froze, frozen) yogurt?
11. Lauren has (given, gave) a good report about Presidential elections.
12. Everyone had (went, gone) home by then.
13. That tree has (grew, grown) several feet this year.
14. I wouldn't have (known, knew) what to do.

15. Our science class has (grew, grown) different plants for an experiment.

16. The team (known, knew) all of the defensive plays.

17. The alarm had (rung, rang) too soon for me.

18. The church bells (rung, rang) at seven.

19. The sun had (rose, risen) early.

20. We (run, ran) the relay races on the indoor track.

21. Bill (seen, saw) two deer.

22. The audience (sang, sung) the chorus of the song.

23. The President has (spoke, spoken) to the reporters.

24. The thief had (stole, stolen) several appliances from the shop.

25. We had never (swum, swam) as far as that.

26. We have (went, gone) skiing every winter.

27. Terry (threw, thrown) the Frisbee to Darcy.

28. Eric has (write, written) a good short story.

29. The pitcher had (threw, thrown) a curve to strike out the batter.

30. Have you (wrote, written) your report for consumer ed?

Say It Right   Hear It Right

A. Say these sentences over until the correct use of *began* and *begun* sounds natural to you.

1. Have you begun yet?
2. Jill hasn't begun.
3. Bill began his job.
4. He began yesterday.
5. Mary began thinking.
6. I began to daydream.
7. I haven't begun the book.
8. Have they begun reading?

B. Say these sentences over until the correct use of *bring* and *brought* sounds natural to you.

1. Did you bring the map?
2. Sam brought an atlas.
3. Did Mike bring the radio?
4. Yes, he brought it.
5. What did Suzi bring?
6. She has brought the food.
7. Claire had brought the soda.
8. I wish I'd brought some too.

Write It Right

Write the correct word from the two words given.

1. Has the movie (began, begun) yet?
2. Yes, it (began, begun) ten minutes ago.
3. I haven't missed that series since it (began, begun).
4. Have you (began, begun) your new book yet?
5. We (began, begun) our day playing tennis.
6. The people (began, begun) to leave the scene of the accident.
7. Jory has (began, begun) to mow the lawn.
8. Patti (bring, brought) me a present for my birthday.
9. The messenger (bring, brought) good news.
10. The jury (bring, brought) in the verdict.
11. Did you (bring, brought) the book I wanted to read?
12. I have (bring, brought) candy for everyone in the class.
13. Did you (bring, brought) sleeping bags for our camp weekend?
14. We have (bring, brought) plenty of food, too.
15. Did you (bring, brought) all the equipment for your experiment?

Say It Right   Hear It Right

A. Say these sentences over until the correct use of *broke* and *broken* sounds natural to you.

1. Pam broke the school record.
2. No one else has broken it.
3. The car broke down in Ohio.
4. Dennis broke the window.
5. Diane had broken the mug.
6. Steve broke his ankle.
7. The mirror was broken.
8. I have broken my watch.

B. Say these sentences over until the correct use of *came* and *come* sounds natural to you.

1. Nathan came yesterday.
2. Your friends have come.
3. They all came together.
4. Janelle should have come.
5. No one came late.
6. Joe came early.
7. He has come early before.
8. Hasn't Heather come yet?

Write It Right

Write the correct word from the two words given.

1. I have (broke, broken) the can opener.
2. Now that it's (broke, broken), we'll need to replace it.
3. The clock is (broke, broken) beyond repair.
4. The VW had (broke, broken) down on the road to the beach.
5. Someone has (broke, broken) into the storeroom.
6. The heat wave (broke, broken) all records for July.
7. Sara (broke, broken) the record for the 100-yard dash.
8. Peter has (came, come) to the game with us.
9. He had (came, come) with us before.
10. My parents (came, come) to our play.
11. Summer has finally (came, come).
12. The coach (came, come) to see me in the hospital.
13. The sailboat (came, come) toward us.
14. We have (came, come) to the parade every Fourth of July.
15. The time has (came, come) for action.

Say It Right   Hear It Right

A. Say these sentences over until the correct use of *chose* and *chosen* sounds natural to you.

1. Have you chosen a book?
2. No, I haven't chosen one.
3. Bill chose his.
4. What has he chosen?
5. He chose a biography.
6. Renée had chosen a novel.
7. Ginny chose a book of poems.
8. Trisha chose a book on sports.

B. Say these sentences over until the correct use of *did* and *done* sounds natural to you.

1. I did my work early.
2. Sue has not done hers yet.
3. Amy has done two sketches.
4. Did you do this diorama?
5. Doug has done his job well.
6. Tom did the dishes tonight.
7. Have you done any hiking?
8. Sue did nothing to help.

Write It Right

Write the correct word from the two words given.

1. Our club has (chose, chosen) a new treasurer.
2. Who was (chose, chosen)?
3. Have you already (chose, chosen) a new president?
4. Yes, we have (chose, chosen) our president.
5. The students have (chose, chosen) good officers.
6. Which rucksack have you (chose, chosen)?
7. I have (chose, chosen) this one and a down sleeping bag.
8. Jonathan has (did, done) a beautiful painting.
9. Do you know how he (did, done) it?
10. He (did, done) it with oil paints.
11. Have you (did, done) your essay?
12. I (did, done) it last night.
13. We (did, done) our work and went skating.
14. Pablo had (did, done) the organizing for the program.
15. He (did, done) the best job of anyone.

Say It Right   Hear It Right

A. Say these sentences over until the correct use of *drank* and *drunk* sounds natural to you.

1. Who drank the milk?
2. Liz must have drunk it.
3. We have drunk all the tea.
4. Tom drank Squirt.
5. Sue drank all the lemonade.
6. I have never drunk Coke.
7. Al drank orange juice.
8. Who drank the soda?

B. Say these sentences over until the correct use of *eat, ate,* and *eaten* sounds natural to you.

1. Have you eaten yet?
2. Yes, I have eaten.
3. Jenny ate quite early.
4. Did you eat at noon?
5. When did you eat dinner?
6. We ate at 6 o'clock.
7. Last night we ate outside.
8. José had eaten with us.

Write It Right

Write the correct word from the choices given.

1. The kittens (drank, drunk) all the milk.
2. Have you ever (drank, drunk) a black cow?
3. No, I've never (drank, drunk) one.
4. We (drank, drunk) the lemonade and went back to work.
5. The patient (drank, drunk) the medicine.
6. Dad has not (drank, drunk) coffee for a month.
7. Jill (drank, drunk) all the chocolate milk.
8. The oranges have all been (ate, eaten).
9. Which one of you has (ate, eaten) all the ice cream?
10. Have you ever (ate, eaten) nectarines?
11. Yes, I have (ate, eaten) them.
12. We (ate, eaten) dinner at the Spaghetti Factory.
13. Carl and I had (ate, eaten) dinner with our grandparents.
14. Mary had (ate, eaten) before we got home.
15. Pam and Sal (ate, eaten) half the watermelon.

Say It Right   Hear It Right

A. Say these sentences over until the correct use of *fell* and *fallen* sounds natural to you.

1. The tree fell last night.
2. The picture fell down.
3. It has fallen before.
4. Have you fallen asleep?
5. Has the temperature fallen?
6. It has fallen ten degrees
7. Al fell on the ice.
8. Leé had fallen yesterday.

B. Say these sentences over until the correct use of *froze* and *frozen* sounds natural to you.

1. The pond froze quickly.
2. It was frozen solid.
3. Rain froze on the window.
4. It had frozen in patterns.
5. The milk has frozen.
6. Rain froze on the walks.
7. The orange crop has frozen.
8. Have you frozen the meat?

Write It Right

Write the correct word from the two words given.

1. Christmas may have (fell, fallen) on a Monday last year.
2. The temperature has (fell, fallen) slightly since noon.
3. Matt (fell, fallen) on the ice during the hockey game.
4. The child thought the clown had really (fell, fallen).
5. Snow has (fell, fallen) steadily for three days.
6. I have (fell, fallen) sometimes at the skating rink.
7. Have you ever (fell, fallen) while skateboarding?
8. That story is about a man who (froze, frozen) to death.
9. Has the lake (froze, frozen) over yet?
10. Are the ice cubes (froze, frozen) yet?
11. The meat has been (froze, frozen).
12. All of the windows were (froze, frozen) shut.
13. The stray dog had almost (froze, frozen) to death.
14. The murderer's heart seemed to have (froze, frozen) into ice.
15. Pedro (froze, frozen) the leftover lasagne.

Say It Right   Hear It Right

A.   Say these sentences over until the correct use of *give, gave,* and *given* sounds natural to you.

1. Who gave you that hat?
2. It was given to me by Amy.
3. Sue gave Al an aquarium.
4. I have given him a book.

5. Did you give your pen away?
6. I have given two pens away.
7. Dick gave me his puzzle.
8. I had given him a model.

B.   Say these sentences over until the correct use of *grew* and *grown* sounds natural to you.

1. The fern grew quickly.
2. The tree hasn't grown.
3. Mr. Smyth grew apples.
4. He has also grown pears.

5. The weather grew colder.
6. It has now grown warmer.
7. The child had grown tired.
8. Have you ever grown herbs?

Write It Right

Write the correct word from the two words given.

1. Jerry has (gave, given) up playing baseball.
2. We have always (gave, given) toys to the orphanage.
3. Maria (give, gave) me a compliment.
4. Pete has (gave, given) two recitals this year.
5. Nancy (give, gave) her brother a sweater.
6. Have you (given, gave) that album away?
7. Our team (give, gave) our rivals a beating.
8. Les has (grew, grown) faster than his cousin has.
9. What have you (grew, grown) in your garden?
10. We've (grew, grown) lettuce and tomatoes.
11. We have also (grew, grown) beans and peppers.
12. The beans have (grew, grown) quite tall.
13. Jean (grew, grown) strawberries in her garden.
14. Alan has (grew, grown) too tall to wear his old uniform.
15. The sapling (grew, grown) into a beautiful tree.

Say It Right Hear It Right

A. Say these sentences over until the correct use of *knew* and *known* sounds natural to you.

1. I knew the results.
2. I have known Jim for years.
3. Who knew the answers?
4. Bret knew the answers.

5. I knew the answers, too.
6. Have you known Josh long?
7. Who knew about the race?
8. Al had not known about it.

B. Say these sentences over until the correct use of *ran* and *run* sounds natural to you.

1. Bill ran a race.
2. He had never run faster.
3. He ran 20 kilometers.
4. The race was run in Chicago.

5. Ed ran the race in an hour.
6. Have you run in the relays?
7. I have never run in a race.
8. Sue ran the raffle.

Write It Right

Write the correct word from the two words given.

1. How long have you (knew, known) the Bernsteins?
2. We have (knew, known) them for a long time.
3. Had you (knew, known) Christmas vacation was extended?
4. Some things are (knew, known) with certainty.
5. I (knew, known) about the airplane accident yesterday.
6. Very few others (knew, known) about it then.
7. Lou had never (knew, known) anyone from Israel before.
8. That calculator is (ran, run) by four batteries.
9. The Lions Club (ran, run) the carnival this year.
10. They had never (ran, run) it before.
11. They (ran, run) for shelter when the tornado alert sounded.
12. Have you ever (ran, run) in a relay race?
13. Our air conditioner (ran, run) for twenty-four hours.
14. Janice has (ran, run) in the Fourth of July race for two years.
15. The thieves (ran, run) when the burglar alarm went off.

Say It Right   Hear It Right

A. Say these sentences over until the correct use of *rang* and *rung* sounds natural to you.

1. Has the telephone rung?
2. I thought it rang.
3. It rang an hour ago.
4. It hasn't rung since.

5. The doorbell rang.
6. Who rang it?
7. I had rung it earlier.
8. The dinner bell rang.

B. Say these sentences over until the correct use of *rode* and *ridden* sounds natural to you.

1. Who rode the horse?
2. The horse was ridden well.
3. Jim rode the horse.
4. I have ridden often.

5. Julie rode her bike.
6. She has ridden it often.
7. Anne rode in our new car.
8. Marla has ridden in it, too.

Write It Right

Write the correct word from the two words given.

1. Sleigh bells (rang, rung) out merrily.
2. All the church bells were (rang, rung) in celebration.
3. Christmas carols (rang, rung) out everywhere.
4. The telephone has (rang, rung) several times.
5. The cries of the hounds (rang, rung) in the air.
6. We have (rang, rung) many doorbells selling magazines.
7. Has the tardy bell (rang, rung) yet?
8. Have you ever (rode, ridden) a snowmobile?
9. I (rode, ridden) one several times last winter.
10. Tammy and Jill (rode, ridden) the bus to Atlanta.
11. Ron has (rode, ridden) in the Goodyear blimp.
12. Do you know anyone who has (rode, ridden) a camel?
13. We (rode, ridden) horseback in the mountains.
14. My family has (rode, ridden) on a DC-10 to Hawaii.
15. Have you (rode, ridden) on a roller coaster?

Say It Right   Hear It Right

A. Say these sentences over until the correct use of *rose* and *risen* sounds natural to you.

1. The sun has risen.
2. It rose at 6:15.
3. The river rose rapidly.
4. It has risen before.
5. The road rose sharply.
6. The moon rose over the hill.
7. The kite rose swiftly.
8. Jo had risen from her seat.

B. Say these sentences over until the correct use of *sang* and *sung* sounds natural to you.

1. Craig sang a solo.
2. He has sung before.
3. The tenor sang softly.
4. Lori also sang a solo.
5. She had sung last year.
6. Has she sung an aria?
7. The birds sang loudly.
8. The violin had sung sadly.

Write It Right

Write the correct word from the two words given.

1. The audience had (rose, risen) from their seats.
2. The official has (rose, risen) to a high rank.
3. The moon (rose, risen) over the mountain.
4. Why hasn't the dough (rose, risen)?
5. The crowd had (rose, risen) to their feet to cheer the players.
6. The divers had (rose, risen) to the surface.
7. The temperature has (rose, risen) to 35° C.
8. Our chorus (sang, sung) in the assembly program.
9. We (sang, sung) a medley of show tunes.
10. We had (sang, sung) them before.
11. Our quartet (sang, sung) at the state competition.
12. They had (sang, sung) last year, too.
13. Has Phil ever (sang, sung) in the choir?
14. The choir has (sang, sung) in many cities.
15. Had Jean (sang, sung) the alto or soprano part?

Say It Right   Hear It Right

A. Say these sentences over until the correct use of *saw* and *seen* sounds natural to you.

1. Have you seen Dan?
2. Yes, I saw him.
3. Ted has seen him, too.
4. Maureen saw him Sunday.

5. I saw that movie.
6. Have you seen it?
7. We saw it Saturday.
8. Bret hasn't seen it yet.

B. Say these sentences over until the correct use of *spoke* and *spoken* sounds natural to you.

1. Jan spoke to us yesterday.
2. She had spoken to us before.
3. Manny spoke first.
4. Has Liz spoken yet?

5. No, she hasn't spoken.
6. Terri spoke at the meeting.
7. She hadn't spoken before.
8. She spoken rather well.

Write It Right

Write the correct word from the two words given.

1. Have you ever (saw, seen) this TV program?
2. It's the best show I've ever (saw, seen).
3. Judy (saw, seen) the President at the airport.
4. Penny (saw, seen) her friends at the library.
5. I have (saw, seen) parachute jumping many times.
6. In the mountains Art (saw, seen) wild horses.
7. Jack had (saw, seen) the Bolshoi Ballet.
8. Dr. Wagner has (spoke, spoken) to me about a job.
9. I have (spoke, spoken) to my parents about it.
10. Everyone in the class has (spoke, spoken) at least once.
11. Rita hasn't (spoke, spoken) to me about her plans yet.
12. Jean has not (spoke, spoken) a word.
13. Our group (spoke, spoken) on energy consumption.
14. Which person had (spoke, spoken) at the meeting?
15. Tracy Austin (spoke, spoken) at our sports banquet.

Say It Right   Hear It Right

A. Say these sentences over until the correct use of *stole* and *stolen* sounds natural to you.

1. Who stole the money?
2. Two gangsters stole it.
3. Why have they stolen it?
4. Had they stolen before?
5. When was it stolen?
6. It was stolen yesterday.
7. They stole it at noon.
8. They stole it wearing masks.

B. Say these sentences over until the correct use of *swam* and *swum* sounds natural to you.

1. I swam in the pool.
2. Have you swum there?
3. Kelly swam all day.
4. We swam in the lake.
5. They have swum in the ocean.
6. Mark swam ten laps.
7. Linda had swum thirty.
8. I swam at the Y. W. C. A.

Write It Right

Write the correct word from the two words given.

1. Someone has (stole, stolen) our spare tire.
2. Why has someone (stole, stolen) it?
3. Lou Brock has (stole, stolen) more bases than anyone else.
4. He (stole, stolen) over 800 bases in his baseball career.
5. Ty Cobb had (stole, stolen) the most bases until Brock broke the record in '77.
6. The thief (stole, stolen) three oil paintings.
7. We know why he might have (stole, stolen) them.
8. Beth (swam, swum) at a very early age.
9. We haven't (swam, swum) much until now.
10. Our team (swam, swum) in the state meet.
11. During vacation, Sally (swam, swum) every day.
12. Have you (swam, swum) in the new pool?
13. Tanya has (swam, swum) there many times.
14. Chuck became ill when he (swam, swum) in the icy water.
15. Our team has often (swam, swum) in the medley relay.

Threw
Thrown

Took
Taken

Say It Right   Hear It Right

A. Say these sentences over until the correct use of *threw* and *thrown* sounds natural to you.

1. Who threw the ball?
2. Carrie threw it.
3. Have you thrown it?
4. Bruce hasn't thrown it.
5. I threw the paper away.
6. Bill threw the door open.
7. Lee has thrown the list away.
8. Chris threw a fast pitch.

B. Say these sentences over until the correct use of *took* and *taken* sounds natural to you.

1. Paula took a walk.
2. Steve took one, too.
3. Lori has taken the book.
4. Craig took three cookies.
5. Who took these pictures?
6. Gene took them.
7. He has taken lots of them.
8. We took a helicopter ride.

Write It Right

Write the correct word from the two words given.

1. The captain had (threw, thrown) the cargo overboard.
2. The runner was (threw, thrown) out at home plate.
3. The quarterback (threw, thrown) a touchdown pass.
4. I had (threw, thrown) cold water over my face.
5. The athlete (threw, thrown) the discus expertly.
6. I have (threw, thrown) those magazines away by mistake.
7. Have you ever (threw, thrown) a horseshoe?
8. Gabe has (took, taken) the wrong route.
9. I have never (took, taken) the expressway.
10. It (took, taken) us an hour to drive downtown.
11. The troops had (took, taken) the enemy by surprise.
12. We (took, taken) our sleeping bags with us.
13. Ms. Miller has (took, taken) our guest speaker to the airport.
14. It has (took, taken) a long time to save money for the party.
15. I have never (took, taken) that kind of medicine before.

Say It Right   Hear It Right

A.   Say these sentences over until the correct use of *went* and *gone* sounds natural to you.

1. Who went skating?
2. Pete has gone home.
3. Julie went to the park.
4. Have they gone swimming?
5. Janice went downstairs.
6. Have they gone yet?
7. They went an hour ago.
8. Everyone has gone.

B.   Say these sentences over until the correct use of *wrote* and *written* sounds natural to you.

1. I've written my paper.
2. Have you written one?
3. I wrote a letter.
4. Sue hasn't written yet.
5. Who has written to you?
6. Paul wrote to me.
7. Donna has written a speech.
8. They wrote the script.

Write It Right

Write the correct word from the two words given.

1. The spacecraft (went, gone) around the earth many times.
2. Another one has (went, gone) into orbit around the moon.
3. We (went, gone) to Disneyland last summer.
4. The Petersons have (went, gone) to New York for a week.
5. My sister has (went, gone) to France to study French.
6. Have you ever (went, gone) skiing?
7. Judy has (went, gone) to Florida for spring vacation.
8. That novel was (wrote, written) by Mark Twain.
9. Jim has (wrote, written) several humorous poems.
10. Melinda (wrote, written) to her friend.
11. Have you (wrote, written) your composition?
12. I've (wrote, written) the first draft.
13. Our class has (wrote, written) letters to the governor.
14. Last year we (wrote, written) to the mayor.
15. Why haven't you (wrote, written) that letter yet?

Part 7   Active and Passive Verbs

One of the interesting things about our language is the great variety of ways in which it expresses ideas. You have seen how many different times the tenses of verbs can show. Now you will see another way in which verbs help you say exactly what you have in mind.

Suppose that a window has been broken. If you know who broke it, you can say something like this:

> My little brother broke the window yesterday.

But suppose you don't know who broke it, or suppose you don't want to say who broke it. You might then say:

> The window was broken yesterday.

In the first sentence, the subject tells who performed the action. When the subject performs the action, the verb is said to be **active.**

In the second sentence, the subject tells what received the action. When the subject tells the receiver or the result of the action, the verb is said to be **passive.** (The word *passive* means "acted upon.")

Forming the Passive

The passive form of the verb is made by using a form of *be* with the past participle.

Active

Megan has finished the project.
Chris has shown the slides.
The store will add the tax.

Passive

The project has been finished by Megan.
The slides have been shown by Chris.
The tax will be added by the store.

Find the direct objects in the sentences in the first column above. What has happened to them in the sentences in the second column? Only verbs that have objects (transitive verbs) can be changed from active to passive.

A verb is active when its subject performs the action stated by the verb.

A verb is passive when its subject names the receiver or result of the action stated by the verb.

Exercises **Use active and passive forms.**

A. Change the verbs in the following sentences from active to passive. Rewrite the sentences.

1. Mr. Harvey cleaned the rug.
2. The digital scoreboard shows the scores and time.
3. Those children fed the ducks.
4. The Art Club decorated the gym.
5. Our team had already won the trophy once before.
6. The fire destroyed five buildings.
7. Almost everybody knows Mr. Walters.
8. Our class had written letters to our Senators.
9. The lawyer will appeal the judge's decision.
10. Bret has found the error.

B. Rewrite each sentence, changing the verb. If the verb is active, make it passive. If it is passive, make it active.

1. One of the boys baked a cake.
2. His plans were affected by inflation.
3. The group discussed playground regulations.
4. The committee held a meeting at one o'clock.
5. Ms. O'Brien read the class an interesting article.
6. The tour had been planned by Aviation Travel company.
7. Several alternatives were considered by the club.
8. The Potter's Wheel also sells ceramic supplies.

Part 8   Troublesome Pairs of Verbs

There are certain pairs of verbs that cause trouble because they are alike in meaning. They are *alike*, but they are not the same. We cannot substitute one of the pair for the other. Learn the differences so that you can use these words correctly.

Sit and set

Sit means "to occupy a seat." The principal parts are *sit, sat, sat*.

Set means "to place." The principal parts are *set, set, set*.

> **Present:** *Sit* on the steps. *Set* the plant here.
> **Past:** We *sat* in the car. Beth *set* the box down.
> **Present Perfect:** We *have sat* for an hour. We *have set* the flag in the middle.

Lie and lay

Lie means "to rest in a flat position" or "to be situated." The principal parts are *lie, lay, lain*.

Lay means "to place." The principal parts are *lay, laid, laid*.

> **Present:** *Lie* down, Pup. *Lay* the blankets here.
> **Past:** Fido *lay* down. We *laid* the blankets here.
> **Present Perfect:** Pup *has lain* down. We *have laid* the blankets on the grass.

Let and leave

Let means "to allow or permit." The principal parts are *let, let, let*.

Leave means "to go away from" or "to allow something to remain where it is." The principal parts are *leave, left, left*.

Present: *Let* me help you. *Leave* your coats here.
Past: Bill *let* us stay. The girls *left* early.
Present Perfect: Dad *has let* the shrubs grow. Sue *has left* for the day.

Rise and *raise*

Rise means "to go upward." The principal parts are *rise, rose, risen.*

Raise means "to lift or to make something go up." The principal parts are *raise, raised, raised.*

Present: The balloon *rises* fast. Please *raise* the window.
Past: The curtain *rose* quickly. Jeff *raised* his voice.
Present Perfect: The moon *has risen.* The recruits *have raised* the flag.

May and *can*

May refers to permission or to something that is possible. *Might* is another form of the word. There are no principal parts. *May* and *might* are used only as helping verbs.

May we go swimming?   You *might* catch cold.

Can refers to ability. *Could* is another form of the verb. There are no principal parts. *Can* and *could* are used as helping verbs.

Janet *can* play the flute.   We *could* see a light.

Learn and *teach*

Learn means "to gain knowledge or skill." The principal parts are *learn, learned, learned.*

Teach means "to help someone learn." The principal parts are *teach, taught, taught.*

Present: *Learn* to swim well. Please *teach* me the trick.

Past: Janet *learned* quickly. My mother *taught* music.

Present Perfect: We *have learned* our lesson. Pam *has taught* us the back jackknife dive.

Exercises   Choose the right verb from the pair.

A.   Number you paper 1–10. Choose the correct verb.

1. The geyser (rose, raised) at least 100 feet up in the air.
2. The sun (rises, raises) over those hills around 6 A.M.
3. (Let, Leave) your books in your locker.
4. (Let, Leave) your assignment on the desk.
5. The audience (rose, raised) and applauded the orchestra.
6. (Lie, Lay) still and listen.
7. You must have (laid, lain) your package down by the fountain.
8. A slow, cool mist had been (raising, rising) off the lagoon.
9. The dog won't (lie, lay) down.
10. They (lay, laid) wall-to-wall carpeting.

B.   Follow the directions for Exercise A.

1. We usually (sit, set) on the porch steps and talk.
2. The moon (sat, set) well before midnight.
3. (May, Can) I use your telephone?
4. (Can, May) I go to the movie tonight?
5. I (set, sat) the box on the big chair.
6. (Teach, Learn) Ryan not to bellyflop, will you?
7. (Can, May) we borrow your tape recorder?
8. They were (sitting, setting) up waiting for Roger.
9. That's a snap. I (could, might) do that easily.
10. Marcia (learned, taught) the speech by heart.

Additional Exercises

Using Verbs

A. Find the verbs.

Find the parts of the verb in each sentence. Put them in two columns labeled *Helping Verb* and *Main Verb*.

1. Where did you buy those socks?
2. Don't take it so hard.
3. Ken should have been the villain in the play.
4. Are Nancy and the others standing in line for hockey tickets?
5. You might have told me about the news report.
6. Can you read the sign?
7. He must have come down the chimney.
8. Our homeroom has decorated the school lobby for the holidays.
9. Do you think so?
10. Shall I make banana nut bread for Friday?

B. Progressive forms.

Copy each sentence, changing each verb to its progressive form.

1. Paul ate the melon.
2. Have you watched the series?
3. We will call my grandparents tonight.
4. Mrs. Levy directs the junior high band.
5. Mandy and Jenny could help us with the gardening.

6. Several volunteers will collect aluminum cans for the recycle center.

7. Jay has worked here since May.

8. Nancy and Marla must have fished here yesterday afternoon.

9. The choir will sing tonight.

10. I had saved my money for a new ten-speed bike.

C. Recognize verb tenses.

Find each verb in the following sentences and tell the tense of each.

1. Have you subtracted correctly?

2. The tickets for the tournament will be available in the main office.

3. Will the new school have air-conditioning?

4. My sister and I flew to Alaska.

5. The Olympic Games will take place in Russia in 1980.

6. Rod Carew is an excellent baseball player.

7. Our music class attended an afternoon performance by the Chicago Symphony Orchestra.

8. Liza Minnelli and Barbra Streisand are exciting performers.

9. We had waited in line for over an hour.

10. With the help of McDonald's, we raised $1000 for the fight against muscular dystrophy.

D. Use passive verb forms.

Change the verbs in the following sentences from active to passive. Rewrite the sentences.

1. Tramco sponsored the program.

2. Everybody in grade nine takes consumer education.

3. Stacy threw the ball out-of-bounds.

4. About fifty people called the radio station.

5. A flat tire delayed the school bus.

6. My little sister designed and painted these covers.

7. This computer will record the sun-spot activity.

8. The Fisher Company is building a condominium on this site.

9. Snow covered the ice rink.

10. Juan developed the photographs.

E. Choose the right verb from the pair.

Number your paper 1–10. Choose the correct verb.

1. (Let, Leave) Craig work by himself.

2. (Raise, Rise) the shelf about another inch.

3. Dan (raised, rose) a sceptical eyebrow.

4. The tool box is (laying, lying) on the workbench.

5. I saw the shovel (lying, laying) out in the rain.

6. Cindy lost her balance and (set, sat) down hard.

7. (May, Can) I use your telephone?

8. Would you (sit, set) the groceries on the table?

9. No one (learned, taught) Laurie to roller skate.

10. How our coach can (sit, set) so calmly is beyond me!

Section 5

Using Modifiers

Nouns and pronouns help us name and identify things and people in the world about us. Verbs help us make statements and ask questions about things and people.

Modifiers—adjectives and adverbs—help us describe what we have seen and heard.

> There was a *brilliant* flash.
> We heard the jet *faintly* in the distance.

In addition, modifiers help us state how we feel about things and people.

> The room was *messy*.
> Our new puppy was *extremely* energetic.

We have already studied nouns, pronouns, and verbs in detail. In this section we shall study modifiers closely.

Part 1   Adjectives

What is the difference between these sentences?

Rain fell.
A cold, hard rain fell.

The difference is in the descriptive words that tell what kind of rain fell. These words are **adjectives.** They are one of the parts of speech.

An adjective is a word that goes with, or modifies, a noun or pronoun.

Some adjectives tell *what kind* about the words they modify:

Look at the *huge, white* balloon.

Some adjectives tell *how many* or *how much* about the words they modify:

Jim found *twenty* dollars.
We have had *little* rain.

Some adjectives tell *which one* or *which ones* about the words they modify:

That door sticks.
These pens work better.

Adjective or Pronoun?

The words *this, that, these,* and *those* can be used as demonstrative pronouns. When used alone, they are pronouns. When followed by a noun, they are adjectives.

These are my sunglasses. (Pronoun)
These problems are easy. (Adjective modifying *problems*)
That is the wrong answer. (Pronoun)
That answer is wrong. (Adjective modifying *answer*)

Predicate Adjectives

Sometimes an adjective is separated from the word it modifies by a linking verb:

Everyone was quiet.

Phil seemed annoyed.

An adjective that follows a linking verb and that modifies the subject is called a **predicate adjective.**

Proper Adjectives

Proper adjectives are adjectives formed from proper nouns. They are always capitalized. Here are some examples of proper adjectives:

an American dollar   the French flag
a Norwegian sardine   an English custom
the Spanish language   an Oriental rug

Exercises   **Find the adjectives.**

A.   Number your paper 1–10. Write the adjectives you find in each sentence. After each adjective, write the word it modifies. Do not write *a, an,* or *the.*

1. The jockey in the blue satin shirt mounted the black racehorse.

2. Jubilant teammates carried the goalie off the muddy field.

3. Two sleek, silver Mercedes were parked in the circular driveway.

4. I feel comfortable in a plaid flannel shirt, corduroy jeans, and brown suede boots.

5. Colonial costumes and decorative furniture were on display at the huge, white Georgian mansion.

6. The red, orange, yellow, and brown leaves on acres of farmland painted a beautiful scene.

7. A tall, wiry player stood at the free-throw line and sank the winning basket.

8. Wicker baskets of white daisies and yellow roses decorated the table.

9. I have worn these old Adidas for two years.

10. The small, brown puppy nestled against me as I sat on the old, rickety bench.

B. Number your paper 1–10. Find the predicate adjectives in these sentences. Write them down.

1. The morning sun was red.
2. Over the lake the mist looked steamy and strange.
3. Gradually the air grew warm.
4. Small birds around us were busy and noisy.
5. The woods seemed full of them.
6. The woods smelled fresh and good in the sunlight.
7. Everyone appeared happy.
8. Our packs felt light.
9. Ahead of us the path was smooth and easy.
10. Life seemed great.

Part 2   Adverbs

In order to make our meaning clear, vivid, and complete, we usually have to tell *how, when, where,* or *to what extent* something is true. Adverbs are used for this purpose.

Adverbs Used with Verbs

Adverbs are used to go with, or modify, verbs to tell *how, when, where,* or *to what extent* an action happened.

Study the following list of adverbs:

How?	When?	Where?	To What Extent?
secretly	then	nearby	often
quickly	later	underground	deep
sorrowfully	afterwards	here	seldom
hurriedly	finally	there	always

Now use some of the above adverbs in this sentence:

The pirates buried their gold.

You can see what a great difference the adverbs make in the above sentence. They make the meaning of the verb *buried* clearer, and they add vividness and completeness to the whole sentence.

Adverbs Used with Adjectives or Other Adverbs

Besides being used to modify verbs, adverbs are also used to modify adjectives and other adverbs. Notice the italicized adverbs in the following sentences:

Niki was happy.
Niki was *extremely* happy.

Rick spoke slowly.
Rick spoke *too* slowly.

Here are some more adverbs that are often used to modify adjectives or other adverbs:

very	nearly	so
just	somewhat	more
quite	rather	most

These adverbs all tell *how much* or *to what extent* something is true.

You can see how useful adverbs are in making clearer, more complete, or more vivid the adjectives or other adverbs that we use.

Adverbs are words that modify verbs, adjectives, and other adverbs.

Forming Adverbs

Many adverbs are made by adding *-ly* to an adjective:

secret + ly = secretly
bright + ly = brightly

Sometimes the addition of *-ly* involves a spelling change in the adjective:

easy + ly = easily (*y* changed to *i*)
capable + ly = capably (final *-le* dropped)
full + ly = fully (*-ll* changed to *-l*)

Many words, like *quite* or *so*, can be used only as adverbs:

This footprint is *quite* recent.
Sue never looked *so* happy before.

Some other words, like *early* or *fast*, can be used either as adverbs or as adjectives:

Bill arrived *early*. (adverb)
He ate an *early* breakfast. (adjective)
Dana can run *fast*. (adverb)
She is a *fast* runner. (adjective)

Exercises **Recognize adverbs.**

A. Number your paper 1–10. Write the adverb in each sentence. After each adverb write the word it modifies. Be ready to explain what the adverb tells about the word it modifies.

Example: The actors usually stay here.

> *usually* modifies *stay*, tells when
> *here* modifies *stay*, tells where

1. The doctor has just left.
2. We have never studied about Greenland.
3. The runners raced vigorously around the track.
4. That movie was quite informative.
5. The newspaper was rather careful about its editorials.
6. The quarterback limped painfully off the field.
7. The runway lights shone brightly at the airport.
8. Our canoe drifted lazily down the river.
9. The summer rain fell heavily.
10. The pounding stopped immediately.

B. Follow the directions for Exercise A.

1. That pounding has started again.
2. It was nearly midnight before the train arrived.
3. The visiting football teams usually stay at the Hilton.
4. Those two cats wander aimlessly from yard to yard.
5. That pitcher seemed somewhat unsure of himself.
6. Alicia smiled weakly.
7. Because the train was ahead of schedule, we arrived early.
8. The play went smoothly until the last act.
9. Mexico City's climate is usually ideal.
10. It is extremely important that you relay the message.

C. Change the following adjectives into adverbs by adding
-ly. Be careful of your spelling.

sure	cruel	terrible	grim
icy	heavy	impatient	careful
full	sad	peaceful	happy
loud	beautiful	dizzy	cool
rough	smooth	crazy	hopeful

An Adverb Tells	An Adjective Tells
∗ **When**	∗ **Which One**
∗ **Where**	∗ **What Kind**
∗ **How**	∗ **How Many**
∗ **How Much**	
About a Verb, Adjective, or Adverb	About a Noun or Pronoun

Part 3 Adjective or Adverb?

Study the following sentences. Which sentence sounds right to you?

> Our team won *easy*.
> Our team won *easily*.

The second sentence is the correct one. An adverb (*easily*) should be used, not an adjective (*easy*).

It is often difficult to decide whether an adjective or an adverb should be used in sentences like the two given above. When you are not sure which form to use, ask yourself these questions:

1. Which word does the modifier go with? If it goes with an action verb (like *won* in the sentences above), it is an adverb. It is also an adverb if it goes with an adjective or another adverb. If it goes with a noun or pronoun, it is an adjective.

2. What does the modifier tell about the word it goes with? If the modifier tells *when, where, how,* or *how much,* it is an adverb. If it tells *which one, what kind,* or *how many,* it is an adjective. In the sentences above, the modifier tells *how* our team won; it must therefore be an adverb: *easily*.

A. List each adjective and adverb, together with the word it modifies. (Do not list *a, an,* or *the*).

Example: The tall runner in the red shirt won easily.

1. Two white puppies walked carelessly through the flowers.
2. Red, white, and blue bunting was decoratively hung around the platform.
3. He paid the bill quite promptly.
4. The suspect answered the questions rather cautiously.
5. The young swimmers dove unhesitatingly into the large pool.
6. The small child cried loudly in the dentist's office.
7. The dancers moved gracefully across the tiny stage.
8. The American ambassador spoke openly and honestly about our foreign policy.
9. The commuters walked briskly toward the long, yellow train.
10. The new puppies are too big for the basket.

B. Choose the correct modifier from the two in parentheses. Tell what word it modifies, and whether it is an adjective or adverb.

1. The bus will arrive (exact, exactly) at eight.
2. My brother drives (careful, carefully).
3. Debbie's drawings were (real, really) good.
4. The leaves turned very (quick, quickly) this year.
5. Mrs. Watson explained the assignment (clear, clearly).
6. Our dog peered (cautious, cautiously) around the sofa.
7. Ted appeared at the door (prompt, promptly) at eight.
8. Everything fitted in place just (beautifully, beautiful).
9. Please work (quiet, quietly) during the test.
10. Renée and Marsha walked (slow, slowly) down the street.

Adverbs and Predicate Adjectives

You will remember that a predicate adjective appears after a linking verb and modifies the subject.

The rose is red. (*red* modifies *rose.*)

The sky became cloudy. (*cloudy* modifies *sky.*)

The pizza tastes good. (*good* modifies *pizza.*)

You also remember that in addition to the forms of *be*, the following can be used as linking verbs: *become, seem, appear, look, sound, feel, taste, grow,* and *smell.*

Sometimes these verbs are action verbs. When they are action verbs, they are followed by adverbs, not adjectives. The adverbs modify the verbs and tell *how, when, where,* or *how much.*

Look at the following sentences to see when adjectives are used and when adverbs are used:

Action Verbs with Adverbs	Linking Verbs with Adjectives
Bob *felt* his way *slowly.*	The *cloth* felt *smooth.*
We *tasted* the fudge *eagerly.*	The *fudge* tasted *good.*
A stranger *appeared suddenly.*	The *dog* appears *sick.*
Erin *looked up.*	The *water* looks *green.*
The plant *grew fast.*	The *horse* grew *tired.*
We *smelled* smoke *suddenly.*	The *flower* smells *good.*

If you are uncertain about whether to use an adverb or adjective after verbs like *sound, smell,* and *look,* try these tests:

1. Does the modifier tell *how, when, where,* or *how much?* If it does, the modifier is probably an adverb.

2. Can you substitute *is* or *was* for the verb? If you can, the modifier is probably an adjective.

Exercise   Choose the right modifier.

Choose the right modifier for the following sentences.

1. The ice looked (thick, thickly).
2. This water tastes (bitter, bitterly).
3. Mother spoke (calmly, calm).
4. At the start of the game we played (badly, bad).
5. Those people were talking rather (loud, loudly) in the library.
6. Carol's idea sounded (reasonable, reasonably).
7. Press (firm, firmly) on the button.
8. The tape stopped (abruptly, abrupt).
9. That house looks (emptily, empty).
10. The music sounded (strange, strangely).

Good and *Well*

The meanings of *good* and *well* are very much alike, but they are not exactly the same. You cannot substitute one for the other in all sentences. Study the following sentences. Can you see the difference between *good* and *well*?

I feel good.	This patient is well.
I feel well.	His health is good.
Betty plays well.	

Good is always an adjective.

Well is sometimes an adjective and sometimes an adverb.

In which of the previous sentences is *well* used as an adverb? In which sentences is it used as an adjective? You can see that when *well* refers to a person's health, it may be used as an adjective.

Exercise **Use *good* and *well* correctly.**

Number your paper 1–10. Choose the right word.

1. Shake the bottle (good, well).

2. That swim felt (good, well).

3. All of the gymnasts did quite (well, good) in the district meet.

4. That looks (well, good) enough to eat!

5. Both teams played (well, good) in the second half.

6. John was sick, but now he's (good, well) again.

7. The new management at the store has worked out quite (good, well).

8. The soup tasted (well, good).

9. Mr. Marks looks (well, good) in his new jacket.

10. Most of the performers did quite (well, good) in last night's production.

Part 4 Articles

The adjectives *a, an,* and *the* are called **articles.**
The is the **definite article.**

Please buy me *the* book ("a particular book").

A and *an* are **indefinite articles.**

Please bring me *a* book ("any book").
Please give me *an* apple ("any apple").

Note that we use *a* before a consonant sound (*a* book, *a* cap, *a* dog). We use *an* before a vowel sound (*an* apple, *an* egg, *an* olive).

The sound, not the spelling, makes the difference. Do we say *a honest man* or *an honest man? a house* or *an house?*

Exercise   **Use the correct article.**

Choose the right article in each of the following sentences.

1. (A, An) elephant supposedly has a good memory.
2. (A, The) best book on that shelf is *Treasure Island*.
3. That is (a, an) heavy chair.
4. I have (a, an) hunch you're right.
5. Joe was wearing (a, an) orange T-shirt.
6. We had (an, a) history test this week.
7. That was (a, the) best thing to do.
8. Don't use (a, an) onion in that recipe.
9. Each of us had to do a report on (a, an) historical event.
10. Tracy made (an, a) honest effort to meet the deadline for the newspaper.

Part 5   Adjectives in Comparisons

Comparing people and things is one way of learning about the world. We compare new things we already know. We say, "This new calculator is *like* a mini-computer. Of course, it is *smaller* and it is *less accurate*." Or we say, "The new girl is *taller* than I am."

Adjectives are very useful in comparing things and people. In comparisons, adjectives have special forms or spellings.

The Comparative

If we compare one thing or person with another, we use the **comparative** form of the adjective. The comparative form is made in two ways:

1. For short adjectives like *sweet* and *happy*, add *-er*.

   sweet + er = sweeter   quick + er = quicker
   happy + er = happier   wise + er = wiser

2. For longer adjectives like *beautiful*, use *more*.

   more beautiful   more capable

Most adjectives ending in *-ful* and *-ous* form the comparative with *more*.

   more healthful   more ambitious

The Superlative

When we compare a thing or a person with all others of its kind, we use the **superlative** form of the adjective. In fact, when we compare a thing or person with more than one other, we use the superlative.

   This is the *best* dinner I have ever tasted.
   Pat is the *smartest* person I know.
   This is the *most interesting* book I have ever read.

The superlative form of adjectives is formed by adding *-est* or by using *most*. For adjectives that add *-er* to form the comparative, add *-est* for the superlative. For those that use *more* to form the comparative, use *most* for the superlative.

Comparative	Superlative
higher	highest
bigger	biggest
stronger	strongest
more agreeable	most agreeable
more expensive	most expensive
more careful	most careful

There are three things to remember in using adjectives for comparison:

1. Use the comparative to compare two persons or things. Use the superlative to compare more than two.

> This car is *wider* than that one.
> Paul is the *thinnest* of the three boys.

2. Do not leave out the word *other* when you are comparing something with everything else of its kind.

> Wrong: New York is larger than any American city.
> (This sentence says that New York is not an American city.)
> Right: New York is larger than any *other* American city.

> Wrong: Claire runs faster than any girl in her class.
> (Is Claire a girl? Is she in her class?)
> Right: Claire runs faster than any *other* girl in her class.

3. Do not use both *-er* and *more* or *-est* and *most* at the same time.

> Wrong: Diamonds are more harder than jade.
> Right: Diamonds are *harder* than jade.

> Wrong: Diamonds are the most hardest of all materials.
> Right: Diamonds are the *hardest* of all materials.

Irregular Comparisons

We form the comparative and superlative of some adjectives by changing the words:

	Comparative	Superlative
good	better	best
well	better	best
bad	worse	worst
ill	worse	worst
little	less *or* lesser	least
much	more	most
many	more	most
far	farther	farthest

Exercises   **Use adjectives correctly in comparisons.**

A.   Number your paper 1–10. Two of the comparisons in the following sentences are correct, but the others are wrong. If a sentence is correct, write *Correct.* If there is an error, write the sentence correctly.

1. These shelves are more high than those over there.
2. The VW Rabbit is the bigger of these three foreign cars.
3. The dictionary was more helpful than the almanac.
4. It was the awfulest storm I had ever seen.
5. Our new dog is much more friendlier than the old one.
6. Of the two plants, the fern is the healthier.
7. It was the most warmest day of the summer.
8. Math is harder than any subject in school.
9. What happened was even surprisinger.
10. The most funniest thing happened yesterday.

B.   Number your paper 1–10. Two of the comparisons in the following sentences are correct, but the others are wrong. If a sentence is correct, write *Correct.* If there is an error, write the sentence correctly.

1. That was the worser of the two jokes.
2. His joke was the goodest of all.
3. Marcy felt worse than she had felt in a long time.
4. He chose the lesser of the two evils.
5. She had littler time than usual.
6. Mine was worse, but Janet's was the worstest.
7. This is the most best I can do.
8. That was a more better game than the one last week.
9. At the leastest noise Prince perked up an ear.
10. Between the grape ivy and the fern, the grape ivy is the healthiest.

Part 6   Adverbs in Comparisons

Adverbs are used to compare one action with another. We say, "This engine runs *smoothly*, but that one runs *more smoothly*."

Or we say, "Julie planned her exhibit *more carefully* than any other student in the class."

Adverbs have special forms or spellings for use in making comparisons, just as adjectives do.

The Comparative

When we compare one action with another, we use the **comparative** form of the adverb. The comparative form is made in two ways:

1. For short adverbs like *soon* and *fast*, add *-er*.

> We arrived *sooner* than you did.
> Kim can run *faster* than Peg.

2. For most adverbs ending in *-ly*, use *more* to make the comparative.

> Bill acted *more quickly* than Jeff.
> The water flowed *more rapidly* than before.

The Superlative

When one action is compared with two or more others of the same kind, we use the superlative form of the adverb.

> Peg and Bill run fast, but Kim runs *fastest*.
> Of the three boys, Scott speaks Spanish the *most fluently*.

The superlative form of adverbs is formed by adding *-est* or by using *most*. Adverbs that form the comparative with *-er* form the superlative with *-est*. Those that use *more* for the comparative use *most* for the superlative.

Comparative	Superlative
harder	hardest
longer	longest
more rapidly	most rapidly
more clearly	most clearly

In using the comparative and superlative forms of adverbs, keep in mind the following three pointers:

1. Use the comparative to compare two actions and the superlative to compare more than two.

It rained *harder* today than yesterday.
Of all the players, Terry tries the *hardest*.

2. Do not leave out the word *other* when you are comparing one action with every other action of the same kind.

Wrong: Tara runs faster than any student in our school.
Right: Tara runs faster than any *other* student in our school.

3. Do not use both *-er* and *more* or *-est* and *most* at the same kind.

Wrong: Tara runs more faster.
Right: Tara runs *faster*.

Exercises **Use adverbs correctly in comparisons.**

A. Write the comparative and superlative forms of these adverbs:

1. fast
2. wildly
3. hard
4. happily
5. closely
6. long
7. bravely
8. slowly
9. recently
10. naturally

B. Some of the following sentences are correct. Others contain errors in comparison of adverbs. Number your paper 1–10. If the sentence is correct, write *Correct*. If there is an error, write the sentence correctly.

1. We drove more carefully after seeing the collision.
2. Vacation ended more soon than we had expected.
3. Write the directions out more completer.
4. These photographs were trimmed more better than those.
5. That fish jumped more higher than any other.
6. This recipe is the more consistently successful of all.
7. Can't you walk more fast than that?
8. You could see the view more clearly from here.
9. He tried more harder than Wayne.
10. Will you read that paragraph again more slower, please?

Part 7 Special Problems with Modifiers

Them and *Those*

Them is always a pronoun. It is used only as object of a verb or as object of a preposition.

Those is an adjective if it is followed by a noun. It is a pronoun if it is used alone.

> We heard *them* in the night. (Pronoun)
> *Those* bikes are too heavy. (Adjective modifying *bikes*)
> *Those* are our gifts. (Pronoun)

The Extra *Here* and *There*

How often have you heard someone say, "This here book" or "That there window"? The word *this* includes the meaning of *here*. The word *that* includes the meaning of *there*.

Saying *this here* is like saying, "This book is my mine," or like repeating your name every time you say *I* or *me:* "Please pass me John Jones the milk."

Kind and *Sort*

Kind and *sort* are singular. Use *this* or *that* with *kind* and *sort*. *Kinds* and *sorts* are plural. Use *these* or *those* with *kinds* and *sorts*.

> We like this kind of dessert.
> Those kinds of food give you energy.

The Double Negative

A **double negative** is the use of two negative words together when only one is needed. Good speakers and writers take care to avoid the double negative.

> **Wrong:** We have*n't no* more tape.
> **Right:** We have*n't any* more tape.
>
> **Wrong:** Jack did*n't* win *nothing* at the fair.
> **Right:** Jack did*n't* win *anything* at the fair.
>
> **Wrong:** She has*n't never* gone there.
> **Right:** She has*n't ever* gone there.

You can see in the sentences above that the first negative word is *not*. When you use contractions like *haven't* and *didn't*, do not use negative words after them.

The most common negative words are *no, none, not, nothing,* and *never*.

After contractions like *haven't* and *didn't*, use words such as *any, anything,* and *ever*. Do not use *no, nothing, never,* or any other negative words after such contractions.

> The club *hasn't any* chairperson.
> We *couldn't* hear *anything*.
> We *haven't ever* seen an eclipse.
> The band *can't* play *any* popular songs.

Hardly, barely, and *scarcely* are often used as negative words. Do not use them after contractions like *haven't* and *didn't*.

Wrong: The cars haven't scarcely moved.
Right: The cars have scarcely moved.

Wrong: They can't barely talk.
Right: They can barely talk.

Wrong: We couldn't hardly breathe.
Right: We could hardly breathe.

Exercises Use modifiers correctly.

A. Choose the right word in these sentences:

1. (Them, Those) are my favorite cookies.
2. Our dog won't eat (them, those) biscuits.
3. (Them, Those) gloves are too small.
4. We chose (those, those there) designs for our posters.
5. I always buy (that there, that) kind of bread.
6. (This, This here) watch needs to be fixed.
7. (Them, Those) are deer tracks.
8. These (kind, kinds) of dogs live a long time.
9. These (sort, sorts) of arguments are pointless.
10. Do you like (this, these) sort of design?

B. Number your paper 1–10. Correct the double negatives in the following sentences. If a sentence contains no double negative, write *Correct* after the corresponding number.

1. The girls couldn't scarcely believe their ears.
2. Bryan hasn't had no piano lessons this year.
3. Rhoda hasn't never been sick.
4. The movers couldn't hardly lift the heavy box.
5. There isn't no time for games.
6. Marguerita couldn't find the stamps.
7. Ms. Ryan won't let nobody use the power tools.
8. We couldn't find the badminton net.
9. Nobody could have had more fun.
10. We had plenty of apples, but Ellen didn't want none.

Additional Exercises

Using Modifiers

A. Find the adjectives.

Number your paper 1–10. Write the adjectives you find in each sentence. After each adjective, write the word it modifies. Do not write *a, an,* or *the.*

1. A blue van was parked next to the large mobile home.
2. The library has a large display of old American flags.
3. A tiny gray kitten perched itself on our roof.
4. A rusty green truck clattered down the alley.
5. The narrow, rocky peninsula has a single road.
6. Tin cans and old shoes hung from the back of the black limousine.
7. Red and white geraniums filled the ceramic pots.
8. The new Japanese policy caused widespread concern.
9. Huge, white seagulls strutted across the sandy beach.
10. The automatic door was controlled by an electric eye.

B. Recognize adverbs.

Number your page 1–10. Write the adverbs in the following sentences. After each adverb write the word it modifies.

1. The students walked quickly through the corridors.
2. Gretchen cautiously opened the box.
3. The two dalmations barked loudly.
4. Nearly forty kegs of nails split open on the highway.
5. The paramedics moved quickly through the crowd.
6. Have you ever found your odometer?

7. The toast finally popped up.

8. We arrived precisely at 8:15 P.M.

9. The children anxiously awaited the clown's arrival.

10. Many tourists strolled casually through the town square.

C. Find the adjectives and adverbs.

Copy each sentence. Draw an arrow from the adjective or adverb to the word it modifies.

1. Enormous waves pounded unmercifully against the tiny boats.

2. The next lookout is the most spectacular.

3. A slight breeze danced lightly through the trees.

4. The weather was only moderately cold.

5. Gary has a very bad cold.

6. A gentle rain danced on the tin roof.

7. Four carolers in colorful costumes sang merrily in the lobby of the store.

8. A large yellow balloon drifted freely above the treetops.

9. A small cloud curled around the top of the mountain.

10. Large, white clouds were scattered across a brilliant blue sky.

D. Choose the right modifier.

Choose the right modifier for the sentences.

1. The afternoon passed (slow, slowly).

2. The guards moved (quick, quickly) up the basketball court.

3. The surface of the water glistened (bright, brightly).

4. Music was playing (quiet, quietly) in the doctor's office.

5. That tar smells (awful, awfully).

6. We felt (bad, badly) about losing the game.

7. Please walk (careful, carefully) across the wet floor.

8. The desk top feels (smooth, smoothly).
9. The operator answered (angry, angrily).
10. Their change of plans seems (sudden, suddenly).

E. Use *good* and *well* correctly.

Choose the right word in parentheses.

1. Prospects for a sunny day were (well, good).
2. You play tennis very (good, well).
3. Her word is always (good, well).
4. The practice went (well, good).
5. Almost everyone dances pretty (good, well).
6. These scissors don't cut (well, good) any more.
7. They don't do it (good, well) enough.
8. This suit fits me (good, well).
9. Does that sewing machine work very (good, well)?
10. Clare and I did quite (good, well) on the history test.

F. Use adjectives correctly in comparisons.

Number your paper 1–10. Two of the comparisons in the following sentences are correct, but the others are wrong. If a sentence is correct, write *Correct*. If there is an error, write the sentence correctly.

1. This lemon is more sourer than others I've eaten.
2. This album is more better than those two.
3. My grandmother feels weller than usual.
4. Their kitchen is the most smallest room in the house.
5. These are the healthiest plants I've ever seen.
6. Always try your bestest.
7. New York is the largest American city.
8. This cake is more better than that one.
9. That was the worstest mistake I ever made.
10. This novel was more easier to read than the other one.

G. Use adverbs correctly in comparisons.

Some of the following sentences are correct. Others contain errors in comparison of adverbs. Number your paper 1–10. If the sentence is correct, write *Correct.* If there is an error, write the sentence correctly.

1. Please hold the wheel more tightly.
2. John arrived more earlier than the others.
3. They weren't the carefulest house painters I've ever seen.
4. That was one of the bestest programs ever shown on TV.
5. Bill plays soccer better than any student in his class.
6. The old man looked at us more thoughtful.
7. Lara waited patienter than Jeff.
8. May is the most nice month of the year.
9. Katharine Hepburn is one of the very bestest actresses on stage or screen.
10. The crowd greeted his next announcement more enthusiastic.

H. Use modifiers correctly.

Number your paper 1–10. If the sentence is correct, write *Correct.* If there is an error, write the sentence correctly.

1. The coaches couldn't hardly believe the final score.
2. Them there rapids look dangerous.
3. The red hawk isn't hardly ever seen around here.
4. Them bikes belong to Roberto and Denise.
5. We like this sort of pie.
6. Them cattle haven't scarcely moved off the road.
7. That sort of behavior could get a player benched.
8. Tricia couldn't hardly talk.
9. Them Scouts couldn't barely finish the hike.
10. Did you think them test questions were difficult?

Section 6

Using Prepositions and Conjunctions

Often we can say what we mean by using short sentences like these:

> The grocer weighed the meat.
> Last night I found a dollar bill.

Frequently, however, what we have to say is more complicated. Perhaps we want to say not merely that we found a dollar bill last night but also that we found it in the driveway.

We may want to tell someone that the grocer weighed not only the meat but also the pears and the potatoes. To express more complicated ideas like these, we use connectives.

Last night I found a dollar bill *in* the driveway.
The grocer weighed the meat, the pears, *and* the potatoes.

This chapter will help you learn to use two important kinds of connectives: prepositions and conjunctions.

Part 1 Prepositions

Connectives are words that are used to join together two or more other words or groups of words. **Prepositions** are one important kind of connective.

Notice the prepositions in the following sentences:

The plane flew *into* the storm.
The plane flew *around* the storm.

In the first sentence, *into* connects *storm*, its object, with the verb *flew*. It points out the relationship between *flew* and *storm*.

In the second sentence, *around* connects *storm*, its object, with the verb *flew*. It points out the relationship between *flew* and *storm*.

You can see that *into* and *around* join parts of each sentence. Like all prepositions, they make clear a certain relationship between the words that they connect.

Now look at the prepositions in the following sentences:

My sister is the person *at* the counter.
My sister is the person *behind* the counter.

You can see that *at* and *behind* join parts of each sentence. They make clear the relationships between *person* and *counter*.

A preposition is a word used with a noun or pronoun, called its *object*, to show the relationship between the noun or pronoun and some other word in the sentence.

Below is a list of 45 words often used as prepositions. Most of these prepositions tell *where*. Others show a relationship of *time*. Still others show such special relationships as *reference*, *separation*, and so on. Study these prepositions and see if you can tell the relationship that each of them can show between words.

Words Often Used as Prepositions

about	before	concerning	like	to
above	behind	down	near	toward
across	below	during	of	under
after	beneath	except	off	until
against	beside	for	on	up
along	between	from	onto	upon
among	beyond	in	over	with
around	but (*except*)	inside	since	within
at	by	into	through	without

Exercises   Find the prepositions.

A. Number your paper 1–10. Find the prepositions in the following sentences. Tell what the objects of the prepositions are.

> Example: On Saturday, Bret and Julie went to the beach.

> Prepositions: *on, to*

> Objects: *Saturday, beach*

  1. The library will hold the book until tomorrow.

2. I hurried up the stairs and into the room.

3. A prop plane with several passengers made an emergency landing in a cornfield.

4. During the night we were awakened by thunder.

5. After the play, we're going to Mike's house.

6. The residents of Franklin Park are concerned about the pollution problem.

7. The football squad huddled around the coach for last-minute instructions.

8. Stack these cartons against that wall and put these books on the shelf.

9. The city was without power for several hours.

10. In the library there are several aquariums and plants on various bookshelves.

B. Follow the directions for Exercise A.

1. In July we are going to Florida for a visit to my grandparents.

2. Student Council will meet before school on Friday.

3. Two sky-writing planes flew over the stadium during the baseball game.

4. The bicycle shop is located on Green Bay Road.

5. On the Island of Oahu we visited the Polynesian Cultural Center.

6. The dog scampered down the stairs with my glove.

7. Tony Dorsett dazzled the crowd in the Coliseum with a 93-yard run.

8. We rode the elevator to the top of the John Hancock Building.

9. Cross-country skiing through forests and across open fields is fun.

10. The pancake house near the expressway is open around the clock.

Preposition or Adverb?

Many words used as prepositions may also be used as adverbs. A preposition never appears alone. It is always followed by its object, a noun or pronoun. If the word has a noun or pronoun following it, it is probably a preposition. If it is not followed by a noun or pronoun, it is probably an adverb.

> I drew a line *across* the paper. (Preposition)
> He dared me to jump *across*. (Adverb)
>
> Ted put his books *down*. (Adverb)
> He ran *down* the street. (Preposition)

Exercises   Recognize adverbs and prepositions.

A. Decide whether the italicized words in these sentences are adverbs or prepositions. Write *Adverb* or *Preposition* for each sentence.

1. Janice turned *around*.
2. There is a new shopping center *near* our house.
3. The committee turned our request *down*.
4. The light bulb burned *out*.
5. The horses trotted *around* the track.
6. All local traffic was allowed *through*.
7. Pete threw his old track shoes *out*.
8. The Frisbee flew *across* the picnic table.
9. The doctor is *in*.
10. We all went *inside*.

B. Follow the directions for Exercise A.

1. Come *around* four o'clock.
2. We waited *outside* the theater.
3. The chain came *off*.
4. The chain came *off* the bicycle.

5. The lion cub rolled *over*.
6. Marsha and Jory went cycling *along* the lakeshore.
7. We heard a noise *below*.
8. John, Vince, and I sat *inside* the tent.
9. That dog always stays *within* the perimeter of his yard.
10. Lew and Niki talked *with* the assistant principal.

Part 2 Prepositional Phrases as Modifiers

A modifier may be a group of words as well as a single word. Frequently a prepositional phrase is a modifier. A **phrase** is a group of words that belong together but do not have a subject and verb.

Notice these phrases used as modifiers:

> The bears hibernated *during the long winter*.
> The player *in the blue jersey* scored.
> The principal's office is *on the first floor*.

The words in italics are **prepositional phrases.**

A prepositional phrase consists of a preposition, its object, and any modifiers of the object.

Preposition	Modifiers	Object
during	the long	winter
in	the blue	jersey
on	the first	floor

Nouns and pronouns are modified by adjectives.
Verbs are modified by adverbs.
Prepositional phrases may modify nouns, pronouns, or verbs.
A phrase that modifies a noun or pronoun is an **adjective phrase.**
A phrase that modifies a verb is an **adverb phrase.**

Regina found a box of *marbles*. (Adjective phrase modifying the noun *box*)

Each of *us* needs a job. (Adjective phrase modifying the pronoun *each*)

Mandy came *into the room*. (Adverb phrase modifying the verb *came*)

Adverbs tell *how, how much, when,* and *where* about verbs. Adverb phrases tell the same thing about verbs.

Often you will find two prepositional phrases in a row. Sometimes the second phrase is an adjective phrase modifying the object of the first phrase.

The cat was sitting *at the top of the stairs*.

(*at the top* is an adverb phrase telling *where* about the verb *was sitting*.)

(*of the stairs* is an adjective phrase modifying *top*. It tells *which top*.)

Cory put the powder *into the can of paint*.

(*into the can* tells where the powder was put.)

(*of paint* modifies *can*. It tells *which can*.)

Diagraming Prepositional Phrases

In diagrams a prepositional phrase is placed below the word it modifies.

The girl *with the red hair* plays *in the band*.

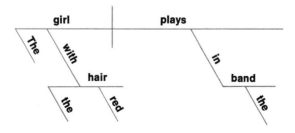

Sometimes two or more nouns or pronouns may be used as objects in a prepositional phrase.

Put butter on the *potatoes* and *squash.*

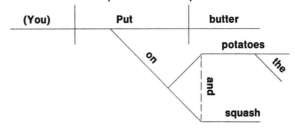

Exercises   **Prepositional phrases used as modifiers.**

A. Copy these sentences. Circle each prepositional phrase. Draw an arrow from the phrase to the word it modifies. Tell whether the phrase is an adjective phrase or an adverb phrase.

Example: He took the book with the pictures of Ireland

with the pictures: adjective phrase modifying *book*; *of Ireland*: adjective phrase modifying *pictures*

1. The man in the navy sport coat plays for the Celtics.
2. A brown terrier sat at the bottom of the staircase.
3. We peered through the windows of the deserted mansion.
4. Patti added some ice to the pitcher of iced tea.
5. That lady in the white suit is my social studies teacher.
6. The sign over the top of the door says "No Exit "
7. The window on the east side of the garage needs repair.
8. The dancer near the back of the stage is Rudolf Nureyev.
9. The sailboat in the water near the dock has a leak.
10. The electric sander is in the cabinet under the workbench.

B. Follow the directions for Exercise A.

1. The passengers on the jet were served a special dinner.

2. The trees in back of the house need pruning.

3. Are you going to the shopping center down the street?

4. The photographer took these pictures with a wide-angle lens.

5. The sign on the door in the office said that school will end at 1 P.M. today.

6. The newspaper article about jogging was very informative.

7. The movie on television features Billy Dee Williams and James Caan.

8. Jane Addams is well known for her contributions in social work.

9. I wrote a composition about my experiences in the Orient.

10. I enjoyed my work with small children last summer.

Part 3   Conjunctions

A second kind of word used to tie the parts of a sentence together is the **conjunction.**

A conjunction is a word that joins words or groups of words.

Notice the conjunctions in the following sentences:

> Lucy *and* Linda look alike. (connects nouns)
> Todd will call his father *or* mother. (connects nouns)
> Mr. Morley hemmed *and* hawed. (connects verbs)
> The cannister smelt spicy *but* damp. (connects adjectives)
> The guide book is either *in the closet* or *on the desk.* (connects prepositional phrases)

Conjunctions are unlike prepositions in that they do not have objects. They are similar to prepositions in that they do show a certain relationship between the words they connect.

Coordinating Conjunctions

To connect single words or parts of a sentence that are of the same kind, we use **coordinating conjunctions.** The most common coordinating conjunctions are *and, but,* and *or.*

> Maya *and* John are here. (*And* connects *Maya* and *John.*)
> We can't see, *but* we can hear. (*But* connects *we can't see* and *we can hear.*)

Correlative Conjunctions

A few conjunctions are used in pairs:

both . . . and	not only . . . but (also)
either . . . or	whether . . . or
neither . . . nor	

Such conjunctions are called **correlative conjunctions.**

> *Both* the benches *and* the tables had been painted.
> *Either* you *or* I have made an error.
> *Neither* football *nor* baseball can be played on that field.
> We need *not only* nails *but also* a hammer.
> Shall I call *whether* it rains *or* snows?

Exercises   Recognize and use conjunctions.

A. Find the conjunctions in the following sentences. Be prepared to tell what words or word groups are connected by the conjunction.

> Example: The Rand Raiders and the Thomas Trojans
> were invited to play in the baseball
> tournament.
>
> *The Rand Raiders* and *the Thomas Trojans*
> are connected by the conjunction *and.*

1. The clowns and magicians entertained the children.

2. Freezing rain and poor visibility delayed most flights.

3. Either the yearbook staff or the newspaper staff will sell refreshments at the home football games.

4. Tom and I couldn't get tickets for the match.

5. The slight breeze, pleasant temperatures, and overcast skies were assets to the marathon runners.

6. At the school picnic, we had corn on the cob and barbecued chicken.

7. Are you going to the movies or to the roller rink?

8. Marcia and I are going either to the water polo game or to the indoor tennis meet.

9. We baked an apple pie and a bundt cake in home economics.

10. The San Diego Zoo and Disneyland were the highlights of my trip to California.

B. Follow the directions for Exercise A.

1. Neither the coaches nor the timekeepers knew the final score.

2. Canoeing and backpacking are my favorite outdoor activities.

3. Either Bob Avelleni or Mike Phipps will be the starting quarterback for the Chicago Bears.

4. You can see an opera with Beverly Sills or the Grand Kabuki by the National Theatre of Japan.

5. Both my brother and my sister are studying medicine.

6. Racquetball, tennis, and squash require speed and endurance.

7. The roadblock and the detour have delayed our trip.

8. Skateboards, painter's pants, Bubble Yum, and Frisbees are fads that characterize the mid-1970's.

9. I like neither avocados nor asparagus.

10. We not only raised enough money for the orphanage, but we also made a donation to the children's hospital.

C. Write two sentences using *and,* two sentences using *or,* and two sentences using *but.* After each sentence write the words or groups of words that are joined by the conjunctions.

D. Write one sentence for each of the following pairs of correlative conjunctions:

both—and   either—or   neither—nor

Part 4   Review of Parts of Speech

As you know, there are eight parts of speech. The eight parts of speech are these:

nouns	**verbs**	**adverbs**	**conjunctions**
pronouns	**adjectives**	**prepositions**	**interjections**

Interjections

Do you remember what interjections are?

An **interjection** is a word or short group of words used to express strong feeling. It may be a real word or merely a sound. It may express surprise, joy, longing, anger, or sorrow.

An interjection is often followed by a special punctuation mark called an **exclamation mark** (!).

Hooray! We won the game.
No way! I'm not riding that roller coaster.

Words Used as Different Parts of Speech

In Part 1 of this section, you learned that words may be used as prepositions or as adverbs. Other words in our language may also be used in different ways.

Since the same word can be used in different ways as different parts of speech, how can you tell what part of speech a word is? Usually you have to see how the word is used in a sentence.

What part of speech a word is depends on how it is used in a sentence.

> Bruce moved the heavy *stone*. (*Stone* is used as a noun.)
> I sat on the *stone* wall. (*Stone* is used as an adjective modifying *wall*.)
>
> Don't *stand* in the doorway. (*Stand* is used as a verb.)
> Bob built a *stand* for his beer can collection. (*Stand* is used as a noun.)
>
> *This* book is exciting. (*This* is used as an adjective modifying *book*.)
> *This* is an interesting book. (*This* is used as a demonstrative pronoun.)

Exercise   Decide the part of speech.

Number your paper 1–12. Write the italicized word in each sentence. After it, write the part of speech that it is in that sentence.

1. Two *fence* posts were wobbly.
2. Joan has gone around to the *back*.
3. We will *plant* a garden in the Spring.
4. I have a couple of *stops* to make on Main Street.
5. The *garage* sale lasted until noon.
6. The harbor is patrolled by the *port* authorities.
7. Put these books *beside* the dictionaries.
8. Everyone *but* Nancy stayed for the entire game.
9. *Hurry!* Here's our train.
10. The *door* hinge creaked.
11. The *plant* shut down yesterday evening.
12. Tricia *backed* the car into the garage.

Additional Exercises

Using Prepositions and Conjunctions

A. Find the prepositions.

Number your paper 1–10. Write the prepositions in the following sentences. Write the object of each preposition.

1. An account of the race will be in the newspaper.
2. Trade-ins are usually accepted at Fernstone Motors.
3. On our doorstep was a lost puppy.
4. There is a new shopping mall near the school.
5. Manny and I went to the bakery for some doughnuts.
6. We rode the subway into the city.
7. In August you can't get in without reservations.
8. The list of winners will be announced in a few minutes.
9. The photographs in the display case were taken by Sue.
10. Rafferty High is beyond the municipal building.

B. Recognize adverbs and prepositions.

Decide whether the italicized words in these sentences are adverbs or prepositions. Write *Adverb* or *Preposition* for each sentence.

1. Dad drove twice *around* the block.
2. Think it *over*.
3. While we waited, it seemed as if days went *by*.
4. The talk show went *on* and *on*.
5. The Statue of Liberty was a gift *from* France.
6. Try their homemade cheesecake *after* dinner.
7. We followed the Freedom Trail *through* Boston.
8. Please turn the radio *off*.

C. Prepositional phrases used as modifiers.

Copy these sentences. Circle each prepositional phrase. Draw an arrow from the phrase to the word it modifies.

1. Look in the drawer with the brass handle.
2. Please give me a hamburger without mustard.
3. The plants in the greenhouse need watering.
4. Some of the books on the table are Kim's.
5. The aquarium in the den needs cleaning.
6. We visited Lincoln's home in Springfield, Illinois.
7. Many French laws originated with Napoleon.
8. The elevator ride to the top of the Sears Tower takes 54 seconds.
9. Carol's expression was too funny for words.
10. Last summer I was on the swimming team with my sister.

D. Recognize and use conjunctions.

Find the conjunctions in the following sentences. Tell what words are connected by the conjunctions.

1. Do you like Jackson Browne or Peter Frampton?
2. Last Saturday, Kathy and I went cycling and bowling.
3. Bob or Jeff can borrow this mitt.
4. "Checagou" or "land of stinking onions" is the Indian name originally given to the city of Chicago.
5. Every marathon race is 26 miles and 385 yards.
6. The origin of marathons and the Olympics can be traced back to ancient Greece.
7. Both Wisconsin and Mississippi were named by the Chippewa Indians.
8. "Ouisconsin" means "grassy place" and "mici zibi" means "great river."
9. We could go to the planetarium or to the zoo.
10. Neither the guitar nor the banjo is difficult to play.

Section 7

Using Compound and Complex Sentences

When you were studying Section 1, you noticed that the section was titled "The Simple Sentence." In that section you studied about subjects, predicates, objects, predicate words, and so on. You may have thought at the time that all of this was far from simple.

The simple sentence has one kind of structure. There are also compound and complex sentences. They have other kinds of structure. The basis for these other kinds of sentences is the simple sentence. It is a good idea to begin your study of the more complicated kinds of sentences by reviewing the simple sentence.

Part 1   Review of the Simple Sentence

The **simple sentence** has two basic parts, subject and predicate.

Subject	Predicate
Days	passed.
Time	flies.
People	asked.
Several people	asked questions.
Many people in the room	asked questions about the movie.

The **subject** of a sentence names the person or thing about which something is said. The **predicate** tells something about the subject.

The **simple predicate** is the verb. The subject of the verb is called the **simple subject.**

In the subject part of the sentence, you will find the simple subject and words that modify it. In the predicate part of the sentence, you will find verbs, objects, predicate words, and their modifiers.

Action Verbs and Linking Verbs

Some **action verbs** are complete in themselves.

The birds *were singing.*
A cold rain *fell.*

Some action verbs are followed by **direct objects,** which name the receiver of the action in the verb.

Bill *washed* the *car.*
Karen *raised* the *window.*

Some verbs do not tell of an action. They tell only that

something is or exists. They are called **linking verbs.** They link a predicate word to the subject.

> The horse *seems* tired.
> Dan *is* the director.

Compound Parts of the Simple Sentence

All of the parts of the simple sentence may be **compound.** That is, they may themselves have more than one part.

> Compound Subject: *Bob* and *I* enjoyed the concert.
> Compound Verb: The crowd *rose* and *cheered*.
> Compound Object: I folded the *napkins* and the *tablecloth*.
> Compound Predicate Word: The show was *long* but interesting.
> The leaders were *Ryan* and *Pam*.

Definition of the Simple Sentence

Now we are ready for a definition of the simple sentence.

A simple sentence is a sentence that contains only one subject and one predicate. The subject and the predicate, or any part of the subject or predicate, may be compound.

Exercises   Analyze Simple Sentences

A. Copy each of the following sentences. Then draw a line between the subject and the predicate.

> Example: Tom Mix and William S. Hart | were famous
> actors in old Western movies.

1. Movie-goers in the 1920's admired such greats as Greta Garbo, Rudolph Valentino, and Douglas Fairbanks, Jr.
2. Slapstick comedy was performed by Charlie Chaplin, Harold Lloyd, and Buster Keaton.
3. "Talkies," or movies with sound, became popular in the late 1920's.

4. The movies in the 1930's starred such people as Shirley Temple, Mae West, and Clark Gable.

5. The city of Hollywood was known as "the celluloid paradise."

6. One of the greatest movies was released in 1939.

7. This particular movie was discussed by hundreds of magazines and newspapers.

8. *Gone with the Wind* swept movie-goers off their feet.

9. The stars, Vivien Leigh and Clark Gable, were recognized by everyone.

10. Their movie became a film classic.

B. Number your paper 1–10. Write the compound subjects, verbs, and objects you find in these sentences.

1. Yesterday's teens and today's youth have had a variety of interests.

2. Mini-skirts, long hair, and Beatlemania were accepted by most young people in the '60's.

3. Young people have danced and have listened to all different kinds of music.

4. Big bands and rock-and-roll music characterized the 1940's and 1950's.

5. Today's youth buys albums and tapes of lots of different musicians.

6. Some fads of the '70's include skateboards, platform shoes, Levis, Adidas, and T-shirts.

7. Popular music and fashion often dictate fads.

8. The Beatles and the Rolling Stones introduced a new kind of music.

9. Since then, radios and stereos have played the music of Elton John, Linda Ronstadt, Diana Ross, the Eagles, and many others.

10. In ten years, what will you and your friends be interested in?

Part 2   Compound Sentences

Sometimes two sentences are so closely related in thought that we join them together. We can join them by using *and,* *but* or *or.*

> We washed the car. Mom took us for a ride.
> We washed the car, *and* Mom took us for a ride.

> The book was long. It was very interesting.
> The book was long, *but* it was very interesting.

A compound sentence is made by joining two or more simple sentences together.

Compound sentences are useful, but they should be written with care. Two ideas should be put into one sentence only if they are closely related. If they are not closely related, the result may be confusing and hard to follow.

> *Wrong*:   Jim painted the barn, and he is nineteen.
>   *Right*:   Jim painted the barn, and John repaired the roof.

Exercise   **Make compound sentences.**

Join each pair of sentences by using *and, but,* or *or.* Place a comma before *and, but,* or *or.*

One of the pairs of sentences should not be joined because the ideas are not related. Can you find that pair?

1. I rode my bike to the gas station. I filled my tires with more air.

2. The car was full. They made room for one more.

3. Look closely at the map. You will see which route to follow.

4. The trap was set. The fox was too crafty.

5. You must watch carefully. You will get lost.

6. It rained all night. The baseball game wasn't cancelled.

7. The assembly was fun. Sit in this chair.
8. We like Jack. We will miss him.
9. Carl painted the picture. Suzi made the frame.
10. The girls bought Ray a sweater. He likes it very much.

Diagraming a Compound Sentence

The diagram of a compound sentence shows one simple sentence above the other. The two sentences are joined by a dotted line with a "step" for the coordinating conjunction. There are two main sentence lines. Each sentence has a subject and a predicate.

The class explored the cave, but they found nothing.

Exercise   **Recognize the parts of a compound sentence.**

Show the two main parts of these compound sentences by diagraming or by copying and underlining.

1. The football game was scheduled for TV tonight, but the President's speech pre-empted all programming.
2. Lucinda and I went cycling, and my brothers did the yardwork.
3. Babe Ruth was a leading contributor to the game of baseball, but Babe Didrikson contributed to women's participation in all sports.
4. Amelia Earhart was a school teacher, but she later became the first woman to fly the Atlantic.

5. I enjoy reading the books of Laura Ingalls Wilder, but my favorite book is *The Good Earth* by Pearl S. Buck.

6. Do you like the modern dance of Martha Graham, or do you like the ballet of Maria Tallchief?

7. We are going to the planetarium tomorrow, and we will see a special slide show there.

8. Betsy Ross may have made the first flag, but little evidence of this is available.

9. Harriet Tubman was a scout for the Union army, and she was also the most celebrated "conductor" of the Underground Railroad.

10. Tanya and I were playing backgammon, but I prefer the game of chess.

Punctuating Compound Sentences

In compound sentences, a comma should be used before the conjunction.

There is a very good reason for using the comma. The comma tells you where to pause. Without a comma, a sentence can be quite confusing:

> I painted the chair and my sister | painted the table.
> Ann watered the flowers and the dog | watched her.

Sometimes the parts of a compound sentence are joined by a **semicolon (;)** instead of by a conjunction and a comma.

> It snowed heavily all night; classes were cancelled the next day.
> The whistle blew; the game was over.

Remember the two ways to join simple sentences:

1. Join them with a comma and one of the conjunctions *and, but,* or *or.* Place the comma before the conjunction.

2. Join them with a semicolon when there is no conjunction. Place the semicolon at the end of the first sentence.

The one way *not* to join simple sentences is to place a comma alone between them. A comma is not powerful enough to hold the sentences together.

Wrong: The symphony was over, we went home.

Right: The symphony was over; we went home.

Right: The symphony was over, *and* we went home.

Exercise   Punctuate compound sentences.

Number your paper 1–10. Write the last word of the *first* part of each compound sentence. Next write the proper punctuation mark. Then write the first word of the second part of the compound sentence.

Example: We called for Ted but he was not ready.
(*Ted, but*)

1. Nancy brought the shovel in she put it behind the door.
2. The new television season has started but I don't care for any of the new shows.
3. Nobody got the answer the problem was too difficult.
4. Anna shimmied up the rope and Sally watched.
5. I must start now or I will be late.
6. My favorite actress is Cicely Tyson and my favorite singer is Carol King.
7. Tina and Miki went to Mardi Gras but Luanne and I went to Florida.
8. There were over eighty people in line I counted them.
9. Our flight to San Diego was delayed and we missed our connection to Hawaii.
10. We drove through northern Michigan last October the fall colors were beautiful.

Part 3 Compound Sentences and Compound Verbs

A simple sentence with a compound verb looks and sounds very much like a compound sentence. It is important to know how *compound verbs* differ from *compound sentences* for two reasons: (1) They must be punctuated differently; (2) Sometimes you can improve your writing by changing a compound sentence to a simple sentence with a compound verb.

A simple sentence, you remember, has only one subject and one predicate. Any part of the predicate may be compound. Here is an example:

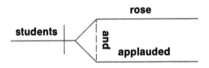
The students rose to their feet and applauded.

In the sentence above, there is one subject: *students*. There are two verbs: *rose* and *applauded*. Both verbs have the same subject: *students rose* and *students applauded*. In this sentence there is only one subject-verb combination. It looks like this:

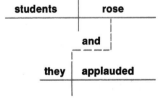

Now let's add a second subject and see what happens.

s.   v.   s.   v.
The students rose to their feet, and *they* applauded.

Now we have two subject-verb combinations. They look like this:

159

You can see that the *simple* sentence has become a *compound* sentence. This has happened because of the addition of the second subject, *they.*

Now let's put the two sentences together to see the difference in the words.

Compound Sentence: The students rose to their feet, and *they* applauded.

Compound Verb: The students rose to their feet and applauded.

By dropping the second subject out of the compound sentence, we make a simple sentence that has a subject-verb combination made up of one subject and two verbs. You can do this whenever the subjects of the compound sentence refer to the same person or thing.

Sam and Andrea arrived, and *they* distributed the uniforms and the equipment.
Sam and Andrea arrived and distributed the uniforms and the equipment.

The *shirt* was dry, but it still looked dirty.
The shirt was dry but still looked dirty.

Do not place a comma between the parts of a compound verb. Study the punctuation of the sentences above.

Exercises **Analyze simple and compound sentences.**

A. Copy the following sentences, adding commas where necessary. After each sentence write *Compound Verb* or *Compound Sentence* to show which it is.

1. I finished my homework and then I cleaned my room.

2. I like all science fiction movies but I really enjoy the old *Star Trek* programs.

3. The dogs barked wildly and ran after the truck.

4. The dogs snarled at the mail carrier but she paid no attention.

5. The jet made an emergency landing but no one on board was injured.

6. The early bird gets the worm but who wants worms?

7. Has Don come or has he been delayed?

8. The lifeguard jumped down and dashed into the water.

9. For an hour we sat by the telephone and just waited.

10. A plane takes off or lands at O'Hare Airport every 45 seconds.

B. Copy these sentences. Underline each subject once and each verb twice. After each sentence write *Simple* or *Compound* to show what kind it is.

1. We saw the King Tut exhibit in New Orleans.

2. The exhibit was a gesture of good will to the people of the United States from the Egyptians.

3. The Wright Brothers flew their plane in Kitty Hawk, North Carolina, on December 17, 1903.

4. A four-cylinder engine and two propellers gave power to their plane, and their glider flew a hundred feet for a total of twelve seconds.

5. Queen Elizabeth II became the monarch of Britain and the Commonwealth at the age of twenty-five.

6. Paper currency is printed at the Bureau of Engraving and Printing in Washington, D.C., but some coins are made at the U.S. Mint in Denver.

7. Elfreth's Alley is the oldest continuously occupied residential street in America.

8. It dates back to the 1690's and is one of the historic landmarks of Philadelphia.

9. Jamestown, Virginia, was the first permanent English colony in the New World.

10. The original Fort James was built in 1607, and today's visitors to the fort may see a full-scale reconstruction.

C. Make a simple sentence with a compound verb from each of the following compound sentences. Be sure to use the correct punctuation in your new sentence.

1. In Acadia National Park in Maine, we went backpacking, and we went horseback riding.

2. Our 4-H Club showed black angus cattle, and we displayed home-grown vegetables.

3. In the late 1800's, immigrants flocked to the United States, and they registered with government officials at Ellis Island.

4. On our vacations, we have visited several Amish villages, and we have seen many Indian reservations.

5. A tree fell during the storm, and it landed on our carport.

6. Snow fell all night, and it buried everything in sight.

7. Our hockey team was victorious in the semifinals, and we finished second in the finals.

8. Paint dripped from the brush, and it fell onto the rug.

9. The waves pounded against the small sailboats, and they lashed against the weatherbeaten dock.

10. Vince, Maria, and Kate attended the Chicago concert, and they went out for pizza afterwards.

Part 4   Complex Sentences

Before you can know what a complex sentence is, you need to know about clauses.

A clause is a group of words that contains a verb and its subject.

According to this definition, a simple sentence is a clause since it has both a verb and subject.

s.   v.
Jerry put the boxes behind the garage.

s.   v.
Sue read the announcements.

It will be easier to understand sentences, however, if we think of a clause as *part of a sentence*. We will think of a clause as *a group of words within a sentence*.

How about compound sentences? Do they contain clauses? Do they contain two or more groups of words that have a subject and a verb? Look at these examples:

    s.   **v.**   **s.** **v.**
Jane hit the ball, and it flew into the bleachers.

    s.   **v.**   **s.** **v.**
We found the box, but it was empty.

The answer is clear. Compound sentences do contain groups of words that have their own subjects and verbs.

Now, let's break up these compound sentences into their main parts and see what happens.

Jane hit the ball. It flew into the bleachers.
We found the box. It was empty.

Each one of the clauses in the compound sentences can become a sentence by itself.

Main Clauses

A clause that can stand as a sentence by itself is a **main clause.** All the clauses in compound sentences are main clauses. They can all stand as simple sentences by themselves. That is why they are sometimes called **independent clauses.**

Subordinate Clauses

Now we will look at clauses of a different kind:

    s.   **v.**
If the mail has come

    s.   **v.**
When the door opened

Neither group of words above makes a complete thought. Each leaves you wondering: *Then what?*

Now, with your finger, cover the first word in each group of words. What happens? Each group of words becomes a complete sentence. You can see, then, that the words *if* and *when* are important.

We say that these words **subordinate** the groups of words they introduce. They are called **subordinating conjunctions.** They introduce **subordinate clauses.**

Words used frequently as subordinating conjunctions are shown below:

Words Often Used as Subordinating Conjunctions

after	because	so that	whatever
although	before	than	when
as	if	though	whenever
as if	in order that	till	where
as long as	provided	unless	wherever
as though	since	until	while

Exercise Make subordinate clauses.

Using *if, because, when, after,* and *since,* make subordinate clauses out of these sentences.

1. It was very foggy.
2. The window is broken.
3. The car stopped.
4. The dog howled.
5. The power went off.
6. You can go.
7. Our packages are ready.
8. The party ended.
9. The crowd had left.
10. It rained on Saturday.

Definition of the Complex Sentence

Now that you know about main clauses and subordinate clauses, you are ready to learn what a complex sentence is.

A complex sentence is a sentence that contains one main clause and one or more subordinate clauses.

We left	before you came.
We'll go to the carnival	unless it rains tonight.
We were on the lake	when the storm began.

Exercises   **Analyze sentences and clauses.**

A. Find the subordinate clause in each sentence. Copy it. Underline the subject once and the verb twice.

1. Before basketball practice begins, the team always runs 25 laps around the gym.

2. Although the heat was on, the room was still quite cold.

3. Stop and see us when you come back.

4. I put the library books in my backpack so that I wouldn't forget them.

5. Where were you when I called for you?

6. The water was colder than I thought.

7. Karen never speaks up, although she usually knows the answers.

8. While we were in Philadelphia, we saw Independence Hall and Betsy Ross's home.

9. Although the land around Denver is flat, it is almost a mile high.

10. We can't start the game until the field is drier.

B. Number your paper 1–10. For each sentence, write *Simple, Compound,* or *Complex* to show what kind it is.

1. Mary and Elyse left in a hurry and forgot their tickets.

2. Close the door when you leave.

3. When the starting quarterback was injured, the substitute showed great talent.

4. Woodworking and weaving are both offered in the fall.

5. Have you finished, or may we help you?

6. Since Chicago is well known for deep dish pizza, we ordered it at a restaurant there.

7. Because of the city's drought, residents had to ration their water carefully.

8. Give us the tools, and we'll finish the job.

9. Jill and I waited in line for over two hours.

10. When we rode the Cog Railway to Pike's Peak, we saw herds of mountain sheep.

Part 5 More About Sentence Fragments

The sentence fragments that you studied in Section 1 were easy to spot. They were fragments because they lacked a verb or the subject of a verb.

Now we meet a new kind of sentence fragment, the subordinate clause. A subordinate clause has both a verb and a subject. It is still a fragment, however, because its meaning is not complete. Look at the groups of words below. Which is a complete sentence? Which is a subordinate clause?

> It is time to leave
> If it is time to leave

A subordinate clause must not be written as a complete sentence. It must always be joined to a main clause.

Fragment: If it is time to leave
Sentence: If it is time to leave, we will say good-bye.

Fragment: When you arrive
Sentence: When you arrive, come in the back door.

You can see that it is important to be able to recognize subordinating conjunctions.

Words Often Used as Subordinating Conjunctions			
after	because	so that	whatever
although	before	than	when
as	if	though	whenever
as if	in order that	till	where
as long as	provided	unless	wherever
as though	since	until	while

Caution: These words are subordinating words only when they introduce a clause. Some of them can be used in other ways.

Exercises   Recognize sentence fragments.

A. Number your paper 1–10. Decide whether the groups of words below are sentences or fragments. Write *S* for *Sentence* or *F* for *Fragment.* Add words to make each fragment a complete sentence. Punctuate and capitalize where necessary.

1. after the shower we saw a rainbow
2. after the show had ended
3. where the school always has its football games
4. where is the box of candy
5. since yesterday morning the air has been clear
6. since we have no food left
7. because of the storm, our lights went off
8. because the doctor advised plenty of rest
9. when are you leaving for Europe
10. when the old mine was closed down

B. Follow the directions for Exercise A.

1. down the mountain rolled a boulder
2. since the beginning of school
3. since you agree, we can go ahead with the plans

4. until the manager came out and stopped the noise
5. where the car went off the road
6. when the wind is from the south, we get rain
7. where is the box for this puzzle
8. before the lifeguard could reach the boat
9. while we waited for our ride
10. although the movie was cancelled, we had a good group discussion

C. On page 167 is a list of subordinating conjunctions. Choose six of the conjunctions that have not been used in Exercise A above. Use each conjunction in an original complex sentence. Underline the subordinate clause in each of your sentences.

Part 6   Adverb Clauses

An **adverb** is a word that modifies a verb, an adjective, or another adverb.

Adverb: Pam sat *down*.

An **adverb phrase** is a prepositional phrase used as an adverb. Adverb phrases usually modify verbs.

Adverb Phrase: Pam sat *in the rocking chair*.

An adverb clause is a subordinate clause used as an adverb.

Adverb clause: Pam sat *where she would be comfortable*.

Adverbs and adverb phrases or clauses tell *where, when, how,* or *how much* about the word they modify.

Remember that a *clause* contains a subject and a verb. A *phrase* has neither a subject nor a verb.

Adverb clauses are always introduced by subordinating conjunctions:

after	because	so that	whatever
although	before	than	when
as	if	though	whenever
as if	in order that	till	where
as long as	provided	unless	wherever
as though	since	until	while

Some of the words above may also be used as prepositions. They are called subordinating conjunctions only when they introduce an adverb clause.

Preposition:	*before* the game
Subordinating Conjunction:	*before* the game started
Preposition:	*after* the party
Subordinating Conjunction:	*after* the food was served
Preposition:	*since* that day
Subordinating Conjunction:	*since* we had already started

Diagraming Adverb Clauses

The adverb clause is placed on its own line below the main clause. A dotted line is drawn from the adverb clause to the word it modifies in the main clause. The subordinating conjunction is placed on the dotted line.

Whenever we arrive on time, we surprise her.

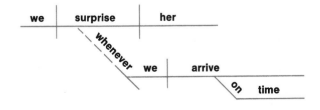

Copy the adverb clause from each sentence. Underline its subject once and its verb twice. Draw a circle around the subordinating conjunction.

Example: Until I was five, I lived in New Mexico.

(Unti)I <u>was</u> five

1. When we arrived in Seattle, it was very cold.

2. Before we could visit the small villages, we had to learn Japanese.

3. There was plenty of ribbon because we had saved it from Christmas.

4. Since the mules were slow, several tourists walked beside them.

5. Two partridges rose and whirred away as we approached.

6. As the mist cleared, Pike's Peak came into view.

7. If South American mail planes are late, search planes are alerted.

8. The geyser erupted again before we left.

9. Although he had lived all his life in England, Rick adjusted quickly to his new American lifestyle.

10. If you had been there on Saturday, you would have seen the precision marching.

Part 7 Adjective Clauses

An **adjective** is a word that modifies a noun or pronoun.

An **adjective phrase** is a phrase that modifies a noun or pronoun:

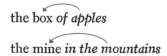

the box *of apples*

the mine *in the mountains*

Clauses as Modifiers

Clauses may be used to modify nouns and pronouns:

I know the mine *that you are talking about.*

Ms. Peters is the one *who asked about you.*

The train, *which had been stopped,* was delayed an hour.

Laura's the one *who telephoned us.*

An adjective clause is a subordinate clause used as an adjective to modify a noun or pronoun.

Usually, the adjective clause comes immediately after the word it modifies. Study the examples above.

Phrases and Clauses

Can you tell the difference between a *phrase* and a *clause?* Look at these examples.

Phrases:	of apples
	in the mountains
Clauses:	s. v. that you are talking about
	s. v. who asked for you

A clause has a subject and a verb. A phrase does not.

Many adjective clauses start with the words *who, whom, whoever, whomever, which,* or *that.* Some adjective clauses start with *where* and *when.*

We passed the place *where you fished.*

It was a time *when everyone was worried.*

It was the day *when half the class was absent.*

Remember: A clause contains both a subject and a verb.

  s.   v.
where *you fish*

  s.   v.
when *everyone was worried*

  s.   v.
when *half* the class *was* absent

Diagraming Adjective Clauses

Both the main clause and the adjective clause are written on main lines. A dotted line goes from the relative pronoun to the word in the main clause that the adjective clause modifies.

Kelly is the girl who won the race.

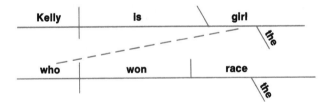

He is the magician of whom we were speaking.

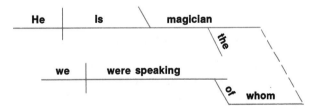

Recognize adjective clauses.

Copy the adjective clause from each sentence. Underline the subject once and the verb twice. Before the clause, write the word it modifies.

> Example: This is the book that I borrowed.
> (*book—that I borrowed.*)
>
> Tom is the one who called you.
> (*one—who called.*)

1. The family who owns the snowmobile lives next door.
2. Burt, who was still awake, smelled the smoke.
3. The new bike that I received for my birthday has a generator light.
4. This is the cookbook that has the best recipes.
5. The mayor is a woman who teaches at the college.
6. The team that wins the game gets the silver cup.
7. We couldn't find anyone who had seen the accident.
8. A lady who was carrying many packages sat down beside me.
9. Sam has the horse that jumps the best.
10. Patti owns a collie that has won several prizes.
11. We lost the picture that you gave us.
12. It was one of those days when everything went wrong.
13. Is this the coat that you want?
14. Your camera is in the closet where we keep the skates.
15. This is the book that explains cloud formations.

Part 8 *Who* and *Whom* in Clauses

The words *who, whose,* and *whom* are often used to begin adjective clauses. They tie the clause to the word it modifies in the main clause. When used in this way, *who, whom,* and *whose* are called **relative pronouns.** They relate the clause (called a **relative clause**) to the word it modifies. *That* and *which* may also be relative pronouns.

Relative Pronouns

who	whose	that
whom		which

Relative pronouns have three jobs:

1. They begin an adjective clause.

2. They relate the adjective clause to a word in the main clause.

3. They act as subject, object, or predicate pronoun of the verb in the adjective clause. They may also be the object of a preposition in the clause.

> Kelly is the girl *who won the race.*
> (*Who* is the subject of *won.*)

> Is Gayle the girl *whom you met?*
> (*Whom* is the object of *met.*)

> He is the magician *of whom we were speaking.*
> (*Whom* is the object of the preposition *of.*)

The subject form is *who.* The object form is *whom.* Which form you use depends upon how the word is used within the clause.

Exercises   Analyze relative clauses.

A. Relative clauses are given below, preceded by the word they modify. Decide whether *who* or *whom* would be used in each clause. Write the pronoun. Then write its use in the clause: subject, object, or object of a preposition.

1. the guide to _____**?**_____ we spoke
2. the doctor _____**?**_____ came to see us

3. the pharmacist from ___?___ we got the prescription
4. the members ___?___ helped us build the float
5. the teacher ___?___ helped us
6. the family with ___?___ I stayed
7. the runner ___?___ always wears a baseball cap
8. the performer ___?___ everyone liked best
9. the miners ___?___ the rescue team found
10. the people ___?___ I counted

B. Follow the directions for Exercise A.

1. the Indians ___?___ once inhabited this area
2. the minister ___?___ performed the ceremony
3. the artist ___?___ painted this mural
4. the construction worker ___?___ handled the jackhammer
5. the relatives ___?___ they visited
6. the astronauts ___?___ the newscaster discussed
7. the journalist ___?___ wrote this article
8. the goalie ___?___ wears a knit cap
9. the gardener ___?___ grew a thousand gardenias last year
10. the grocer ___?___ sponsors our hockey team

Part 9 Noun Clauses

You will remember that nouns can be used as subjects, as objects of verbs, as predicate words after linking verbs, and as objects of prepositions.

A **noun clause** is a clause used as a noun in a sentence. The noun clause can be used in any way that a noun is used. Noun clauses do not modify anything because nouns are not modifiers.

Uses of Noun Clauses

Subject:	*What we wanted* was food.
Subject:	*What the magician did* astonished us.
Object:	We saw *that you were in a hurry.*
Object:	We know *whom you mean.*
Object of Prep.:	Give the clothes to *whoever can use them.* (The clause is the object of the preposition *to.*)
Object of Prep.:	Jack works hard for *what he gets.* (The clause is the object of the preposition *for.*)
Predicate Noun:	The answer was *what we had expected.*
Predicate Noun:	The responses were *what we anticipated.*

Words That Introduce Noun Clauses

A great many noun clauses are introduced by *that* and *what.* Some are introduced by *whatever, whoever,* and *whomever.* Other noun clauses are introduced by *who, whose,* and *whom.* Still others are introduced by *where, when,* and *how.*

You cannot tell the kind of clause from the word that introduces it. You can tell the kind of clause only from its use in the sentence. If the clause is used as a noun, it is a noun clause. If the clause is a modifier, it is an adverb or adjective clause.

Wherever he went was a mystery. (Noun clause as subject)
No one knew *where we hid.* (Noun clause as object)

He left pieces of paper *wherever he went.* (Adverb clause)
This is the cave *where we hid.* (Adjective clause)

Diagraming Noun Clauses

A noun clause is diagramed on a bridge at the place where the clause is used in a sentence. The word that introduces the clause is placed on a horizontal line above the clause.

1. Noun clause as subject

That she wasn't coming was certain.

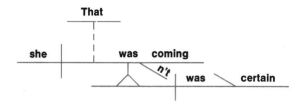

2. Noun clause as object of the verb

Donna could see *who was coming.*

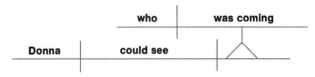

3. Noun clause as object of a preposition.

We were surprised by *what happened.*

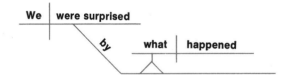

Exercises   Analyze noun clauses.

A. Copy the noun clauses in these sentences. Underline the subject once and the verb twice. Tell how the clause is used. Your teacher may ask you to diagram the sentences.

1. I will do whatever you decide.
2. Whoever wins gets this trophy.
3. Do you remember who told you that?
4. I don't know where the Marcuses live.

5. Whoever appeared was put to work.
6. I was just thinking about what you said.
7. Show this card to whoever is at the door.
8. Paula didn't know where Kevin was going.
9. Our class will support whatever candidate is chosen.
10. Where we go on our class trip hasn't been decided.

B. Follow the directions for Exercise A.

1. Whoever finds Kathy's watch will receive a reward.
2. Why they chose me is hard to understand.
3. Whatever you decide is all right with me.
4. Save these coupons for whoever wants them.
5. Whoever wins the tournament deserves great recognition.
6. We didn't know who was in charge of the ballot box.
7. I was wondering how you did that.
8. Sally doesn't know where the supplies are.
9. Sign the papers for whoever needs them.
10. How you finished so quickly is beyond me.

Exercise   **Analyze adverb, adjective, and noun clauses.**

Copy the subordinate clauses in these sentences. Tell whether they are adverb, adjective, or noun clauses. Underline the subject once and the verb twice.

1. We arrived when Dr. Jordan was speaking.
2. Is this the coat that you want?
3. Can you study while the TV is on?
4. We did not know who the man was.
5. Jeff ducked before the snowball hit him.
6. The plane that leaves at 7:00 P.M. has a feature movie.
7. I don't believe that the experiment is possible.
8. Someone said that we would have a holiday tomorrow.
9. Dad lived in Colorado when he was growing up.
10. How the dog got out is beyond me.

Additional Exercises

Using Compound and Complex Sentences

A. Analyze simple sentences.

Label four columns *Subject, Verb, Object* and *Predicate Word.* For each sentence fill in the appropriate columns. Some sentences may have compound parts.

> Example: Their confidence and determination impressed and surprised the other team.

Subject	Verb	Object	Predicate Word
confidence	impressed	team	
determination	surprised		

1. Their supply of butane gas was low.
2. The sky looks brighter and clearer to the east.
3. The fields and meadows were covered with daisies.
4. The entire week was hot and muggy.
5. The hot sun and the humidity made football practice impossible.
6. Mariners watch the wind and clouds carefully.
7. The shutters and doors flapped and banked.
8. Darnell and I baked cookies for our picnic.
9. The books and the china were all ready for shipment.
10. The librarian ordered some new encyclopedias and a new atlas.

B. Make compound sentences.

Join each pair of sentences by using *and, but,* or *or.* Place a comma before *and, but,* or *or.* One pair of sentences should not be joined because the ideas are not related. Can you find that pair?

1. Jim groomed four horses. He didn't have time for the fifth.

2. Trudy went at 10 o'clock. The store was still not open.

3. Do you want to make lunch? Do you want to go to Burger King?

4. The short circuit in the toaster blew the fuse. The iron did it.

5. The tide was in. The beach in the cove was covered.

6. We were going to the motocross races. The heavy rain delayed them until next week.

7. Do you enjoy ice skating? Do you prefer toboganning?

8. Our class collected aluminum cans. We took them to the recycling center.

9. Marsha counted fourteen hawks. Sara saw eighteen.

10. The bus was full. The driver was nowhere to be seen.

C. Punctuate compound sentences.

Number your paper 1–10. Write the last word of the *first* part of each compound sentence. Next write the proper punctuation mark. Then write the first word of the second part of the compound sentence.

1. Bill opened the door and two dogs rushed in.

2. I like to read short stories but I really enjoy long, detailed mysteries.

3. The helicopter flew over the park that's its usual route.

4. Mrs. Stuart has about fifty different kinds of plants in her windows you can hardly see out.

5. Our field trip to Knotts Berry Farm was fun but I liked the tour at Universal Studios the best.

6. Should we buy Tim a birthday present or should we make him something?

7. The great auk is a diving bird it is almost 30 inches long.

8. Jeff stood close to the house and Pete got on his shoulders.

9. Sandy pitches best but Lana is the best batter.

10. I'll lend you some money you can pay me tomorrow.

D. Analyze simple and compound sentences.

Copy these sentences. Underline each subject once and each verb twice. After each sentence write *Simple* or *Compound* to show what kind it is.

1. The key was on the table, and I hung it up.

2. He took the receiver off the hook and forgot about it.

3. I threw the trash into the basket, but I didn't notice any magazines.

4. The trees lined the avenue and shaded it.

5. Foreign newspapers come in at noon, and Lee buys them on her way home.

6. A wind started about suppertime and blew hard.

7. I washed the dishes, and Rhonda dried them.

8. José washed the dishes and cleaned the kitchen.

9. Joan and Tom made a hollow around each little tree and watered it.

10. It rained all afternoon, and my sister and I stayed in and played chess.

E. Recognize adverb clauses.

Copy the adverb clause from each sentence. Underline its subject once and its verb twice. Draw a circle around the subordinating conjunction.

1. If the shelf is too low, move it up.

2. When the alarm sounded, all classes left the building.

3. Wherever he went, he took his Spanish-English dictionary.

4. Since we had lots of time, we stayed for dessert.

5. Juanita hurt her ankle as she was running the hurdles.

6. If you want my opinion, it's available.

7. When you go to Philadelphia, see Independence Hall.

8. Lauren talked as if she would run for vice-president of the French Club.

9. When the trumpet fanfare began, the audience returned to their seats.

10. When the bobsled finally stopped, we could barely crawl out.

F. Recognize adjective clauses.

Copy the adjective clause from each sentence. Underline the subject once and the verb twice. Before the clause, write the word it modifies.

1. This is the store that I had in mind.

2. We enjoyed the postcards that you wrote from South America.

3. Mount Vernon is the home where George and Martha Washington lived.

4. The book that you wanted has been checked out.

5. The speaker whom they want charges $400.

6. Do you remember the time when you fell out of the chestnut tree?

7. This is my friend Tracy, whom I was telling you about.

8. Bob, who had just come back from the dentist, looked rather uncomfortable.

9. It was Ben Franklin who invented bifocals, the electrical generator, and the Franklin stove.

10. This is the album that I want.

G. Analyze relative clauses.

Decide whether *who* or *whom* would be used in each clause. Write the pronoun. Then write its use in the clause: subject, object, or object of preposition.

1. the jockey _____?_____ you picked
2. the pilots _____?_____ United Airlines hires
3. the clerk _____?_____ answered your question
4. the sculptor _____?_____ designed this piece of art
5. the newsboy from _____?_____ she usually buys her paper
6. the singer _____?_____ did that TV special
7. The caterers _____?_____ the mayor hired
8. the mail carrier _____?_____ was on duty yesterday
9. the police officer with _____?_____ you were walking
10. the teacher to _____?_____ you talked

H. Recognize noun clauses.

Copy the noun clause in each sentence. Tell how the clause is used.

1. Whoever wins the tennis finals goes to the state meet.
2. The plaque commemorates what she did for the school.
3. How this sewing machine works is what I would like to know.
4. Nancy told me that Maurita wasn't coming.
5. Most of us did not agree with what the speaker said.
6. Coach Larson could see that the defense was tiring.
7. Zebulon Pike was ill prepared for whatever his expedition would face.
8. He did not know that his men would encounter a bitter winter.
9. Carol said that her report was about Renaissance painters.
10. Whoever told you that was wrong.

Section 8

Making Subjects and Verbs Agree

Part 1   Making Subjects and Verbs Agree in Number

When a word refers to one thing, it is singular. When it refers to more than one thing, it is **plural.** When we speak of the **number** of a word, we are talking about whether it is singular or plural.

A verb must agree in number with its subject.

If the subject is singular, the verb must be singular. If the subject is plural, the verb must be plural.

Singular	Plural
The bird *sings*.	The birds *sing*.
She *listens*.	They *listen*.
It *whistles*.	They *whistle*.

You can see that the third person singular of the verb ends in *s*. The *s* disappears in the plural.

You will have problems in agreement of subject and verb only when you are not sure what the subject is. *Remember:* To find the subject, first find the verb. Then ask *who?* or *what?* before it.

One of the players is sick.

Verb: is   Who is?: one   Subject: one

The subject of the verb is never found in a prepositional phrase.

Watch out for phrases that lie between the verb and the subject.

One of the eggs *was* broken.

The *pictures* on the desk *were* torn.

Phrases beginning with the words *with, together with, including, as well as,* and *in addition to* are not part of the subject.

The *principal*, in addition to the teachers, *is* here.

Mr. *Bard*, together with his children, *has* left.

Exercises   Make verbs agree with their subjects.

A. Choose the verb that agrees with the subject.

1. One of my front teeth (are, is) loose.

2. The captain, together with his crew, (look, looks) after the ship.

3. Several pages in the book (is, are) missing.

4. The drawings on display (was, were) done by the art classes.

5. The bus with all the players (arrives, arrive) at three.

6. The schedule for all the sports events (is, are) on the bulletin board.

7. The choice of the judges (was, were) not very popular.

8. All the signs along the road (has, have) been taken down.

9. A popcorn stand in the lobby (was, were) open.

10. The new schedule for the suburbs (has, have) more trains.

B. Follow the directions for Exercise A.

1. The doctor, together with her staff, (are, is) often here.

2. The edges of the playing field (was, were) still wet.

3. My jacket, as well as my ski pants, (is, are) wet.

4. Each of the homerooms (contribute, contributes) to the Toys-for-Tots campaign.

5. Those antique cars in the driveway (belongs, belong) to the Hadleys.

6. A request for money and provisions (was, were) granted.

7. The members of the swim team (report, reports) to the pool every morning.

8. Two of my teachers (coaches, coach) the volleyball team.

9. The girls on the team (like, likes) the coach.

10. The attendants at the airport (requires, require) passengers to check their luggage.

Part 2 Compound Subjects

Compound subjects joined by *and* require a plural verb.

The truck and the trailer *were* badly damaged.
The walls and the ceiling *are* soundproofed.

When the parts of a compound subject are join by *or* or *nor*, the verb agrees with the part nearer to it.

Either Mom or the boys *have* come home.

Neither the boys nor Mom *has* been home yet.

Either the musicians or their leader *has* your music.

Exercises **Make verbs agree with their subjects.**

A. Choose the verb that agrees with the subject.

1. Al and Ken (hasn't, haven't) finished repairing their old car.

2. Either the coach or the co-captains (call, calls) the time-outs.

3. Both winter and summer (is, are) mild here.

4. Either a raccoon or some dogs (has, have) gotten into the garbage.

5. The evening news and the late newspaper (report, reports) the sports results of the day.

6. Neither the tent nor the sleeping bags (arrive, arrives) until tomorrow.

7. Both the tugs and the Loganville ferry (dock, docks) here.

8. Corrine and her family (is, are) arriving tomorrow.

9. Neither my gym shoes nor my uniform (need, needs) to be laundered.

10. The players and the referee (are, is) arguing about the call.

B. Follow the directions for Exercise A.

1. Either Phil or his sister (is, are) bringing us home.

2. Neither the cookies nor the cake (taste, tastes) burnt to me.

3. The water and the beach (look, looks) inviting.

4. Neither complaints nor threats (has, have) any effect on the umpire.

5. Buildings or billboards often (obscures, obscure) the horizon.

6. Neither fishing nor hunting (is, are) permitted.

7. Both the German Club and the Spanish Club (help, helps) decorate the lobby for Christmas.

8. Both the ordinary frogs and the bullfrog (tune, tunes) up at sundown.

9. Either the dog or the cat (stay, stays) home.

10. Either our local newspaper or our local radio stations (publicize, publicizes) our school's sporting events.

Part 3   Indefinite Pronouns

The indefinite pronouns in the list below are singular:

Singular Indefinite Pronouns		
another	either	nobody
anybody	everybody	no one
anyone	everyone	one
anything	everything	somebody
each	neither	someone

Each of the cars *was* given a number.
Everybody *has* a job to do.
Neither of us *has* a good enough report.

The words *some, all,* and *most* are singular if they refer to one part of something. They are plural if they refer to several things.

Singular	Plural
all of the paper	all of the people
most of the work	most of the books

The pronoun *you* is always followed by a plural verb.

We know you *have* been working hard.
Is it true that you *were* in Europe last summer?

Exercises Make verbs agree with their subjects.

A. Choose the verb that agrees with the subject.

1. Another of those talk shows (come, comes) on tonight at 10 o'clock.
2. Many of Debbie's friends (were, was) away.
3. Most of the boathouse (need, needs) painting.
4. Either Michelle or Ted (is, are) ushering.
5. Some of the students (earn, earns) extra money as ushers.
6. No one told me that Mike (were, was) moving to South Carolina.
7. Another of her reports (compare, compares) the prices of sporting goods.
8. Everyone in Rock Hill (was, were) here.
9. All of the books (have, has) been shelved in alphabetical order.
10. Each of the ensemble members (play, plays) at least two instruments.

B. Follow the directions for Exercise A.

1. All of the honeydew melons (is, are) ripe.
2. One of my brothers (is, are) in the navy.

3. Neither of the maps (show, shows) Rainbow Springs.

4. These bundles of newspapers (go, goes) to the recycling plant.

5. Neither of us (is, are) ready to give our speech.

6. Most of the hay (dry, dries) in a week.

7. Everyone in the audience (was, were) captivated by the performances.

8. All of the telephones (is, are) busy right now.

9. Most of the players (practices, practice) in the morning and the afternoon.

10. Somebody (is, are) responsible for writing up the club's minutes.

Part 4   Other Problems of Agreement

The pronouns *it, he,* and *she* are used with *doesn't.* All other personal pronouns are used with *don't.*

> It *doesn't* look like rain now.   I *don't* dance.
> She *doesn't* need more money.   You *don't* sing.
> He *doesn't* swim well enough.   They *don't* know.

In sentences beginning *Here is, There is,* and *Where is,* the subject comes after the verb.

> Here *is* your ticket.
> Where *is* the projector?
> There *are* the keys for the cottage.

Exercises   Make verbs agree with their subjects.

A. Choose the verb that agrees with the subject.

1. It (doesn't, don't) look as if the sky will clear before noon.

2. Where (was, were) she taking those packages?

3. Here (is, are) the tube socks and T-shirts the team ordered.

4. There (go, goes) the siren.

5. That idea (doesn't, don't) make any sense.

6. Where (is, are) the box for these ornaments?

7. Here (is, are) all the sheet metal that I could find.

8. Beth (don't, doesn't) want to go apple-picking with us.

9. There (are, is) several deer on the front lawn.

10. There (are, is) the new batteries for the flashlight.

B. Choose the verb that agrees with the subject.

1. There (come, comes) the other team onto the ice.

2. (Don't, Doesn't) Jennie want to ride with us?

3. There (is, are) the float we built for the homecoming parade.

4. Erica (doesn't, don't) agree with us.

5. Here (are, is) the magazine you wanted.

6. There (was, were) few skiers on the chairlift.

7. Where (do, does) these cartons go?

8. There (are, is) a fawn and its mother in our yard.

9. Where (is, are) my Disney World T-shirt?

10. Here (is, are) some of the pictures we took last winter.

Additional Exercises

Making Subjects and Verbs Agree

A. Make verbs agree with their subjects.

Choose the verb that agrees with the subject.

1. The sandbars in the Mississippi (cause, causes) many accidents.

2. Some sections of the city (has, have) no bus service.

3. Three students, including my sister, (was, were) chosen for the state art fair.

4. That lady in the gray sweat suit (jog, jogs) five miles a day.

5. The new books in the library (is, are) on a special shelf.

6. The answers to the exercise (is, are) in the back of the textbook.

7. The evidence on these films (looks, look) convincing.

8. The photographers on the yearbook staff (is, are) Raul and Patti.

9. The price of the German binoculars (are, is) too high.

10. Our team, including the coach and the cheerleaders, (take, takes) the bus from here.

B. Choose the right verb.

Choose the verb that agrees with the subject.

1. Neither the fenders nor the license plate (was, were) dented.

2. The principal and the teachers (organize, organizes) a student-faculty softball game every year.

3. Either my alarm clock or the clock in the den (is, are) wrong.

4. The principal or one of the secretaries (telephone, telephones) the radio station if school is cancelled.

5. Both Chico and his brother (was, were) there.

6. Neither porcupine quills nor skunks (stop, stops) our dog Rusty.

7. Either Sean or his grandparents usually (pick, picks) up the mail.

8. Yogurt and frozen yogurt (come, comes) in a variety of flavors.

9. Both the Hershey Company and Sara Lee Kitchens (has, have) tours of their food processing plants.

10. Either a van or a truck (suit, suits) our purpose quite well.

C. Choose the right verb.

Choose the verb that agrees with the subject.

1. Some of these stamps (don't, doesn't) stick.

2. (Wasn't, Weren't) you ready when the whistle blew?

3. Not one of the newscasts (has, have) publicized our candy sale.

4. Most of the time (was, were) wasted.

5. Everything on the two bottom shelves (belong, belongs) to David.

6. All of the fenceposts (has, have) snow on them.

7. Anything made of metal (was, were) immediately magnetized.

8. Neither of the gas pumps (is, are) working.

9. Nobody in the bleachers (cheer, cheers) louder than our Pep Club.

10. Most of our supplies (come, comes) from the school store.

D. Choose the right verb.

Choose the verb that agrees with the subject.

1. Here (is, are) the fire trucks.
2. Here (is, are) what the newspaper says about the eclipse.
3. There (goes, go) the runners.
4. Sam (doesn't, don't) ever take his eyes off the TV.
5. Here (is, are) the photographs that Heather picked out.
6. Where (is, are) the envelopes for these letters?
7. There (isn't, aren't) any time to waste.
8. (Don't, Doesn't) the Orient Express run any more?
9. Here (is, are) your tickets for the carnival.
10. She (doesn't, don't) know how to swim the butterfly stroke.

Section 9

Using Verbals

You have learned that there are eight parts of speech. The eight parts of speech are these:

nouns	verbs	adjectives	conjunctions
pronouns	adverbs	prepositions	interjections

In addition to the eight parts of speech, our language contains three other kinds of words. These are **infinitives, participles,** and **gerunds.** These words are called verbals. A **verbal** is a word that is formed from a verb but acts as another part of speech.

In this chapter you will study the three kinds of verbals, and learn how they are used in the sentence.

Part 1 Infinitives

The **infinitive** is the name of the verbal that usually appears with the word *to* before it. *To* is called the **sign of the infinitive.**

> to go   to see   to run   to walk

The word *to* is often used as a preposition. It is a preposition if it is followed by a noun or pronoun that is its object. *It is the sign of the infinitive if it is followed by a verb.* Notice these examples:

> We went *to the park.* (*Prepositional phrase*)
> We wanted *to swim.* (*Infinitive*)
>
> We stayed *to the end.* (*Prepositional phrase*)
> We tried *to dive.* (*Infinitive*)

Because the infinitive is formed from a verb, it is like a verb in several ways. The infinitive may, for example, have an object. It may also be modified by adverbs.

> Chris learned *to run a lathe.*
>   (*Lathe* is the direct object of the infinitive *to run.*)
> We tried *to give the dog a bath.*
>   (*Dog* is the indirect object and *bath* is the direct object of *to give.*)
> You will need *to work fast.*
>   (*Fast* is an adverb modifying *to work.*)
> Linda wanted *to drive the car to the station.*
>   (*Car* is the object of *to drive; to the station* is an adverb phrase modifying *to drive.*)

The infinitive with its objects and modifiers is an **infinitive phrase.**

Uses of the Infinitive Phrase

Infinitives and infinitive phrases can be used (1) as nouns, (2) as adjectives, or (3) as adverbs.

You remember that nouns are used as subjects and objects of verbs. Infinitives and infinitive phrases can be used as subjects, as objects, and in other ways that nouns are used.

Subject: *To leave early* is sometimes impolite.
           (*To leave early* is the subject of *is.*)

Object: Sue wanted *to leave.*
           (*To leave* is the object of *wanted.*)

Infinitives and infinitive phrases can be used as modifiers. If the infinitive or infinitive phrase modifies a noun or pronoun, it is used as an adjective. If it modifies a verb, adjective, or adverb, it is used as an adverb.

Adverb: Rick went *to see the doctor.*
           (*To see the doctor* modifies the verb *went.*)

Adverb: Tickets for the big game are hard *to get.*
           (*To get* modifies *hard.*)

Adjective: The catcher is the player *to watch.*
           (*To watch* modifies *player.*)

The Split Infinitive

Sometimes a modifier is placed between the word *to* and the verb. A modifier in this position is said to split the infinitive. Usually, a split infinitive sounds awkward and should be avoided.

Awkward: Ann expects to *easily* win.
Better: Ann expects to win *easily.*

Exercises   Find the infinitives and infinitive phrases.

A. Find the infinitives and infinitive phrases in these sentences. Write each infinitive or infinitive phrase. Be prepared to tell how it is used in the sentence.

Example: They were ready to drop the whole thing.

Infinitive phrase: *to drop the whole thing*

1. Mary and I plan to watch the Neil Diamond TV special.
2. Mr. Anderson wants to explain the new procedures.
3. To finish this project by Monday is my goal.
4. We tried to remember the address.
5. We plan to visit Washington.
6. Judy and I were told to bring our registration cards to orientation.
7. The vet came to see our horses.
8. This is the best book to use.
9. Bill ran to get a flashlight.
10. Sue still has homework to do.

B. Follow the instructions for Exercise A.

1. This is the path to follow.
2. The best thing to do is to wait.
3. Would you like to eat breakfast at the pancake house?
4. To read the first two chapters of this book is our assignment.
5. Amy has someone to help her to finish the job.
6. Do you want to go shopping tomorrow?
7. He wanted to sail up the coast to Alaska.
8. Did you remember to buy film?
9. Remind me to fill out the application form tonight.
10. Do you want to play tennis after school?

Part 2   Participles

You remember that one of the principal parts of the verb is the **past participle.** The past participle is formed by adding

-d or *-ed* to the present tense: *walk-walked.* The past participles of irregular verbs do not follow this rule and have to be learned separately: *bring-brought, ring-rung.*

There is another kind of participle, called the **present participle.** All present participles are formed by adding *-ing* to the present tense of the verb: *bring-bringing, ring-ringing, walk-walking.* Participles are always used as adjectives. They can modify nouns or pronouns:

> *Smiling,* Jan accepted the award.
> (*Smiling* is a present participle modifying the noun *Jan.*)
> Lunging, he hit the fence.
> (*Lunging* is a present participle modifying the pronoun *he.*)

Because participles are formed from verbs, they can have objects and be modified by adverbs. The participle with its objects and modifiers forms a participial phrase.

> *Turning the pages,* Barb found an old letter.
> (*Turning the pages* is a participial phrase modifying Barb; *pages* is the object of the participle *turning.*)
> *Turning suddenly,* Jean bumped into Mrs. Wood.
> (*Turning suddenly* is a participial phrase modifying *Jean.* The word *suddenly* is an adverb modifying the participle *turning.*)
> *Exhausted,* the last swimmer crawled out of the pool.
> (*Exhausted* is a participial phrase modifying *swimmer.*)

Exercises   **Find the participles and participial phrases.**

A. Write down the participles and participial phrases in these sentences. Show which word the participle modifies.

> Example Flipping the switch suddenly, Ron picked up two possums in the flashlight beam.
>
> Participle: *flipping* modifies the noun *Ron.*
> Participial phrase: flipping the switch suddenly

1. Exhausted, the cross-country runners crossed the finish line.

2. Moving effortlessly, the skaters danced across the ice.

3. Jumping clear, Jim opened his parachute.

4. Crossing the old bridge, she passed the old general store.

5. Frozen, the pie tastes even better.

6. Tested in our laboratories, the parts are guaranteed.

7. Spread thin, the glue dries in an hour.

8. Looking through binoculars, Jim cold see the skyline quite clearly.

9. Concentrating deeply, the center sank the free throw.

10. Moving quickly, the goalie blocked the kick.

B. Follow the directions for Exercise A.

1. Seeing the rain, Mr. Mill waited.

2. Clutching the receiver tightly, she listened.

3. The ball ricocheted, hitting the taillight.

4. Waiting patiently, the passengers stood in line at the gate.

5. Driving hard, the running back dove over the goal line.

6. Holding her pigeon, Lisa showed us the leg band.

7. Watch for gravel trucks leaving the quarry.

8. Fascinated by the talk, we listened without a sound.

9. He forgot that paperback lying on the table.

10. Breathing hard, Nancy crossed the finish line.

Part 3   Gerunds

A **gerund** is a verb form that is used as a noun. Gerunds can be used in any way that nouns are used:

> *Swimming* is good exercise.
> (*Swimming* is a gerund, the subject of *is*.)

Karen likes *riding*.
(*Riding* is a gerund, the object of *likes*.)

The time for *wrestling* is changed.
(*Wrestling* is a gerund, the object of the preposition *for*.)

Because gerunds are formed from verbs, they can have objects and can be modified by adverbs. Because they are used as nouns, they can also be modified by adjectives.

Riding a horse scares Kitt.
(*Riding* is a gerund; *horse* is the object of *riding*.)

Running cross-country is difficult.
(*Running* is a gerund; *cross-country* is an adverb modifying *running*.)

Careful *reading* requires concentration.
(*Reading* is a gerund; *careful* is an adjective modifying *reading*.)

Gerunds can also be modified by prepositional phrases:

Cycling in city traffic is frustrating.
(*Cycling* is a gerund; *in city traffic* is a prepositional phrase modifying *cycling*.)

A **gerund phrase** consists of a gerund with its modifiers and objects.

Exercises Find the gerunds and gerund phrases.

A. Find the gerunds and gerund phrases. As your teacher directs, show how the gerund is used.

Example: Planning the sports meet was fun.

Planning: gerund, subject of *was*.
Planning the sports meet: gerund phrase

1. Skydiving takes nerve.
2. Skiing is an invigorating sport.

3. Cleaning the attic was not my idea of a good time.
4. Washing that wall took all afternoon.
5. Painting the scenery took more time than we thought.
6. Running has become a popular activity.
7. Putting on a play takes teamwork.
8. Chris enjoys baking.
9. Skating on the lake in winter is fun.
10. That dog specializes in digging.

B. Follow the directions for Exercise A.

1. Joe learned fencing last summer.
2. Writing that essay was a difficult assignment.
3. Learning Russian requires homework.
4. Visiting Dallas was interesting.
5. Jack has always liked reading.
6. Wearing sunglasses rests her eyes.
7. They got sick from overeating.
8. Clare likes walking in the rain.
9. Eating outside was cooler.
10. Driving to Alaska was a long, interesting journey.

Distinguishing Between Gerunds and Participles

The gerund, like the present participle, is formed by adding *-ing* to the present tense of the verb. How can you tell whether a word is a gerund or a participle? It depends upon how the word is used. If it is used as a modifier, it is a participle. If it is used as a noun, it is a gerund.

> Walking is good exercise.
> (*Walking* is a gerund, the subject of *is*.)
> Walking fast, we overtook the boys.
> (*Walking* is a participle modifying *we*; *fast* is an adverb modifying *walking*.)

Trying is half the battle.

(*Trying* is a gerund, the subject of *is*.)

Trying, Brenda pushed harder.

(*Trying* is a participle modifying *Brenda*.)

Exercise **Distinguishing between gerunds and participles.**

For each sentence, write down the gerund or participle and say which it is. Be prepared to explain why it is a gerund or a participle.

1. Watching television bothers his eyes.

2. Watching television, Terry noticed the colors were wrong again.

3. Fixing steps was Mr. Buswell's specialty.

4. Fixing a sandwich, Gerry listened to the sportscast.

5. Cleaning is done every Saturday.

6. Cleaning the car, Pat found her notebook.

7. Removing the tree was difficult.

8. Panning for gold, the old man waded into the stream.

9. Moving quickly, the paramedics aided several of the victims.

10. Swimming is good for most people's health.

Additional Exercises

Using Verbals

A. Find the infinitives and infinitive phrases.

Find the infinitives and infinitive phrases in these sentences.

1. We hope to visit Washington this summer.
2. To satisfy his curiosity is impossible.
3. Ask them to come with us.
4. We hope to go to the movie on Sunday.
5. I still have a couple of windows to wash.
6. We were just starting to eat the other half of the pizza.
7. Jill proceeded to explain her proposal.
8. Andy is teaching us to float.
9. To go around by the bridge takes too long.
10. Wendy was planning to go to the beach.

B. Find the participles and participial phrases.

Write down the participles and participial phrases in these sentences.

1. Flopping frantically, the trout got off the wharf.
2. Speaking quietly, the librarian explained the reference book to me.
3. Look at the cat carrying its kitten in its mouth.
4. Racing wildly, the horses cross the finish line simultaneously.
5. Elated, Beth told us the news.
6. Cleaning the garage, John found some interesting old newspapers.
7. Bought second-hand, the motor lasted three years.

8. Snorting and kicking, the pinto refused to wear a saddle.

9. Walking slowly, Laura and her dog watched the sunset.

10. Made in Japan, the tape recorder was an instant money-maker.

C. Find the gerunds and gerund phrases.

1. Tracy likes making pottery.
2. Skydiving requires skill and an adventurous spirit.
3. Talking on the phone tires Mr. King.
4. Walking is good exercise and a time to think.
5. Reading is my favorite pastime.
6. Have you forgotten about mowing the lawn?
7. Panelling the den was Dad's idea.
8. You will never get rich by wishing.
9. In basketball, quick thinking is essential.
10. Driving over Highland Pass takes about an hour.

D. Distinguish between gerunds and participles.

Write down the gerund or participle for each sentence, and say which it is. Be prepared to explain why it is a gerund or a participle.

1. Swimming fast is all right for short spurts.
2. Swimming fast, he reached the dock first.
3. Talking a mile a minute, Jan explained her tardiness.
4. Thinking on your feet is not always easy.
5. Talking doesn't take any effort for Pat.
6. Thinking fast, he avoided the collision.
7. Waiting on tables is not hard work.
8. We saw the plow coming up the hill.
9. Finishing the last question on the test, Maria's pen ran out of ink.
10. Playing tennis is Michelle's favorite sport.

Section 10

Capitalization

There are many rules for the use of capital letters. You already know some of them well.

Here are the rules for capitalization. They are organized so that you can study them in a systematic way. They are also organized so that you can refer to them anytime during the year if you are not sure whether a word or phrase should be capitalized or not.

Proper Nouns and Adjectives

Capitalize proper nouns and proper adjectives.

A **common noun** is the name of a whole group of persons, places, or things. A **proper noun** is the name of an individual person, place, or thing. A **proper adjective** is an adjective formed from a proper noun.

Common Noun	Proper Noun	Proper Adjective
person	Elizabeth	Elizabethan
country	Spain	Spanish
city	Paris	Parisian

Proper nouns occur in great variety. The following rules with their illustrations will help you solve the capitalization problems that proper nouns present.

Names of Persons

Capitalize the names of persons and also the initials or abbreviations that stand for those names.

> **J. R. R.** Tolkien   John **R**onald **R**evel **T**olkein
> **E**lla **T.** Grasso   **E**lla **T**ambussi **G**rasso

Capitalize titles used with names of persons and also the initials or abbreviations that stand for those titles.

> **R**ev. M. R. Eaton   **P**resident Carter
> **L**t. Patricia Smith   **D**r. John J. DeBender

Do not capitalize titles used as common nouns:

> Have you seen your doctor?
> She is the company president.

Capitalize titles of people whose rank is very important, even when these titles are used without proper names.

The President of the United States

The titles *Mr., Mrs., Ms.,* and *Miss* are always capitalized.

Family Relationships

Capitalize such words as mother, father, aunt, and uncle when these words are used as names.

Note that when the noun is modified by a personal pronoun, it is not capitalized.

Hello, Mother. Is Dad home yet?
My aunt is going to visit us next week.

The Pronoun *I*

Capitalize the pronoun *I*.

Is he taller than I?

The Deity

Capitalize all words referring to the Deity, to the Holy Family, the Bible, and to religious scriptures.

God	the Lord	the Bible
Allah	the Virgin Mary	the Book of Exodus

Capitalize personal pronouns referring to the Deity.

God spoke to His prophets.

Exercises   Use capital letters correctly.

A. Number your paper 1–10. Copy the following sentences. Change small letters to capital letters wherever necessary.

1. I told my mother that i had a doctor's appointment.
2. She said, "Please ask dr. hernandez to call me."
3. The new teacher is from paris, france.
4. He is a parisian.
5. Would you tell mom i'll be a little late for dinner?
6. The first book of the bible is the book of genesis.
7. My mother asked aunt rose if tad and maria could stay for lunch.
8. Please take this message to the principal, lynn.
9. She says that ms. holchak is not in her office.
10. Some names for god are jehovah, the lord, and the almighty.

B. Follow the directions for Exercise A.

1. There are seven cities named springfield.
2. The largest is in massachusetts.
3. Our country is sometimes called a jeffersonian democracy.
4. The new student is toshio kitagawa. His sister is mieko.
5. Both of them were born in japan.
6. Which cairo do you mean?
7. Is it the one in egypt or the one in illinois?
8. Speakers were mr. s. f. paulson, mrs. j. p. perez, and ms. p. d. cardelo.
9. All of my aunts and uncles live in california.
10. It was captain sherman who gave sue and ted the booklets on bicycle safety.

Geographical Names

In a geographical name, capitalize the first letter of each word except articles and prepositions.

The article *the* appearing before a geographical name is not part of the geographical name and is therefore not capitalized.

Continents: Europe, Asia, Africa, Australia

Bodies of Water: the Pacific Ocean, Puget Sound, the Columbia River, Hudson Bay, the Straits of Magellan, Lake Superior, the English Channel, the Arabian Gulf

Land Forms: the Mississippi Delta, the Cape of Good Hope, the Mojave Desert, the Atlas Mountains, Pike's Peak, Dismal Swamp

Political Units: the Village of Oak Park, the City of Los Angeles, Commonwealth of Puerto Rico, First Congressional District, the State of Utah, Great Britain, the Azores

Public Areas: Badlands National Monument, Grant Park, Shawnee National Forest, the Battery, the Black Hills, Zion National Park

Roads and Highways: Oregon Trail, Lincoln Highway, Broad Street, 34th Avenue, Tri-State Tollway, Riverside Freeway, Drury Lane, Route 23

Directions and Sections

Capitalize names of sections of the country but not of directions of the compass.

Industrial production was high in the **N**orth.
We headed **s**outh for our vacation.
The pioneers moved **w**est over the Oregon Trail.
The first English settlements were along the **E**ast **C**oast.
The frontier moved **w**estward.
The school is **s**outhwest of our home.
The **S**outhwest is our fastest-growing region.

Capitalize proper adjectives derived from names of sections of the country. Do not capitalize adjectives derived from words indicating direction.

an **E**astern school   a **n**orth wind
a **W**estern concept   a **s**outherly course

Exercises   Using capital letters correctly.

A. Number your paper 1–10. Find the words in the following sentences that should be capitalized. Write the words after the proper number, using the necessary capital letters.

1. Many wagon trains left from independence, missouri.
2. The trail took them first to fort kearney, nebraska.
3. Then they followed the north platte river to fort laramie.
4. The pioneers crossed the rocky mountains at south pass, wyoming.
5. After they crossed the rockies, the trail split into three parts.
6. The oregon trail went to the pacific northwest.
7. The mormon trail went to salt lake city, utah.
8. A third trail crossed the great basin of nevada and utah.
9. It crossed the sierra nevada mountains at donner pass.
10. Many frontiersmen followed these trails westward.

B. Follow the directions for Exercise A.

1. The trans-canada highway crosses the entire width of canada.
2. Of the seven continents, asia and africa are the two largest.
3. Next week we elect the representative from the eighth congressional district.
4. The track championships will be held in morton township.
5. The island of capri is in the bay of naples.
6. The blue grotto is a famous tourist attraction on capri.
7. Lake baikal is the world's deepest freshwater lake.
8. The lake is in siberia, in the soviet union.
9. We had our family picnic at the lincoln park zoo.
10. Last summer, we drove along the gulf of mexico to new orleans and then north to memphis.

Names of Organizations and Institutions

Capitalize the names of organizations and institutions, including political parties, governmental bodies or agencies, schools, colleges, churches, hospitals, clubs, businesses, and abbreviations of these names.

General Motors Corporation Children's Hospital
Oakwood High School St. Mark's Church
University of Southern California **U.S.C.**

Do not capitalize such words as *school, college, church,* and *hospital* when they are not used as names:

the basketball team of our school

Names of Events, Documents, and Periods of Time

Capitalize the names of historical events, documents, and periods of time.

Battle of Hastings Treaty of Paris Age of Discovery
World War II Bill of Rights Middle Ages

Months, Days, and Holidays

Capitalize names of months, days, and holidays, but not the names of seasons.

March Labor Day summer
Friday Fourth of July Feast of the Passover

Races, Languages, Nationalities, Religions

Capitalize the names of races, languages, nationalities, and religions and adjectives derived from them.

Caucasian African Lutheranism
French Buddhism Episcopalian

School Subjects

Do not capitalize the names of school subjects, except course names followed by a number.

Algebra I   History of Civilization II
social studies   physical education

Remember that the names of languages are always capitalized.

English   Spanish
Hebrew   German

Ships, Trains, Airplanes, Automobiles

Capitalize the names of ships, trains, airplanes, and automobiles.

U.S.S. Constitution   Cutlass
Santa Fe Chief   *Spirit of St. Louis*

B.C., A.D.

Capitalize the abbreviations *B.C.* and *A.D.*

The first Olympic Games were held in 776 **B.C.**
The Norman Conquest took place in **A.D.** 1066.

Exercises   **Use capital letters correctly.**

A. Number your paper 1–10. Write the words in each sentence that should be capitalized. Use the necessary capital letters.

1. Our car was made by american motors corporation.

2. We saw a ford pinto, a chevy monza, and a ford fairmont before buying the buick skyhawk.

3. My sister is class president at pulaski high school.

4. I registered for ancient history I, algebra II, social studies, english, and music.

5. In 1898 the treaty of paris ended the spanish-american war.

6. The fourth of july is an important date in american history.

7. The declaration of independence was signed on july 4, 1776.

8. My favorite subjects are home economics, english, and physical education.

9. The first woman to fly across the atlantic ocean was Amelia Earhart.

10. In 44 b.c. Julius caesar was assassinated.

B. Follow the directions for Exercise A.

1. The island of hispaniola was discovered in a.d. 1492 by Columbus.

2. The prophet muhammad founded the religion of islam.

3. His followers are called moslems or muslims.

4. The *u.s.s. constitution* is also called *"old ironsides."*

5. The *broadway limited* runs between New York and Chicago.

6. The new head of brookston hospital is dr. margaret allen.

7. The new social studies teacher is from munich, germany.

8. the head nurse in the emergency room at st. luke's hospital is jeffrey adams.

9. The spanish, russian, french, and german clubs at hersey high school sponsored an international bazaar.

10. My sister is studying russian at u.c.l.a., and my brother is a european history major at u.s.c.

First Words

Sentences and Poetry

Capitalize the first word of every sentence and the first word in most lines of poetry.

My sister likes tennis. She is the captain of her team.

Lines of poetry:

Grow old along with me!
The best is yet to be . . .

Sometimes, especially in modern poetry, the lines of a poem do not always begin with a capital letter.

Quotations

Capitalize the first word of a direct quotation.

Ralph Waldo Emerson said, "Hitch your wagon to a star."

Do not capitalize the first word of the second part of a divided quotation unless it starts a new sentence.

"Well," he said, "what you say is quite true."
"I agree," he said. "What you say is quite true."

Letters

Capitalize the first word, words like *Sir* and *Madam*, and the name of the person addressed in the greeting of a letter.

Dear Mrs. Gomez   Dear Miss Perkins   Dear Mr. Castillo

In the complimentary close, capitalize the first word only.

Yours very truly   Sincerely yours

Outlines

Capitalize the first word of each line of an outline.

   I. Improve your handwriting.

      A. Form letters carefully.

         1. Watch *a, e, r, l,* and *t.*

Titles

Capitalize the first word and all important words in the titles of books, poems, short stories, articles, newspapers, magazines, plays, motion pictures, works of art, and musical compositions.

Articles (the words *a, an,* and *the*), conjunctions, and prepositions are not usually considered important words. However, note that an article, a conjunction, or a preposition used as the first word of a title must be capitalized.

        Book: *The Good Earth*
        Poem: "Chicago"
        Play: *The Miracle Worker*
  Magazine: *Sports Illustrated*

Exercises   **Use capital letters correctly.**

A. Number your paper 1–10. Write the words that should be capitalized. Use the correct capital letters.

    1. eleanor roosevelt said, "no one can make you feel inferior without your consent."

    2. walt whitman wrote a famous poem about lincoln entitled "o captain! my captain!"

    3. the famous humorist will rogers, who was of indian descent, said, "my forefathers didn't come over on the *mayflower,* but they met the boat."

4. I. american history
    A. the war for independence
        1. battle of bunker hill

5. "don't go," he said. "i haven't explained yet."
6. for my birthday I got a subscription to *seventeen*.
7. the morning paper is the *herald tribune*.
8. very sincerely yours,
9. "hurry up!" father said. "if we don't leave soon, we'll be late."
10. We went to see the play *fiddler on the roof*.

B. Follow the directions for Exercise A.

1. dear mrs. weiss:
2. Robert Frost wrote "the death of the hired man."

3. I. business letters
    A. correct business letter form
        1. heading

4. The recent issue of *sports illustrated* has complete coverage of all the hockey teams.

5. he would answer to "Hi!" or to any loud cry
   such as "Fry me!" or "Fritter my wig!"
   to "What-you-may-call-um!" or "What-was-his-name!"
   but especially "Thing-um-a-jig!"

6. The article "images of youth past" appeared last fall in an issue of *life* magazine.
7. Meg finally got to the airport. she asked, "has the plane left?"
8. "i'm afraid so," Janet replied. "we're too late."
9. i have always enjoyed *the wizard of oz*, but I was thoroughly entertained by the stage production of *the wiz*.
10. i think *the call of the wild* is jack london's best book.

Additional Exercises

Capitalization

A. Use capital letters correctly.

Number your paper 1–10. Find the words in the following sentences that should be capitalized. Write the words beside the proper numbers and capitalize them correctly.

1. Warren e. burger was appointed chief justice of the supreme court by president nixon on may 21, 1969.

2. My aunt theodosia has always been dad's favorite sister.

3. The reverend doctor martin luther king, Jr. received the Nobel Peace Prize in 1964.

4. Our drama class went to see carol channing in the musical *Hello, Dolly!*

5. Most people think i look like mom, but actually i have my dad's brown eyes and hair.

6. The poet hilda doolittle was known by her initials h. d.

7. Indian civilizations flourished in both peru and mexico before the arrival of the spanish.

8. Allyson would like to become a doctor.

9. Should I send the invitation to ms. anita schilling in care of mr. and mrs. albert romani?

10. Tadeusz kosciuszko, a famous polish army officer, fought on the side of the american colonists.

B. Use capital letters correctly.

Number your paper 1–10. Copy the following sentences, changing small letters to capital letters wherever necessary.

1. The gaspé peninsula in canada is part of the province of quebec.

2. My parents were delighted to see the chicago skyline as we drove south along lake shore drive.

3. Which are taller, the rocky mountains or the andes mountains?

4. In the last presidential election, the republicans won every state except the commonwealth of massachusetts and the district of columbia.

5. The isthmus of panama in central america was a likely place to build a canal.

6. At that spot, the distance between the caribbean sea on the north side and the gulf of panama on the south is only forty miles.

7. Have you noticed that people from the midwest speak differently than people from the east?

8. If you are interested in civil war history, be sure to visit vicksburg national park when you're in the south.

9. By the time we got off of that hot beach, my mouth felt like the gobi desert, the sahara desert, and death valley rolled into one.

10. Lake geneva borders switzerland on the north and france on the south.

C. Use capital letters correctly.

Number your paper 1–10. After the proper number, copy the words from each sentence that should be capitalized. Use the necessary capital letters.

1. Those three blue fords are still parked in front of rosemont baptist church.

2. So far only six students have signed up for algebra I.

3. The period from a. d. 500 to a. d. 1000 is sometimes called the dark ages.

4. The five countries involved in the six-day war were israel, egypt, syria, jordan, and iraq.

5. Next year rosemont high school will have a winter break during the second week of january.

6. We have to memorize the gettysburg address for our history assignment.

7. A big company like legrow, inc., probably has two or three doctors who work for it.

8. Most of the people in green bay, wisconsin, are catholic.

9. The gregory art museum is closed on memorial day and christmas.

10. The people of switzerland speak either french, german, or italian.

D. Use capital letters correctly.

Number your paper 1–10. Find the words in the following sentences that should be capitalized. Write the words after the proper numbers, using the necessary capital letters.

1. "there will be a quiz tomorrow," said Mr. Sims, "and it will cover Chapters 1 and 2."

2. have you ever read the poem "song of myself" by walt whitman?

3. my teacher says that *the adventures of huckleberry finn* is a more enjoyable book than either *tom sawyer* or *the prince and the pauper*.

4. I. shakespeare's plays
    A. comedies
       1. *as you like it*
       2. *much ado about nothing*

5. our school library subscribes to *newsweek, time,* and *u.s. news and world report.*

6. death, be not proud, though some have called thee
    mighty and dreadful, for thou are not so . . .

7. because I was raised in the city of chicago, I really enjoy reading the poem "chicago" by carl sandburg.

8. both sculptures, *moses* and *david,* are by michelangelo.

Section 11

Punctuation

When you read, you probably do not think much about the punctuation used. But if it were not there, you would be bothered by its absence! You might not be sure, for example, when the writer meant to end one sentence and begin another.

Punctuation marks are signals for a reader. They indicate pauses and show points of emphasis. If you want your readers to understand the exact meaning of what you write, give them the right signals by using punctuation marks correctly.

End Marks

The punctuation marks that show where sentences end are called **end marks.** They include *periods, question marks,* and *exclamation points.*

The Period

Use a period at the end of a declarative sentence.

A **declarative sentence** is a sentence that makes a statement. It is the kind of sentence you use when you want to tell something.

My brother plays the piano.

A declarative sentence is often shortened to one or two words; for example, in answering a question.

Where are you going to put this macramé planter?
Over there. (*I am going to put it over there.*)

Use a period at the end of an imperative sentence.

An **imperative sentence** is a sentence that requests or tells someone to do something.

Please close the door.

If the imperative sentence also expresses excitement or emotion, an exclamation point is used after it.

Look out!

Use a period at the end of an indirect question.

She asked us whether we liked strawberries.

An *indirect question* is the part of a statement that tells what someone asked, but that does not give the exact words of the person who asked the question.

Use a period after an abbreviation or after an initial.

Dr. Marla E. Corona   Trenton, N.J.
Rev. John L. Haeger, Jr.   2:30 P.M.

Periods are omitted in some abbreviations. If you are not sure whether an abbreviation should be written with or without periods, look up the abbreviation in your dictionary.

FM (*frequency modulation*)
UN (*United Nations*)
FBI (*Federal Bureau of Investigation*)

Use a period after each number or letter that shows a division of an outline or that precedes an item in a list.

(An Outline)   (A List)

I. Poets   1. eggs
    A. American   2. milk
       1. Robert Frost   3. butter

Use a period in numerals between dollars and cents and before a decimal.

$18.98   2.853

The Question Mark

Use a question mark at the end of an interrogative sentence.

An **interrogative sentence** is a sentence that asks a question.

Has anyone seen my dog?

The above sentence gives the exact words of the person who asked the question. It is called a *direct question*. A question mark is used only with a direct question.

Do not use a question mark with an indirect question. Instead, use a period.

An *indirect question* is the part of a statement that tells what someone asked, without giving the exact words.

Kelly asked whether anyone had seen her dog.

The Exclamation Point

Use an exclamation point at the end of an exclamatory sentence.

Tim, look out!

Use an exclamation point after an interjection or after any other exclamatory expression.

An **interjection** is a word or group of words used to express strong feeling. It may be a real word or simply a group of letters used to represent a sound. It is one of the eight parts of speech.

Hurrah!   Wow!

Exercises   Use end marks correctly.

A. Copy the following sentences, adding the necessary punctuation. Be prepared to tell what punctuation marks you used and why you used them.

1. Where did I put my new sweater
2. Wow that was quite a football game
3. What is Dr Harrigan's phone number
4. Where is Sgt Leslie's office located
5. Help I can't get this door open
6. I was supposed to meet Tom at 10:30 A M.
7. Dr James Coogan, Jr is going to talk about lifesaving
8. Mary, look out
9. Our art supplies will cost more than ten dollars, and I have only $825
10. My appointment with Dr Wagner is at 1115 A M on Friday

B. Follow the directions in Exercise A.

1. Dr Elizabeth McMinn is our school principal
2. Please send your requests to Franklin's, Ltd, P O Box 552, New York, NY
3. While in Washington, DC, where did you stay
4. One mile is equal to 16 kilometers
5. Luis asked if he could help me with my homework
6. I have two broadcast bands on my radio: AM and FM
7. UNICEF is the children's organization of the UN
8. My parents were born in Buffalo, NY
9. Rev James M Butler, Jr will be the guest speaker at the ceremonies
10. Will you mail these coupons to the Clark Company, Inc, 301 E Walton Place, Chicago, Illinois 60611

The Comma

Commas are used to separate words that do not belong together. In speaking, we can keep words apart by pausing. In writing, we must use commas.

Commas in a Series

Use a comma after every item in a series except the last.

The items in a series may be single words, or phrases, or clauses.

Words:	The flag is red, white, and blue.
Phrases:	The dog ran out the door, down the steps, and across the lawn.
Clauses:	How kangaroos run, what jumps they can take, and how they live are explained in this book.

Use commas after the adverbs *first, second, third,* and so on, when these adverbs introduce a series of parallel items.

There are three ways to get good marks: first, pay attention; second, take notes; third, study.

When two or more adjectives precede a noun, use a comma after each adjective except the last one.

They drove away in a bright, shiny, expensive sports car.

Sometimes two adjectives are used together to express a single idea made up of two closely related thoughts. Adjectives so used are not usually separated by a comma.

Our house is the little green one.
Look at the big round moon.

When you say the two sentences above, notice that you do not pause between the adjectives.

Exercises   Use commas correctly to separate items.

A. Number your paper 1–10. Copy the following sentences and add commas where necessary.

1. A strong northerly wind swept the snow against the front door.

2. That little green TR7 belongs to my sister.

3. Red white and blue bunting decorated the speaker's stand.

4. We went to the store and bought Fritos potato chips pretzels and Coke.

5. The race car skidded did a complete turn-around and blew out its right front tire.

6. At the movies, I like fresh salty buttery popcorn.

7. Strong gusty winds blew across the lake.

8. My sister can play the guitar the banjo and the mandolin.

9. In order to finish the scenery, do the following: first nail the supports together; second paint the backdrop; and third put away all unnecessary tools and paint.

10. Sue finished her homework made a telephone call and went to bed.

B. Follow the directions for Exercise A.

1. The committee discussed analyzed and accepted the proposal.

2. A fluffy tiger-striped cat was sitting on our porch swing.

3. A small rabbit scooted across our doorstep through the evergreens and under our back porch.

4. Handball racquetball and squash are similar sports.

5. Bowling tennis and jogging are my favorite activities.

6. A long sleek black limousine pulled up in front of the bank.

7. James Joan and Greg helped design the posters.

8. We need crepe paper balloons and tape to decorate the gym.

9. The speaker stated the hard clear facts.

10. The magician pulled a green scarf out of the air spread it flat on the table and pulled a pigeon out from under it.

Commas after Introductory Words, Phrases, or Clauses

Use a comma to separate an introductory word, phrase, or clause from the rest of the sentence.

Yes, I will go.
After circling twice, the airplane landed.
Although Dick needed help, he said nothing.

The comma may be omitted if there would be little pause in speaking.

At first I didn't know what to do.

Commas with Interrupters

Use commas to set off words or groups of words that interrupt the flow of thought in a sentence.

Anne, to tell the truth, was quite happy.
The report, moreover, is altogether inaccurate.

Exercises   Use commas to set off words correctly.

A. Number your paper 1–10. Copy the following sentences and add commas where necessary.

1. No I don't think the library is open on Sundays.
2. After circling the airport for an hour we finally landed.
3. Although the game was postponed until Friday we had practice every morning.
4. Yes I have finished the dishes.
5. The exam however will be given as scheduled.
6. Mrs. Cassini to tell the truth was quite pleased with our panel discussion.
7. Since the Cubs lost their last ten games they will not be in the play-offs.
8. The results of the student survey however will not be revealed until next week.
9. No the mail has not been delivered.
10. Even though we arrived early we still didn't get good seats for the basketball game.

B. Follow the directions for Exercise A.

1. After we went on the hayride we had a barbecue and played volleyball.
2. Yes the garage has been cleaned out.
3. The game consequently was postponed.
4. The latest weather report however has predicted rain for the weekend.

5. Although the heavy snow tied up most of the morning traffic most companies and businesses were open as usual.

6. Yes the intramural track meet is tomorrow.

7. Since Mardi Gras is such a celebrated occasion in New Orleans most schools there take a holiday.

8. It is doubtful however that the weather will change our plans.

9. No the garage sale isn't until next week.

10. If you look carefully at these old tintypes you will see how different dress and housing used to be.

Commas with Nouns of Direct Address

Use commas to set off nouns of direct address.

The name of someone directly spoken to is a **noun of direct address.**

> If you look, Peggy, you will see the book I mean.
> Your firefighters did well, Captain.
> Be careful, children, when you cross the street.

Commas with Appositives

Use commas to set off most appositives.

An **appositive** is a word or group of words used directly after another word to explain it.

> The speaker, a famous explorer, told about New Guinea.

An appositive phrase may have a prepositional phrase within it.

> The leader, *the person on horseback,* moved away.

Nouns used as appositives are called **nouns in apposition.** When the noun in apposition is a short name, it is not usually set off by commas.

> This is my friend Rhoda.

Commas with Quotations

Use commas to set off the explanatory words of a direct quotation.

The "explanatory words" used in giving a direct quotation are such brief statements as *Tina said, Christie answered,* or *Bill asked.*

Kate shouted, "Keep your eye on the ball!"

In the sentence above, the explanatory words come *before* the quotation. A comma is then placed after the last explanatory word.

Now look at this quotation:

"I can't find the key," said Patty.

If the explanatory words come *after* the quotation, as in the example above, place a comma within the quotation marks after the last word of the quotation.

Sometimes a quotation is separated into two parts by the explanatory words. This is often done to add variety to the sentence construction. Here is an example:

"The spacecraft," the announcer said, "has just been launched."

The sentence above is an example of a *divided quotation.* A comma is used after the last word of the first part. Another comma is used after the last explanatory word.

Do not confuse direct and indirect quotations. Indirect quotations are *not* set off from the rest of the sentence by commas.

Sylvia said that she had studied for at least an hour.

The Comma in a Compound Sentence

Use a comma before the conjunction that joins the two main clauses in a compound sentence.

Kimberly seemed to agree, and no one else objected.

In a very short compound sentence with the clauses joined by *and*, it is not necessary to use a comma if there is no turn or change in the thought. Always use a comma before *or* or *but*, since these words do change the direction of the thought.

> Pete finally arrived *and* we started off.
> Pete arrived, *but* it was too late to go anywhere.

Do not use a comma before the *and* that joins a compound subject or a compound predicate.

> Sally turned on the radio and sat down to read a magazine.

Exercises **Use commas correctly.**

A. Number your paper 1–10. Copy the following sentences, adding commas where they are needed.

1. "Cheerleading tryouts will be held tonight" began the announcement "and all students are invited to participate."
2. The team captain the player in the blue jersey is a good student.
3. I read *Roots* but I preferred the television series.
4. I enjoy reading science fiction novels but I also enjoy reading mysteries.
5. She ran down the stairs and raced down the sidewalk.
6. Ms. Leoni our new science teacher was born in Italy.
7. Sir Georg Solti the famous conductor directs the Chicago Symphony Orchestra.
8. When you are finished Kurt will you help with this project?
9. Maria finished her tennis practice and then went directly to play rehearsal.
10. John Hancock one of the signers of the Declaration of Independence was from Massachusetts.

B. Follow the directions for Exercise A.

1. The First Lady Mrs. Rosalynn Carter visited Latin America.

2. Linda showed me her present a cassette tape recorder.

3. I will wash the car but I don't have time to wax it.

4. I asked Mrs. Wright our science teacher about lasers.

5. Andrés Segovia the classical guitarist will play at Orchestra Hall in May.

6. Will you come with me or would you rather stay here?

7. Mrs. Watkins our P. E. teacher was a member of the U. S. Olympic swim team.

8. We saw the end of "The Hardy Boys" and then we watched the "ABC Movie of the Week."

9. "Please take the dog for a walk" said Dad.

10. Pam this is my brother Paul.

Commas in Dates

In dates, use a comma between the day of the month and the year.

July 4, 1776   December 7, 1787

In a sentence, a comma follows the year.

The postmark read September 10, 1978, but we didn't receive the letter until yesterday, October 2.

Commas in Locations and Addresses

Use a comma between the name of a city or town and the name of its state or country.

Miami, Florida
Munich, Germany

In writing an address as part of a sentence, use a comma after each item.

Forward our mail to 651 Sentinel Drive, Wilmette, Illinois 60091, where we will be moving next month.

Note that you do *not* place a comma between the state and the zip code.

Commas in Letter Parts

Use a comma after the salutation of a friendly letter and after the complimentary close of a friendly letter or a business letter.

Dear Tim,   Yours sincerely,

Exercises   Use commas correctly

A. Copy the following sentences. Add commas where necessary.

1. The bombing of Pearl Harbor on December 7 1941 marked the beginning of World War II.

2. On August 14 1945 Japan surrendered to the Allies.

3. The stock market crash on October 29 1929 marked the beginning of the Great Depression.

4. On August 20 1974 Nelson A. Rockefeller was nominated for the office of Vice President.

5. Send your requests to Mr. R. Joseph Laya 180 North Capitol Avenue Denver Colorado 80202.

6. The first state, Delaware, entered the Union on December 7 1787.

7. The first Transcontinental Railroad was completed on May 10 1869 in Promontory Utah.

8. In 1874 Joseph Glidden of DeKalb Illinois invented barbed wire.

9. The President of the United States lives at 1600 Pennsylvania Avenue Washington D. C. 20500.

10. George Washington was inaugurated in New York City on April 30 1789 at Federal Hall.

B. Follow the directions for Exercise A.

1. Because my parents work for the government, I have lived in Fairbanks Alaska and Madrid Spain.

2. The Lewis and Clark expedition began on May 14 1804 in St. Louis Missouri and returned there on September 23 1806.

3. John H. Glenn, Jr. became the first American to orbit the earth on February 20 1962 aboard the *Friendship* 7.

4. We ordered our uniforms from the J. C. Wood Company P. O. Box 5835 Richmond Virginia 23220.

5. The 1984 Olympics will be held in Los Angeles California.

6. The charter flight will visit Helsinki Finland and Stockholm Sweden.

7. My sister was born in Tokyo Japan on January 1 1965 and I was born in Frankfurt Germany on January 1 1968.

8. On August 26 1920 the amendment that gave women the right to vote was adopted.

9. The Great Chicago Fire of 1871 supposedly started in the barn at Mrs. O'Leary's 558 DeKoven Street Chicago Illinois.

10. Dear Jill

    Would you please send me the Harrisons' new address? I'd appreciate it.

                Your friend

                Tom

Commas with Nonrestrictive Clauses

Use commas to set off nonrestrictive clauses.

A **nonrestrictive clause** is one that merely adds an idea to the sentence. The sentence would be complete and the meaning would be definite without it.

A **restrictive clause** is one that is essential to the meaning of a sentence. If a restrictive clause is dropped out of the sentence, the meaning changes.

Nonrestrictive:	Cheryl White, whom I have known for years, will go to Purdue in the fall.
	Cheryl White will go to Purdue in the fall.
Restrictive:	Cheryl White is the only person in our school who is going to Purdue.
	Cheryl White is the only person in our school.

Restrictive clauses are often used to identify or point out the person or thing they modify. Without this identification, the meaning of the sentence would not be clear. Nonrestrictive clauses, on the other hand, add no essential meaning to the sentence.

Restrictive:	Janice is the girl *who found the money.*
	(which girl?)
Restrictive:	This is the book *that has the map.*
	(What book?)
Nonrestrictive:	Janice, *who is very alert,* found the money.
	Janice found the money.
Nonrestrictive:	This book, *which has pictures,* is my choice.
	This book is my choice.

Commas To Prevent Misreading

When no specific rule applies, but there is danger of misreading, use a comma.

Who she is, is a mystery.

Exercises   Use commas correctly.

A. Number your paper 1–10. Decide where commas should be used in the following sentences. Write the word before the comma, add the comma, then write the word after the comma. If no commas are necessary, write *Correct* after the appropriate number.

1. My grandparents who are very active people have just completed a tour of South America.

2. Our dog who recently had puppies is very protective of her litter.

3. This is the bicycle that I repaired and painted.

4. The speed limit which is strictly enforced has reduced traffic accidents.

5. This is the autobiography that I read for class.

6. Mrs. Kruse is the person who owns that flower shop.

7. Those students who are finished with the test may leave.

8. Kyle who is my best friend is moving to Japan next month.

9. The Wades who live next door are well known oceanographers.

10. The bus that I told you to take stops at that corner.

B. Follow the directions for Exercise A.

1. This camera which has many features is the best buy.

2. Ms. Larson is the teacher who coaches the volleyball team.

3. The letter you were waiting for has finally arrived.

4. Our neighbor who is an excellent gardener helped us with our rock garden.

5. The coach who anticipated a tough defense shifted her team to a zone offense.

6. This Super Suds detergent which is heavily advertised on television has had increased sales.

7. Mr. Hansen who is our club sponsor will be my English teacher next year.

8. Tomoko Pham is the only student in our school who is from Southeast Asia.

9. That is the book that has all the color photographs in it.

10. Rita Coolidge who is touring with Kris Kristofferson will be in Dallas next week.

The Semicolon

Use a semicolon to join the clauses of a compound sentence when no coordinating conjunction is used.

Dan has finished his homework; Darcy has not begun hers.

When there are many commas in the clauses of a compound sentence, separate the clauses themselves with a semicolon.

McCurdy of Illinois made the most spectacular shot of the game, a toss from mid-court; and Indiana, which had been favored to win, went down to defeat.

When there are commas within items in a series, use semicolons to separate the items.

Hartford, New Haven, and Norwich, Connecticut; Springfield, and Worcester, Massachusetts; and Pine Bridge, Mt. Kisco, and Chappaqua, New York, have all tried this experiment.

Use a semicolon before a conjunctive adverb that joins the clauses of a compound sentence.

Conjunctive adverbs commonly used are *therefore, however, hence, so, then, moreover, besides, nevertheless, yet,* and *consequently.*

It was a sunny day; however, it was quite cool.

The Colon

Use a colon after the greeting of a business letter.

Dear Sir or Madam: Ladies and Gentlemen:

Use a colon between numerals indicating hours and minutes.

10:00 P.M.

Use a colon to introduce a list of items.

> If you are trying out for the team, bring the following things: a pair of gym shoes, your P.E. uniform, and your consent form.

If there would be no pause in speaking, no colon is used before the list of items.

> If you are trying out for the team, bring a pair of gym shoes, your P.E. uniform, and your consent form.

Exercises   **Use semicolons and colons correctly.**

A. Copy the word before and after each missing punctuation mark and add the correct punctuation mark.

1. Jon prepared dinner Paula set the table.

2. Grinning broadly, Lee crossed the finish line 10 feet ahead of the others however, the grin faded when the judges told her she had been disqualified.

3. San Francisco, Los Angeles, and Oakland, California Dallas and Houston, Texas and New York and Buffalo, New York, have professional teams.

4. It was a clear day moreover, it was perfect for swimming.

5. Allen, wash the car Jenny, clean up the yard Joan, take the dog for a walk.

6. New animals in the collection include a cheetah, an okapi, and a harpy eagle from Africa a tiger, two peacocks, and a rhinoceros from India a snow leopard from Tibet and two caribou, a Kodiak bear, and an arctic fox from Alaska.

7. Bring three things to class tomorrow your text, paper, and a blue or black pen.

8. You will need to meet me between 830 and 845 A.M.

9. Dear Madam

   This letter will confirm your reservation.

10. It was a cold autumn day however, it was quite sunny.

B. Follow the directions for Exercise A.

1. Please stop at the store and bring these items home a gallon of milk, a can of tomatoes, and a box of crackers.

2. Tracy was reading a mystery Sandy was hooking a rug.

3. I know that there is not much time nevertheless, the work must be finished by 530.

4. Mother's plane arrives at 655 P.M. Dad's will land at 715 P.M.

5. Jim studied hard for the test yet he thought it was one of the hardest ones he'd ever taken.

6. The Pep Club will handle ticket sales the cheerleaders will help with the ushering.

7. Our bus leaves at 715 A.M. my sister's bus doesn't leave until 830 A.M.

8. The snow was blinding however, the school bus arrived on time at 815 A.M.

9. The running back made a spectacular drive to the goal, a 47-yard run and the defense, which couldn't get organized, was stunned.

10. Bring these items to sewing class on Monday tracing paper, your pattern, thread, and pins.

The Hyphen

Use a hyphen if a syllable of a word must be carried over from one line to the next.

> In the library you will find several authorita-
> tive books on solar energy.

Only words of two or more syllables can be divided at the end of a line. Never divide words of one syllable, such as *height* or *worse*.

A single letter must not be left at the end of a line. For example, this division would be wrong: *a-waken*. A single letter must not appear at the beginning of a line, either. It would be wrong to divide *sanitary* like this: *sanitar-y*.

Use a hyphen in compound numbers from twenty-one through ninety-nine

twenty-three cents   forty-two students

Use a hyphen in fractions used as modifiers.

We won a two-thirds majority.

Use a hyphen or hyphens in such compound nouns as great-aunt and commander-in-chief.

Use a hyphen or hyphens between words that make up a compound adjective used before a noun.

This is an up-to-date edition.
But: This edition is up to date.

Exercise   Use hyphens correctly.

Number your paper 1–15. After the proper numbers, write the words that should be hyphenated. Add the necessary hyphens. Use your dictionary if you need to.

1. We received the store's new, up to date catalog.
2. In ten years I will be twenty three years old.
3. We saw that the lawn was half cut.
4. One sixth of the students voted for Pam.
5. Ninety three students in all voted in the election.
6. Maurita won the election by a three fourths majority.
7. You must write out the amount of the check:
one hundred twenty three dollars and fifty six cents.
8. Our great grandmother celebrated her ninety fifth birthday.

9. The postage for this package is sixty two cents.

10. About sixty eight percent of the residents voted in the special election.

11. When were your great grandparents born?

12. The man had a well to do look about him.

13. Thirty two students were chosen to go to the speech contest.

14. Chester A. Arthur was the twenty first President.

15. The President of the United States is the Commander in Chief of the Armed Forces.

The Apostrophe

One of the most frequent uses of the apostrophe is its use in forming the possessive of nouns. Before you form the possessive of a noun, be sure to notice whether the noun is singular or plural.

To form the possessive of a singular noun, add an apostrophe and an s.

girl + 's = girl's   man + 's = man's
boy + 's = boy's   Ross + 's = Ross's

When a singular noun of more than one syllable ends in s, the possessive may be formed by adding only the apostrophe.

the waitress' apron   Dickens' novels
the hostess' dress   the witness' testimony

To form the possessive of a plural noun that does not end in s, add an apostrophe and an s.

men's   women's

To form the possessive of a plural noun that ends in s, add only an apostrophe.

drivers + ' = drivers'   pilots + ' = pilots'

Use an apostrophe and an *s* to form the possessive of indefinite pronouns.

someone + 's = someone's   anybody + 's = anybody's

Never use an apostrophe in a possessive pronoun.

ours   yours

Use an apostrophe in a contraction.

In a contraction, the apostrophe simply replaces one or more omitted letters.

he's = he is	aren't = are not	I'm = I am
it's = it is	isn't = is not	I've = I have
won't = will not	don't = do not	we've = we have

Use an apostrophe to show the omission of numbers in a date.

the class of '80 (the class of 1980)

Use an apostrophe and *s* to form the plurals of letters, figures, and words used as words.

two m's   four 6's   and's and but's

Exercises   Use apostrophes correctly.

A. Copy these sentences, inserting apostrophes where they are needed.

1. Weve heard that there wont be an assembly until next week.

2. Beatrix Potters most famous work is *Peter Rabbit*.

3. Her writings and illustrations are well known in childrens literature.

4. Billie Holidays life and music were portrayed in the movie *The Lady Sings the Blues*.

5. Diana Rosss performance as the jazz musician earned her an Oscar nomination.

6. Soichiro Hondas company has been producing motorcycles and cars in Japan since the 1940s.

7. Ive always liked the silent movies of Mary Pickford and Charlie Chaplin.

8. All of the teachers meetings are held in the library.

9. Babe Didrikson Zahariass autobiography reveals her intense love for athletics and her zest for life.

10. *The Miracle Worker* is a play about Helen Kellers childhood and Annie Sullivans efforts to help the blind and deaf Helen.

B. Follow the directions for Exercise A.

1. The *1s* and the *7s* in this ledger are difficult to distinguish.

2. The graduating classes of 79 and 80 are buying a new digital scoreboard.

3. Although she was the first woman to go into space, Valentina Tereshkovas name is not well known.

4. Weve heard Beverly Sillss performance at the opera.

5. Someones moped is parked in the Burtons driveway.

6. Isnt the girls gymnastics meet on Saturday?

7. Clara Bartons dedication in a volunteer nurse corps led to her founding of the American Red Cross.

8. S. E. Hintons novel, *That Was Then, This Is Now,* is one of the best books weve read this year.

9. Jennys sister and Paulas brother are both interns at St. Marys Hospital.

10. Nurses training programs are extensive and demanding.

Quotation Marks

Quotation marks tell your reader that you are quoting directly the exact spoken or written words of another person.

Use quotation marks at the beginning and at the end of a direct quotation.

Donna said, "My cat's eyes shine in the dark."

Quotation marks are *not* used with indirect quotations:

Donna says that her cat's eyes shine in the dark.

Sometimes a direct quotation is broken into two or more parts by explanatory words. In such a case, each part of the quotation is enclosed in quotation marks.

"Do you think," Bill asked, "that you could help me with the dishes?"

The second part of a divided quotation starts with a small letter, as in the example above, unless it begins a new sentence or unless it is a proper noun.

"We got drenched," said Bob. "We had no umbrellas."

The first part of a divided quotation is followed by a comma that is placed *inside* the quotation marks.

"Before you leave," said Mrs. Lazar, "I want to talk to you."

Explanatory words in a divided quotation are followed by either a comma or a period *outside* the quotation marks. A comma is used after the explanatory words if the second part of the quotation does not begin a new sentence. A period is used after the explanatory words if the second part of the quotation is a new sentence.

"When you arrive," said Carol, "ring the doorbell."
"I can't go," said Janet. "I have to study."

Explanatory words at the beginning of a sentence are followed by a comma *outside* the quotation marks. The period at the end of the sentence is placed *inside* the quotation marks.

Mother said, "There is someone to see you."

Explanatory words at the end of a sentence are followed by a period. The quoted words at the beginning of the sentence are followed by a comma *inside* the quotation marks.

"There is someone to see you," Mother said.

Place question marks and exclamation points inside quotation marks if they belong to the quotation itself, but outside if they do not belong to the quotation.

Dad asked, "Has Mike closed the garage doors?"
Did Mother say, "Be home by five o'clock"?
"Look out!" Terry shouted.

You may wonder how to use quotation marks when you are quoting *two or more sentences of a single speaker.* Notice how the following quotation is punctuated.

"Is the club going to meet tomorrow?" asked Sue. "I wasn't sure whether we had decided to meet tomorrow or the next day. We have important things to discuss."

Only one set of quotation marks would be needed if the example read as follows:

Sue asked, "Is the club going to meet tomorrow? I wasn't sure whether we had decided to meet tomorrow or the next day. We have important things to discuss."

When a quotation is long, it may consist of two or more paragraphs. In such a case, open each of the paragraphs with a quotation mark, but do not use an end quotation mark until the whole speech is finished.

"There are many ways in which every individual can conserve energy on a daily basis," began the speaker.
"For example, turning off lights, radios, stereos, or televisions when we're really not using them saves a lot of electrical power.
"Being conscientious about our means of travel is beneficial to energy conservation, too. Do we unnecessarily travel by car

when we could walk, cycle, or use public transportation? All of these considerations seem minor, but if *everyone* made an effort to conserve a little energy every day, we'd all benefit enormously."

When you are writing *dialogue* (conversation), begin each speaker's part with a new paragraph, even if the speeches are quite short.

> "It's Saturday again, and here we all are," said Larry.
> "Yes, it's Saturday all day today," Ted joked.
> "It's a wonderful day!" said Anne, happily.

With a quotation *inside another quotation*, single quotation marks are used. Here is an example:

> "It was Patrick Henry," declared Liz, "who said, 'Give me liberty or give me death!'"

Notice that the whole quotation is enclosed in quotation marks. The quotation within the quotation is enclosed in single quotation marks. A comma precedes the single quotation marks at the opening of the inner quotation. Notice how the quotation marks (' ") come together at the end of the sentence.

Exercises   Use quotation marks correctly.

A. Copy the following sentences. Add the necessary quotation marks and other punctuation marks. Use capital letters where necessary.

1. Have the committee members come yet asked Molly they are supposed to set up the tables and chairs

2. It was Martin Luther King, Jr. reported Tanya who said Injustice anywhere is a threat to justice everywhere.

3. Would you mind asked Cindy if I borrowed your bicycle

4. Didn't the teacher say we'll meet in the gym at 10:30

5. Andrea Sally said may I borrow your camera this weekend

6. Our history teacher told us John Paul Jones is supposed to have said I have not yet begun to fight

7. Kristen inquired was it Amelia Earhart who said Courage is the price that life exacts for granting peace

8. Bill kept saying It's just one of those things said Nancy.

9. In his inaugural address said Sherry John Kennedy stated: And so, my fellow Americans, ask not what your country can do for you; ask what you can do for your country

10. Will you organize the committee asked Sara and order the decorations

B. Follow the directions for Exercise A.

1. In her autobiography said Anne Eleanor Roosevelt wrote Life was meant to be lived, and curiosity must be kept alive. One must never, for whatever reason, turn his back on life

2. Isn't it getting too late Roger asked for us to start making plans for an all-school play

3. In what ways have you, as an individual, conserved energy began our guest speaker

4. There's the doorbell said Uncle Thomas will you answer it, Ramon

5. That's the game yelled the announcer The Yanks have won the Series

6. There's someone to see you my sister said and it looks as if he's bringing back the jacket you lost

7. Is it Burger King or McDonald's whose motto is You deserve a break today asked Debbie

8. Bill said I will drive you to school explained Peg.

9. Joan, have you seen that movie yet asked Dan

10. I never heard of such a thing said my mother quietly are you sure that is what he said

Using Quotation Marks for Titles

Use quotation marks to enclose chapter titles, titles of magazine articles, titles of short stories, essays, or single poems, titles of television and radio programs, and titles of songs or short pieces of music.

Chapter title:	Chapter 3, "Americans in London"
Magazine article:	"Images of Youth Past"
Short story:	"The Lottery"
Essay:	"My First Article"
Poem:	"The Raven"
Television Program:	"Happy Days"
Song:	"The Star-Spangled Banner"

When you write the titles of whole books or of plays, magazines, newspapers, works of art, long musical compositions, and motion pictures, do not use quotation marks. Instead, underline the titles, like this: <u>Light in the Forest</u>. Such titles should be underlined when you are writing in longhand or when you are typing. Use a single underlining, not a double one. Written or typed words that are underlined are set in a special style of type in printing. This style of type used is called *italics*.

Exercises   Use quotation marks and underlining correctly.

A. Number your paper 1–10. Copy the following sentences, adding quotation marks around titles or underscoring titles where necessary.

1. I liked the story The Monkey's Paw.

2. For my poetry assignment, I read Macavity: The Mystery Cat.

3. Read the first chapter, Discovery in the New World, for tomorrow.

4. The television program Family deals with problems and pleasures of everyday life.

5. Some of James Thurber's stories are The Very Proper Gander, The Shrike and the Chipmunks, and The Owl Who Was God.

6. Our band played the theme from Rocky and the theme from Star Wars.

7. The Charlie Chaplin movie The Gold Rush and Harold Lloyd's film Safety Last are two well known silent comedies.

8. Did you see the movie One on One?

9. Read Chapter 2, How We Came to the River.

10. The Love Bug is a movie about a Volkswagen.

B. Follow the directions for Exercise A.

1. God Save the Queen and America have the same melody.

2. Two of Jack's favorite programs are Welcome Back, Kotter and M*A*S*H.

3. We read the novel The Call of the Wild and the short story Brown Wolf by Jack London.

4. Adjö Means Good-Bye by Carrie A. Young is the story of a friendship.

5. My essay entitled Youth Today won an honorable mention in the poetry and prose contest.

6. One Flew over the Cuckoo's Nest won the Academy Award for the best picture in 1976.

7. Old Man River is a song from the musical Showboat.

8. Last week's editorial was entitled The Mess in City Government—What Are You Doing about It?

9. Barry Manilow, who has recorded such songs as I Write the Songs and Mandy, has also written many popular advertising slogans and jingles.

10. My favorite poem is The Revolt of the Machines by Stephen Vincent Benét.

Additional Exercises

Punctuation

A. Use end marks correctly.

Copy the following sentences, adding the necessary punctuation.

1. The order was issued by Capt Thomas E Conklin
2. Marty watch out
3. Tomorrow night Dr Linda Surprenant and Mr Mark Leopold will lecture on law enforcement
4. Our tour of the new FBI Building in Washington, D C begins at 8:00 A M sharp
5. Did you know that Prof Stevens is teaching in St. Louis
6. Wow That relay race was exciting
7. Rev Martin T McDaniel will speak at the lecture hall at 9:00 P M
8. Marcia's report for U S history is on the subject of NATO
9. Be careful There's broken glass in that bag
10. Mr and Mrs Barrett will chaperone the canoe trip

B. Use commas correctly.

Number your paper 1–10. Copy the following sentences. Add commas where necessary.

1. If I know David, he would beg borrow or even work to go on that camping trip.
2. That long sleek silver Jaguar belongs to Dr. Weston.
3. Leaves and branches were strewn all over the front yard the driveway and the flower bed.

4. While searching the ground for clues, the detectives discovered a thin razor-sharp knife.

5. A feisty mischievous poodle dashed across the newly seeded lawn.

6. Are you sure that only Ginny Pat and Terry need rides?

7. I washed the car waxed it and polished all of the chrome.

8. To get to the ice rink, go two blocks north turn right and park in the junior high school lot.

9. If you want to conserve gasoline, do the following: first start and stop your car gradually; second drive at a steady speed; third don't keep the engine running unnecessarily.

10. While in New Orleans, we visited the French Quarter rode down the Mississippi on a riverboat and heard many jazz bands perform.

C. Use commas correctly.

Number your paper 1–10. Copy the following sentences and add commas where necessary.

1. Yes I've read several Agatha Christie mysteries.

2. After the photographs have been developed we can choose one for the newspaper.

3. Gary to tell the truth was quite satisfied with the test results.

4. The results of the election however will not be posted until tomorrow morning.

5. No the test will not be given until Monday.

6. Although the game had to be postponed the dance went on as planned.

7. The office fire was consequently a setback for the business.

8. Your decision moreover will affect our plans.

9. After running fifteen laps around the gym the team practiced its defensive plays.

10. Yes the wrestling meet will be held at the high school.

D. Use commas correctly.

Number your paper 1–10. Copy the following sentences, adding commas where they are needed.

1. Bruce Jenner the Olympic decathlon champion was the guest speaker at our school.

2. If you look closely into the microscope Barb you will see thousands of living organisms.

3. Margaret Hillis the famous conductor directed the symphony at Carnegie Hall.

4. "Weather patterns are changing" explained Mrs. Hammill "and no one is quite sure why."

5. Maria Tallchief and Martha Graham ladies famous in the world of dance have performed all over the world.

6. Severe drought the worst in twenty years hit the Great Plains last summer.

7. Joyce would you please start a fire in the fireplace?

8. Los Angeles has been chosen to be the host city for the 1984 Olympics and the city is already making plans for the games.

9. Curling a sport played on ice with brooms is a rigorous game.

10. Running and swimming are physically demanding activities but they are the top two sports for staying in shape.

E. Use commas correctly.

Copy the following sentences. Add commas where necessary.

1. Please have the package sent to Ms. Kathy Murphy 2439 North Granville Avenue Marion Ohio 43302

2. All letters must be postmarked by January 1 1979 to be considered.

3. Dear Mrs. Brannstrom

Thank you for the birthday gift. It was greatly appreciated.

Yours sincerely

Michael Flynn

4. We visited Bellingrath Gardens in Theodore Alabama and the capitol buildings in Jackson Mississippi while vacationing last summer.

5. The Omni International Hotel in Atlanta Georgia has a huge indoor ice rink six movie theaters and countless shops and restaurants.

6. My father was born on February 6 1929 in Duluth Minnesota and I was born on February 6 1951 in Evanston Illinois.

7. The Superdome in New Orleans Louisiana and the Astrodome in Houston Texas are phenomenal structures.

8. When you say "Kansas City" do you mean Kansas City Missouri or Kansas City Kansas?

9. On July 4 1876 celebrations for our nation's one hundredth birthday were held in Philadelphia Pennsylvania.

10. Ray Kroc opened his first McDonald's restaurant on April 15 1955 in Des Plaines Illinois.

F. Use commas correctly.

Number your paper 1–10. Decide where commas should be used in the following sentences. Write the word before the comma, add the comma, and then write the word after the comma. If no comma is necessary, write *Correct* after the appropriate number.

1. Whatever you do do well.

2. Janice and Laura are the ones who started the ski club.

3. This magazine which has beautiful color photos is one of my favorites.

4. Laura Eaton who has been my friend for years has moved to Arizona.

5. Franklin Delano Roosevelt was the only American President who was elected to four straight terms in office.

6. Before eating my goldfish darts rapidly around its bowl.

7. After we ate the horses had to be cared for.

8. Paul's camera which has a telephoto lens is ideal for sports pictures.

9. While moving our family stayed at a motel.

10. Mrs. Hogan is the teacher who sponsors the German Club.

G. Use semicolons and colons correctly.

Copy the word before and after each missing punctuation mark and add the correct punctuation mark.

1. Jack passed the history test I failed it.

2. The guidebook suggested buying these items leather from Barcelona, Spain, or Florence, Italy wool from London, England, or Edinburgh, Scotland and crystal from Waterford, Ireland, or Stockholm, Sweden.

3. When he finally decided to buy Mrs. Daniels' old car, Ted was happy however, he was miserable when the transmission fell apart three months later.

4. The concert tickets went on sale at 900 A.M. by 945 A.M. they were all sold.

5. Dear Sir

Enclosed you will find your refund check for nine dollars.

6. Keith cleaned out the garage I painted the storm windows.

7. To make the punch, you will need the following ingredients lime sherbet, lemon juice, and ginger ale.

8. At 830 A.M. the following students are to report to the gym Doug Smith, Beth Schleker, and Lynn Kimball.

9. Please bring these items to the testing room two #2 pencils, an eraser, and a spiral notebook.

10. At 730 A.M. Mary jumped out of bed and started getting dressed then she remembered that it was Saturday.

H. Use hyphens correctly.

Copy the following sentences. Add hyphens wherever they are needed.

1. Ninety two is the best golf score Julie has ever shot.

2. Mr. Perez's daughter in law is an up and coming politician.

3. Jake's still life paintings are much better than his portraits.

4. The save the trees resolution passed the City Council with a three fifths vote of approval.

5. Last week Louis saw an accident involving twenty two vehicles.

6. Gina's great great grandfather founded the town of Chenoa.

7. Kelly's Lake, once a quiet, out of the way resort, is now a dirty, evil smelling swamp.

8. Eighty eight children applied to the camp; once forty one were accepted.

9. My great aunt and my great grandmother are both ninety one years old.

10. Eighty five percent of the student population participated in the Toys-for-Tots campaign.

I. Use apostrophes correctly.

Number your paper 1–10. Copy the following sentences. Add apostrophes where they are needed.

1. The head coachs decision to have two extra practices was helpful.

2. The actresss jeweled costume looked as if it weighed at least fifty pounds.

3. I dont think that the art supplies we ordered will be enough.

4. Scott wondered if a stewardesss salary is as high as a nurses.

5. The *ms* and *ns* in this note look alike.

6. Its supposed to snow this weekend, so well probably be able to go skiing.

7. Dont you think it would have been fun to grow up during the 50s?

8. The girls swimming meet and the boys basketball game are on the same day.

9. Since the municipal parks tennis courts were being used, Sandy and Lisa played on the high school courts.

10. The junior high schools choir and orchestra, and the high schools freshmen chorale, will perform at the new shopping mall.

J. Use quotation marks correctly.

Number your paper 1–10. Copy the following sentences. Add the necessary quotation marks and other punctuation marks. Use capital letters where necessary.

1. Will the student council sponsor the car wash asked our principal or should another club be responsible

2. If we win tonight said Coach Strand we'll definitely play in the holiday tournament

3. I think it was Ben Franklin replied David who said A penny saved is a penny earned

4. Who said The test is really easy asked Pat

5. I wonder said Wendy if anyone wants to go to the art fair.

6. Trisha asked was it Tolstoi who wrote If you want to be happy, be

7. Juanita inquired What time is play rehearsal tomorrow

8. Yolanda said It was Mark Twain who wrote Always do right. This will gratify some people, and astonish the rest

9. Did you see the movie with Katherine Hepburn and John Wayne asked Debbie It was on television last night

10. Mr. Pierce said Do the first eight questions said Nancy he didn't say anything about the last two

K. Use quotation marks and underlining correctly.

Number your paper 1–10. Copy the following sentences, adding quotation marks around titles or underlining titles where necessary.

1. The movie Gone with the Wind appeared on television for the first time in 1976.

2. Many adults enjoy watching Sesame Street as much as their children do.

3. The prize-winning student essay was entitled The Future Belongs to Me.

4. Our class read two of Poe's short stories: The Tell-Tale Heart and Murders in the Rue Morgue.

5. Have you ever read the poem Paul Revere's Ride by Longfellow?

6. Eve Merriam's two poems Thumbprint and Sometimes are two of my favorites.

7. The first chapter of David Copperfield is called I Am Born.

8. The March issue of National Geographic has an interesting article about the Sahara entitled Caravaning Through the Desert.

9. My Fair Lady is based on a play called Pygmalion.

10. The television program Little House on the Prairie is based on a novel by Laura Ingalls Wilder.

Section 12

Spelling

It is important for you to have good spelling skills. You will use these skills when you write friendly and business letters. You will use them when you write reports on all subjects at school. You will use them when you flll out job applications. If you care what others think of you, you will need to be able to spell words correctly.

There is no simple way to teach you how to spell. However, there are several methods you can use to attack your spelling problems. These methods are discussed in this chapter.

How To Become a Better Speller

1. Find out what your personal spelling demons are and conquer them. Go over your old composition papers and make a list of the words you misspelled on them. Keep this list and master the words on it.

2. Pronounce words carefully. It may be that you misspell words because you don't pronounce them carefully. For example, if you write *probly* for *probably*, you are no doubt mispronouncing the word.

3. Get into the habit of seeing the letters in a word. Many people have never really looked at the word *similar*. Otherwise, why do they write it *similiar?*

Take a good look at new words, or difficult words. You'll remember them better. Copy the correct spelling several times.

4. Think up a memory device for difficult words. Here are some devices that have worked for other people. They may help you, either to spell these words or to make up your own memory devices.

> ac**q**uaint (*cq*) To get ac**q**uainted, I will *seek* you.
> princi**pal** (*pal*) The princi**pal** is my *pal*.
> princi**ple** (*ple*) Follow this princi**ple,** please.
> bus**i**ness (*i*) I was involved in big bus**i**ness.

5. Proofread everything you write. In order to learn how to spell, you must learn to examine critically everything you write.

To proofread a piece of writing, you must read it slowly, word for word. Otherwise, your eyes may play tricks on you and let you skip over misspelled words.

6. Learn the few important spelling rules given in this chapter.

How To Master the Spelling of Particular Words

1. Look at the word and say it to yourself. Be sure you pronounce it correctly. If it has more than one syllable, say it again, one syllable at a time. Look at each syllable as you say it.

2. Look at the letters and say each one. If the word has more than one syllable, divide the word into syllables when you say the letters.

3. Write the word without looking at your book or list.

4. Now look at your book or list and see whether you spelled the word correctly. If you did, write it again and compare it with the correct form again. Do this once more.

5. If you made a mistake, note exactly what it was. Then repeat 3 and 4 above until you have written the word correctly three times.

Rules for Spelling

The Final silent *e*

When a suffix beginning with a vowel is added to a word ending in a silent *e*, the *e* is usually dropped.

create + ion = creation   grieve + ing = grieving
graze + ing = grazing   relate + ive = relative
fame + ous = famous   continue + ing = continuing

When a suffix beginning with a consonant is added to a word ending in a silent e, the e is usually retained.

spite + ful = spiteful	taste + ful = tasteful
state + ment = statement	move + ment = movement
voice + less = voiceless	wide + ly = widely

The following words are exceptions:

truly   argument   judgment   ninth   wholly

Words Ending in y

When a suffix is added to a word ending in y preceded by a consonant, the y is usually changed to i.

crazy + ly = crazily	puppy + s = puppies
seventy + eth = seventieth	silly + ness = silliness
hilly + est = hilliest	marry + age = marriage

Note the following exception: When -ing is added, the y does not change:

scurry + ing = scurrying	carry + ing = carrying
ready + ing = readying	worry + ing = worrying

When a suffix is added to a word ending in y preceded by a vowel, the y usually does not change.

employ + ed = employed	stay + ing = staying
play + er = player	relay + ing = relaying

Exercises   Words and their suffixes.

A. Find the misspelled words in these sentences and spell them correctly.

1. Who is driveing us home today?
2. After writeing the letter, I hurryed to mail it.
3. Let's end the arguement before leaving.
4. Ice skating must be done gracefully.
5. My homework was done sloppyly and hastily.

6. That's the sillyest program I've ever seen.
7. You had me almost believeing your story!
8. Grandpa remembers horse and carryage days.
9. The shiny new car is as noisey as our old rattletrap.
10. Have you truly considered the judgement?

B. Add the suffixes as shown and write the new word.

1. write + ing
2. amaze + ment
3. care + ful
4. dirty + er
5. happy + ly
6. stay + ing
7. spray + er
8. relate + ion
9. hurry + ing
10. glory + ous
11. pray + er
12. employ + er
13. lazy + est
14. shiny + ness
15. enjoy + ment
16. skinny + er
17. mystery + ous
18. thirty + eth
19. bounty + ful
20. sleepy + er

The Addition of Prefixes

When a prefix is added to a word, the spelling of the word remains the same.

re + elect = reelect
mis + spell = misspell
im + moderate = immoderate
il + legible = illegible
mis + direct = misdirect
re + enter = reenter
dis + satisfy = dissatisfy
ir + regular = irregular

The Suffixes -*ness* and -*ly*

When the suffix -*ly* is added to a word ending in *l*, both *l*'s are retained. When -*ness* is added to a word ending in *n*, both *n*'s are retained.

normal + ly = normally
real + ly = really
open + ness = openness
thin + ness = thinness

Words with prefixes and suffixes.

Find the misspelled words in these sentences and spell them correctly.

1. The cast imobilized my leg.
2. Our garden is carefuly tended.
3. An ireplaceable vase was broken.
4. The uneveness of the road is annoying.
5. We are learning about iregular verbs in French class.
6. The teacher remphasized the point.
7. I have spent money unecessarily.
8. That was an ilegitimate move.
9. The mispelling was totaly unnecessary.
10. That painting is beautifuly framed.

Words with the "Seed" Sound

Only one English word ends in *sede: supersede.*
Three words end in *ceed: exceed, proceed, succeed.*
All other words ending in the sound of *seed* are spelled *cede:*

    concede   precede   recede   secede

Words with *ie* and *ei*

When the sound is long e ($\bar{e}$), the word is spelled *ie* except after *c.*

I Before E

relieve	grieve	field	pierce
belief	piece	pier	reprieve

Except After C

conceit	conceive	perceive	
ceiling	receive	receipt	deceive

The following words are exceptions:

either   weird   species
neither seize   leisure

**Exercise   Words with the "Seed" Sound and
Words with _ie_ and _ei_**

Find the misspelled words in these sentences and spell
them correctly.

1. When was Louisiana ceeded to the United States?
2. Hercules' sheild was made of gold.
3. There's one peice of pecan pie left.
4. Nixon preseeded Carter as president.
5. Will aspirin releive this headache?
6. The town was siezed after a fierce battle.
7. The clerk proceded to write a receipt.
8. My leisure hours excede my work hours.
9. The paint on the cieling is chipped.
10. I babysit for my neice every weekend.

Doubling the Final Consonant

**Words of one syllable, ending in one consonant preceded
by one vowel, double the final consonant before adding a
suffix beginning with a vowel.**

1. Words of one syllable ending in one consonant:

near   treat   loot   feel

The rule does not apply to these one-syllable words because
two vowels precede the final consonant.

2. Words of one syllable ending in one consonant preceded
by one vowel:

slim   grab   dig   drug

These words are the kind to which the rule applies.

These words double the final consonant if the suffix begins with a vowel.

grab + ing = grabbing   drug + ist = druggist
dig + er = digger   slim + est = slimmest

3. The final consonant is doubled in words of more than one syllable:

When they end in one consonant preceded by one vowel.
When they are accented on the last syllable.

re·gret′   per·mit′   de·ter′

The same syllable is accented in the new word formed by adding the suffix:

re·gret′ + ed = re·gret′ted
per·mit′ + ing = per·mit′ting
de·ter′ + ence = de·ter′rence

If the newly formed word is accented on a different syllable, the final consonant is not doubled.

re·fer′ + ence = ref′er·ence
pre·fer′ + ence = pref′er·ence

Exercise   Doubling the Final Consonant

Add the suffixes as shown and write the new word. Indicate with an accent mark (′) where each word is accented.

1. plug + ing   11. sleep + ing
2. prefer + ing   12. swim + er
3. control + er   13. hot + est
4. prefer + ence   14. trim + ed
5. big + est   15. fat + est
6. remit + ance   16. heat + ing
7. slim + er   17. scoot + er
8. tug + ing   18. motor + ist
9. permit + ing   19. slug + er
10. treat + ing   20. drag + ing

Additional Exercises

Spelling

A. The final silent e and words ending in y.

Add the suffixes as shown and write the new word.

1. enjoy + able
2. ice + y
3. carry + ing
4. early + est
5. waste + ful
6. believe + able
7. hurry + ed
8. continue + ing
9. employ + er
10. create + ing

B. The addition of prefixes.

Find the misspelled words in these sentences and spell them correctly.

1. It's unecessary to change your plans.
2. If you mispell more than two words, you must retake the test.
3. Sharon was dissappointed with the test results.
4. All traffic was imobile after the heavy snowfall.
5. Several cars were parked ilegally in the loading zone.

C. The suffixes -ness and -ly.

Find the misspelled words in these sentences and spell them correctly.

1. Jill's openess made her an easy person to talk to.
2. I realy don't believe Mike actualy said that!
3. The van was illegaly parked by the fire hydrant.

4. The uneveness of this book's pages is hardly acceptable.

5. Eventualy the rain stopped.

D. The "seed" sound; words with *ie* and *ei*.

Find the misspelled words in these sentences and write them correctly.

1. Mrs. Barnett succeded Mr. Smyth as corporate treasurer.

2. The janitor believed that the cieling needed to be repainted.

3. After we receive all of the reciepts, we will procede with payment.

4. All cars must yeild to the workmen and not excede the limit of 40 M.P.H.

5. The Johnsons' neice and nephew were here for a breif visit.

E. Doubling the final consonant.

Add the suffixes as shown and write the new word.

1. drop + ed
2. run + ing
3. put + ing
4. slug + er
5. begin + ing
6. refer + ing
7. run + er
8. plant + ing
9. big + est
10. control + ing

Index

Abbreviations
  in *B.C.* and *A.C.*, 216
  in names of persons, 210
  periods in, 227
  for time, 227
Abridged dictionaries, 185-186
Action verbs, 74, 152
Addressing letters, 142-143
Adjective clauses, 170-172
Adjective phrases, 140-141
Adjectives
  adverbs modify, 113
  in comparisons, 121-123
  defined, 110, 116
  predicate, 110, 118
  pronouns as, 110
  proper, 110
  in a series, 229
Adverb clauses, 168-170
Adverb phrases, 140-141
Adverbs
  comparison of, 125-126
  defined, 113, 116
  forming, 114
  in a series, 230
  used with verbs, 113
Agreement, in subjects and
  verbs, 185-191
Almanacs, 191
Antecedents of pronouns, 65
Antonyms, 13
Apostrophe, 245-246
Articles, 120
  definite, 120
  indefinite, 120
Atlases, 191
Author card, 179-180

Biographical references, 192
Body of business letters, 133
Body of compositions, 84,
  98-101
Body of friendly letters, 121
Bread-and-butter notes, 126
Business letters, 130-139
  addressing of, 143
  body of, 133
  closing of, 133
  folding of, 141
  forms for, 130
    block, 130, 131
    modified block, 130, 132
  heading of, 133
  inside address in, 133
  parts of, 133-134
  salutation of, 133
  signature on, 134
  types of, 134-139

Capitalization, 209-219
  of abbreviations, 216
  A.D., *B.C.*, 216
  of the Deity, 211
  of documents, 215
  of events, 215
  in direct quotation, 248
  of family relationships used as
    names, 211
  of geographical names and
    locations, 212-213
  of *I*, 211
  of initials, 210-215
  of languages, 215
  in letters, 218
  of months, days, and

holidays, 215
of names and abbreviations of
  names, 210
of nationalities, 215
of organizations and
  institutions, 215
in outlines, 219
of periods in time, 215
in poetry, 218
in proper adjectives, 210
of proper nouns, 35, 210
of races, 215
of religions, 215
school subjects, 216
in sentences, 218
of ships, trains, cars, etc., 216
of titles of people, 210
of titles of written works, 219
Card catalog, 179-183
Cause and effect, in logical
  reasoning, 164-165, 166-167
Clause, defined, 162, 171
Clear thinking. See Thinking
  clearly.
Closing of a letter, 121, 133
Colons, 241-242
Common nouns, 34-35
Commas
  with appositives, 233
  to avoid confusion, 239
  in compound sentences,
    234-235
  in dates, 236
  in geographical names and
    locations, 236
  with interrupters, 232
  with introductory words, 231
  in letters, 121, 237
  in locations and addresses,
    236

with nonrestrictive clauses,
    238-239
  with nouns of direct address,
    233
  with quotations, 234
  in a series, 229-230
Comparative
  in adjectives, 121-122
  in adverbs, 125
Complex sentences
  defined, 165
  independent clauses in, 163
  main clauses in, 163
  subordinate clauses in,
    163-164
Composition writing, 83-101
  conclusion, 101
  defined, 83
  ideas for, 89, 90-92, 93-94
  introduction for, 95-96
  middle or body of, 98-101
  narrowing topic for a, 88
  parts of, defined, 83-84
    conclusion, 84
    introduction, 83-84
    middle or body, 84
    planning, 87-94
    subjects for, 84-86
Compositions, kinds of, 103-116
  descriptive, 109-110
  explanatory, 111-116
    the "how" composition,
      111-112
    the "what" composition,
      113-114
    the "why" composition,
      115-116
  narrative, 104-107
    first-person, 105-106
    third-person, 106-107

Compound personal pronouns, 62-63
Compound sentences
  commas in, 157
  and compound verbs, 159-160
  defined, 155
  diagraming, 156
  semicolons in, 157
Compound subjects, 188
Conclusion, in composition development, 84, 101
Conjunctions
  coordinating, 144
  correlative, 144
  defined, 143
Connectives, 136
Connotation, 149-150
Context clues, 2-10
  comparison, 8
  contrast, 9
  definition, 3-4
  examples, 6-7
  restatement, 4-5
Coordinating conjunctions, 144
Correlative conjunctions, 144
Cross reference cards, 182-183

Denotation, 149-150
Descriptive compositions, 109-110
Descriptive paragraph, 67-72
  choosing words and details for, 68-71
  following logical order in, 71-72
Dewey Decimal System, 174-175
Diagraming (of sentences)
  adjective clauses, 172
  adverb clauses, 169
  compound objects of verbs, 25

compound phrases, 141-142
compound predicate words, 25
compound sentences, 156, 159
compound subjects, 25
compound verbs, 25, 159
imperative sentences, 16
indirect objects, 20
noun clauses, 177
predicate words, 23
subjects and predicates, 10
with There, 14
Dictionaries, 185-188
  abridged, 185-186
  general, 185
  about languages, 186-187
  pocket, 186
  specific-subject, 187-188
  thesaurus, 187
  unabridged, 185
Dictionary usage, 17-31
  accent marks, 26
  alphabetical order, 18
  definitions, 29
  diacritical marks, 26
  finding a word, 23-24
  pronunciation, 25-28
  respellings, 26
  synonyms, 30-31
  synonymys, 30
Direct objects, 18, 25, 152
Double negatives, 128-129

Either-or thinking, 168-169
Encyclopedias, 188-189
  general, 188
  specific-subject, 188-189
Envelopes, how to address, 142-143
Exclamation points, 228

Explanatory compositions, 111-116
  the "how" composition, 111-112
  the "what" composition, 113-114
  the "why" composition, 115-116
Explanatory paragraph, 75-81
  the "how" paragraph, 75-76
  the "what" paragraph, 77-78
  the "why" paragraph, 78-81

Facts, (in clear thinking)
  checking, 153-154
  clarifying, 156-157
  logical reasoning, 159-169
  sources for, 158
  being specific, 156-157
Facts and opinions, separation of, 146-147
Fallacies, 165-166
Formal group discussion, 201-202
Friendly letters, 120-129
  body of, 121
  closing of, 121
  forms of, 120
  guidelines for, 122
  headings for, 121
  salutation of, 121
  signature on, 121
  social notes, 124-129
    bread-and-butter notes, 126
    notes of invitation, acceptance, and regret, 126-129
    thank-you notes, 124-125

Generalizations, 159-162
Gerunds, 191, 202-203
  defined, 202

and participles, 204-205
as phrases, 203
good and well, 119
Group discussions, 200-202
  formal, 201-202
  informal, 200-201
  responsibilities in, 204-207
    chairperson, 204-205
    clarifier, 206
    evaluator, 207-208
    initiator, 205-206
    summarizer, 206-207
Guide cards, 183

Heading of a letter, 121, 133
Helping verbs, 11-12
here and there, 127
Hyphens, 243-244

Imperative sentence, 16
Indefinite pronouns, 189-190
Indirect objects, 19-20, 25
Infinitives, 191, 198
  defined, 198
  as phrases, 198
  split, 199
Informal group discussion, 200-201
Interjections, 146
Interviews, 197-199
  guidelines for, 198-199
Intransitive verbs, 18
Introduction, in composition development, 83-84, 95-96

Judgment words, 148-149

kind and sort, 128

Letters (correspondence), 119-143

addressing, 142-143
business, 130-139
capitalization in, 121
friendly, 120-123
parts of, 121
punctuation in, 121
social notes, 124-129
See also Business letters *and*
Friendly letters.
Libraries, 173-194
card catalogs in, 179-183
classification of books in,
174-178
reference materials in,
185-194
Linking verbs, 22, 74-75,
152-153
Logical reasoning, 159-169
cause and effect, 164-165
clarifying in, 166-167
either-or thinking, 168-169
fallacies, 165-166
one-cause fallacy, 166
wrong-cause fallacy,
165-166
generalizations, 161-162
giving evidence for,
161-162
qualifying, 161
generalizing, 159-160
errors in, 160

Magazines, 193-194
Main clauses, 163
Main verbs, 11-12
Middle or body, in composition
development, 84, 98-101
Modifiers, 109-129. *See also*
Adjectives *and* Adverbs.

Narrative compositions, 104-107

first-person, 105-106
third-person, 106-107
Narrative paragraph, 64-67
first-person, 64-65
third-person, 66-67
Nonrestrictive clause, 238-239
Noun clauses, 175-177
Nouns, 33-40
common, 34-35
defined, 34
forming plurals, 36-37
forming possessives, 39-40
proper, 34-35

Paragraph development, 49-60
definitions in, 57-60
examples in, 55-57
facts and figures in, 53-54
specific details in, 50-52
Paragraph writing, 35-45
definition of a paragraph,
35-37
narrowing the topic, 43-44
topic sentence in, 39-40, 43-45
unity in, 36
Paragraphs, kinds of, 63-80
descriptive, 67-72
choosing words and details
for, 68-71
following logical order in,
71-72
explanatory, 75-81
the "how" paragraph, 75-76
the "what" paragraph,
77-78
the "why" paragraph, 78-81
narrative, 64-67
first-person, 64-65
third-person, 66-67
Participles, 191, 200-201
and gerunds, 204-205

past, 200-201
present, 201
Parts of speech, 34, 146-147
Periods
  in abbreviation and initials,
    227
  at ends of sentences, 226
  in outlines and lists, 227
  with quotations, 247-248
Plurals of nouns, 36-37
Possessive of nouns, 39-40
Predicate adjectives, 22-23,
  118-119
Predicate nouns, 22-23
Predicate pronouns, 22-23
Predicate words, 22-23, 25
Predicates, 6-7, 8, 9-10
Prepositional phrases, 140-142
Prepositions
  defined, 136
  nouns as objects of, 140-141
  pronouns as objects of, 139
  words used as adverbs and,
    137, 139
Pronouns, 45-65
  used as adjectives, 110
  adjectives modify, 110
  antecedents of, 65
  cases of, 53-55
    nominative, 54
    objective, 54
    possessive, 55
  compound personal, 62-63
  confusion in use of, 62-63
  defined, 45-46
  demonstrative, 52
  genders, 47
  indefinite, 50
  interrogative, 52, 59
  as objects of prepositions, 57
  personal, 48

possessive, 55, 61
predicate, 22-23, 111
  them and *those*, 63
  we and *us*, 63
  who and *whom*, 59
  you, 46
Proper adjectives, 111
Proper nouns, 34-35
Punctuation, 225-252
  apostrophes, 245-246
  colons, 241-242
  commas, 229-239
  defined, 225
  exclamation points, 228
  hyphens, 243-244
  in letters, 121
  periods, 226
  question marks, 227
  quotation marks, 247-252
  semicolons, 241

Question marks, 227
Quotation marks, 247-250, 252

*Readers' Guide to Periodical
  Literature*, 193-194, 195
Reading vocabulary, 2
Reference materials, 185-194
  almanacs, 191
  atlases, 191
  biographical references, 192
  dictionaries, 185-188
  encyclopedias, 188-189
  magazines, 193-194
  Readers' Guide, 193-194, 195
  thesaurus, 187
  vertical file, 193
  yearbooks, 191
Restrictive clause, 238-239
Role playing in group discussions
  chairperson, 204-205

clarifier, 206
evaluator, 207-208
initiator, 205-206
summarizer, 206-207
R.S.V.P., defined, 128

Salutations,
in business letters, 133
in friendly letters, 121
Semicolons, 241
Sentence diagraming. See
Diagraming of Sentences.
Sentence fragments, 4-5,
166-167
Sentences
complex, 162-165
compound, 155-160
simple, 3-26, 152-153
Signature, in letter writing, 121,
134
Simple sentences, 3-26, 152-153
Slanting, 151-152
Social notes. See Friendly letters.
Speaking vocabulary, 1
Spelling rules
doubling the final consonant,
269
a plan to master, 264-265
of plural nouns, 36-37
for prefix addition, 267
for the suffix -ly, 267
for the suffix -ness, 267
for words ending in y, 266
for words with the final silent
e, 265-266
for words with ie and ei,
268-269
for words with "seed" sounds,
268
State-of-being verbs. See Linking
Verbs.

Subject card, 181
Subject of a sentence, 6-7
agreement of verb and,
185-186, 189-190, 191
compound, 25, 188
defined, 6-7
with Here, 15
nouns used as, 34-35
pronouns used as, 46-47
in questions, 16
simple, 8-9
with There, 13-14
understood, 16
in unusual position, 13-16
Subordinate clauses, 163-164
Subordinating conjunctions,
163, 167
Superlative
in adjectives, 122-123
in adverbs, 125-126
Synonyms, 11-12, 30-31

Thank-you notes, 124-125
them and those, 63, 127
Thesaurus, 187
Thinking clearly, 145-169
checking your facts, 153-154
connotations, 149-150
denotations, 149-150
facts vs. opinions, 146-147
clarifying facts, 156-157
judgment words, 148-149
logical reasoning, 159-169
slanting, 151-152
Title card, 180
Topic sentence, in paragraph
writing, 39-45
Transitive verbs, 18

Unabridged dictionaries, 185

Verbals, 191-205

Verbs,
  action and linking, 74,
    152
  active, 100-101
  agreement of subjects and,
    185-191
  compound, 25
  confusing, 102-103
  defined, 8, 74
  finding of, 9-10, 15-16
  helping, 11-12, 76
  in inverted sentences, 15-16
  irregular, 82-99
  linking, 22, 74-75, 152-153
  main, 11-12, 76
  modified by adverbs, 113
  objects of, 17-20, 152
  parts of, 11-12, 81
  passive, 100-101
  progressive forms, 78
  in questions, 16
  regular, 82
  tenses of, 79-80
  transitive and intransitive, 18
  in unusual position, 15-16
  with *There*, 13-14
Vertical file, 193
Vocabulary development, 1-13
  antonyms, 13
  context clues, 3-10
  in reading, 2
  in speaking, 1
  synonyms, 11-12
  in writing, 2

we and *us*, 63
who and *whom*, 59, 173-174
Writing vocabulary, 2

Yearbooks, 191
you, understood as subject, 16

Acknowledgements

Page 20–21, 30, 31, and 38; William Collins + World Publishing Company, for entries from *Webster's New World Dictionary of the American Language,* Students Edition; copyright © 1976 by William Collins + World Publishing Company, Inc.

Illustrations

Joseph D. Jachna: alphabet photographs. Pamela Greenfield: design production. Ken Izzi: all diagrams and charts. Jeanne Seabright: handwritten letters.